The Kingfisher That Rocked

in abundance

MARY xxx

A SPIRITUAL TRIUMPH
THE ROAD TO PEACE
LOVE
SUCCESS
AND FREEDOM

i

First published in the United Kingdom by

Mary L Curtis October 2015

Copyright © 2015 Mary L Curtis

The right of Mary L Curtis to be identified as the author of this book
has been asserted by her in accordance with the Copyright, designs
and patents Act, 1988

All additional material Copyright ©

All rights reserved.

No part of this publication may be reproduced, distributed or
transmitted in any form or by any means without the permission of
the author, except in the case of brief quotations for articles & book
reviews.

First edition

ISBN 978-0-9933734-0-4

Published by Mary L Curtis

The Kingfisher That Rocked

A SPIRITUAL TRIUMPH
THE ROAD TO PEACE
LOVE
SUCCESS
AND FREEDOM

Contents

Part One   *THE GOLDFISH FLIES*

Part Two   ROCKING WITH THE DIAMOND

FOREWORD BY PETER SANDERSON

It was Mark Twain who said the two most important days in your life are the day you are born and the day you realise why. It took me 36 years of lolloping around in the mortal fog, looking and feeling more lost and confused than the Littlest Hobo, before I finally twigged at what Twain was getting at. We all have a reason for being here – we just need to find our path.

That is exactly what this book is all about; helping you find your way. After her gripping first book – The Goldfish that Jumped – Mary Curtis, a gifted psychic, healer and writer, invites us all back into her world and takes us on a captivating and spiritually enchanting journey of her life since the goldfish so gracefully leapt from its bowl. This time the fish has shapeshifted into a Kingfisher but, for anyone fearing Mary has become carnivorous since penning her second book, fear not. She has merely evolved in every aspect of her fascinating life and, like the Kingfisher totem, she has now spread her wings and found peace and prosperity in her life. From Brian Weiss to Wayne Dyer, from Doreen Virtue to Louise Hay, I've read hundreds of books within this genre but nobody makes the journey feel more than real than Mary. And I have her to thank for showing me how to escape the shackles of my ordinary existence after a gentle nudge in the spiritual proverbials from an old school mate.

It was my friend James who introduced me to her first book. At that point, I knew Mary only through the miracles she had achieved with him after the medical world had run out of ideas. Here was a man who had once run marathons but was now struggling to run a bath after being struck down by Chronic Fatigue Syndrome. Until he hit the wall, he was completely closed off from the spiritual world but, after trying every conventional medicine to free himself of an illness which had plagued his life for over a decade, he decided to contact Mary.

The next time I saw James was in Portugal; he looked and acted 20 years younger. A man reborn. I remember joking with him that I wanted a prescription for whatever drugs he was on. That's when he told me about Mary and how she had changed his life and been given fresh hope by her incredible powers of healing. I downloaded her book on my kindle as soon as I returned to my home in Switzerland and absorbed every last word on a weekend break on the shores of Lake Como in Italy – a place which, by complete coincidence, Mary spoke about in great depth during the book. There was a lot to take in but I knew I HAD TO MEET THIS WOMAN. The next weekend I booked a flight to England.

When I finally got to meet her in the flesh, Mary gave me my 'Mark Twain moment' as she helped wake me up and smell the spiritual bacon, turning my outlook on the world on its head – the full 360 degrees. I felt like a new man as my world opened up to so many possibilities. I'd worked at the top level in sport and broadcasting for so many years supposedly 'living the dream' and yet suddenly there was something even better out there, something which made sport pale into insignificance.

When somebody changes your life so radically, it's difficult to find a present which comes even close to showing the gratitude you think they deserve. I noticed photos of lakes and mountains all over her house and, when she divulged her love of Switzerland, I invited her over to Geneva – the place I have lived for 12 years – and organised appointments for Mary. The locals thought she was incredible - but it wasn't just people she was healing. I had the pleasure of watching her working with the energies of the Swiss Alps as well as the wonderful waters of Lake Geneva. It was like Mary had come home. She was in her absolute element and, such was her popularity here, I could have booked her out for the next year with appointments.

Some of the things which happened in those few days and next few months left me gobsmacked but I'll let Mary reveal those in the later chapters.

One thing I did learn by spending time with her was that being born with the gift of seeing auras and hearing voices in your head, like Mary, means very few things are straightforward. That's what makes this book so riveting. With her high-level guides pushing her hard to make the most of her psychic gifts, Mary meets some weird and wonderful people as she jet-sets around the United Kingdom and Europe healing spiritual hotspots, trying to find her true path as well as trying to get to grips with some past life experiences which have left their scars on her current lifetime. But what makes Mary's books so extra special is her ability to speak from the heart and to wear her heartache like a badge of honour instead of pretending the bad things never happen. Whereas most writers hold back the full truth, Mary puts her heart, soul and her chakras on the line throughout this book giving it an extra level of pizzazz.

Not only will this book help you to trust more in the universe and have faith that it truly does have a bigger plan for you, it will also teach you how to make the necessary changes in your life so you are in full control of your own destiny. Perhaps the most crucial lesson you will learn from Mary's wisdom in this book, however, is how to live life through the heart using unconditional love. If you have always wondered what, beyond any other thing, makes your heart tick and what is the secret behind keeping that heart chakra spinning then please do not miss any of the pages which follow. Mary will teach you to learn how to love yourself and, once you have achieved this vital lesson in your life, the rest will take care of itself.

Anyone who picks up this book is simply destined to read it as part of their big plan. Strap yourself in because you're about to embark on a magical journey. Not only will it make you laugh and cry at the heart-warming and heart-wrenching stories of love, healing and sadness as they unfold, but, crucially you will learn from Mary's infinite wealth of knowledge and advice along the way which, quite simply, can only come from someone who has experienced life beyond this dimension.

Mary Curtis changed my life. And, if you open your heart and soul to this book, she is about to change yours.

Enjoy the ride.

Peter Sanderson

Journalist, Television Producer & Spiritual Writer

BBC, UEFA & IUCN

THE KINGFISHER

A Personal Note

Over eight years ago, when I left my partner George, I was in a place of inner despair and confusion. When the relationship broke down I was still very much in love with him and he left the beautiful farmhouse to allow me space, whilst I sorted out new living accommodation for me and my three sons.

I spent much time alone and was deeply saddened at the relationship breakdown yet knew inside that it had to be so. One afternoon I got out my daughter's art pencils and began to draw a Kingfisher. To be honest I cannot recall what had inspired me to draw this beautiful bird but I knew enough to follow my heart.

My daughter is the artist of the family and she would no doubt have drawn one in a few minutes and it would have looked amazing. I set to and started sketching the outline. It actually looked like a Kingfisher which was a surprise in itself! I was really chuffed as it began to feel real and alive. As I began to colour it in I felt a real connection with this majestic creature. I coloured in all but the red breast that morning and couldn't bring myself to finish the bird.

I was still wet behind the ears and learning rapidly about spiritual awareness. It was several days later when I actually coloured in the breast. The red colours represent fire energy which is necessary to bring to life all projects. When we refer to "Fire in the belly" we mean that someone has motivation, innovation, passion and drive, not to mention many other qualities too. The relationship meltdown meant that my fire energy was certainly non – existent!

I still have the picture and I'm looking at it as I type the final chapters of the book. It's been a heck of a journey from despair to peace over the last eight years and it was only this evening that I pieced another chunk of the jigsaw together. I was sat researching the book when the Kingfisher spoke to me and said he was here to clear the final clutter so that I can really stand in my power and move on in life. Quite a revelation to be honest! It certainly explained a lot and felt real.

On Sunday 14th June I decided that I would change the title to "The Kingfisher That Rocked." This meant leaving the theme of the Goldfish….Gary and I had originally thought that it would be great to do the Goldfish series…The Goldfish That Jumped, then Flew, Then Tango'ed, Then Rocked.

In the last eight years EVERY time I have seen a Kingfisher there has been a hugely monumentous significance to its being there. It has signified to me that I was realising something of huge importance, letting go of something or moving into a time of inner peacefulness. Very often over those years my guides have said "Today is very important and you will know the importance of the Kingfisher and see one today"….and, guess what? I always have.

Many dear friends know my love of them. My dear friend Julie and I were out walking a few years ago when we came across a kingfisher which just stayed in the trees for several minutes and both of us at that time were going through huge personal transformations. We both recognised its' significant and sent a quiet prayer of thanks. I have seen them several times by the canal at Chorley and each time I am drawn to tears.

Just over two years ago I was working through issues where I have allowed people to control and manipulate me. One particular event had brought much awareness of the power and control which I have previously allowed into my life. Whilst walking in a local country park I saw one flying by the river. My eyes filled with tears, allowing my emotional release and surrender, as I watched in awe and was so touched that I knew the bird was a sign of my leaving old habits behind.

My dear mother and father have just bought me a beautiful birthday card with a picture of the Kingfisher on the front. Mum said she had spotted it months before and knew she had to give it me in June. Many clients have randomly and I must add, very kindly bought me presents of Kingfisher cards, book marks, fridge magnets, etc.

My thanks indeed to you all.

Matthew, my son out in Oz, recently said that he regularly saw a kingfisher in the local park and thought of me every time.....further confirmation that the title needed to change.

Several months ago, my dear friend Karen wrote to me, when I returned from Salou to say that she thought I should include the Kingfisher in the title of my new book. Well Karen, here's to you my sweet and a very big THANK YOU.

For your interest, I have included some references to the Kingfisher as a totem/power animal. This book is all about how I have learnt to stand in my power, with wisdom and integrity. You can judge for yourself, how relevant the Kingfisher is and always has been, without my knowing for the last eight years and maybe earlier than that too?

I hope you enjoy the read and I truly hope that this book inspires you upon your life's journey towards completion and whole-heartedness. Good luck in all you do; now and always.

Mary x

POWER ANIMAL: KINGFISHER/KOOKABURRA.

Also known as the Holycon, the Kingfisher is a symbol of peace and prosperity, many legends and superstitions surround it, with many originating in Greece.

The promise of abundance, new warmth, prosperity and love that is about to unfold within your life.
Matthew James (mara-gamiel.blogspot.co.uk)

Blue plumage associated with Jupiter, the planet of abundance. People with a totem of kingfisher need to live near water and kingfisher is about diving into the new – head-first – sunshine, love and abundance await.

Increased mental and spiritual abilities and activity. Time to connect to Mother Earth is important – grounding and centering. He knows how to strike with determination. Listen to dreams and visions.

Time to move forward, forget and forgive the past. The kingfisher medicine is about balancing male and female, showing your depths as you dive deep into newfound peace of mind too.

www.rainbow Of Spirituality.org

Beauty, Dignity, speed, agility, serenity & peace in life.
Symbolic of success and prosperity coming MY WAY.

www.buzzle.com

Symbolic of ancient wisdom and lore for centuries, intelligence, strength, watchfulness, counselling, truth.
The Wild Wood Tarot Mark Ryan and John Matthews

TESTIMONIALS

"The Kingfisher that rocked is an exceptionally honest and open book written by an exceptionally honest and open healer.

As a powerful healer Mary continues to demonstrate that she walks the walk as well as talks the talk. On her journey Mary faces gruelling past lives filled with strong and overwhelming emotions, but she never backs away and faces them head on, and it's this willingness and determination that makes her the healer she is today.

Whether you're a healer, an enthusiast or someone who is awakening to the world around them, there are so many lessons that can be learned throughout her writings.

The big lesson for me is that regardless of who we are, we all have unconscious blocks from our past that have to be faced before we can learn, heal and move forward in life.

So follow Mary's triumphant journey on the road to peace, love, success and freedom, and if you find yourself, laughing, crying or punching the air triumphantly as you read, then all power to you."
Chris Gelder

"In this book, Mary continues on her spiritual journey, it's a story of courage, determination and self-discovery. Mary is a healer & teacher, but above all, a remarkable woman.

This story of her own journey is written from the heart. It is candid, honest and inspirational. She doesn't pull her punches. It's a story of tears as well as triumph....And her unstoppable desire to discover... There is much to learn from this book.

It's a work that serves as an invitation to us all. To take hold of the steering wheel of our own lives, as we begin our own journey to find out just how special we all are...

This wonderful book contains all you need to make that journey. It's definitely a book to stir the soul."
Brian Catterall. Musician and Artist

"Once again Mary Curtis delivers a further profoundly, captivating read. After completing Mary's first book, 'The Goldfish That Jumped', I was hooked!

In the same manner 'The Kingfisher That Rocked' is so beautifully written, with Mary continuing to bare her heart and soul, her numerous life challenges, of which she has so courageously overcome. I consider myself extremely blessed to now know Mary personally; her vitality and zest for life are reflected so decorously here, as is her infinite determination in helping others. Mary's true compassion allows us beings to evolve in a similar manner, whilst supporting us with the re - balancing of our mental, spiritual, physical and emotional equilibrium.

Thank you Mary, from the bottom of my heart, for sharing such a candid account of your life and congratulations on your 'Spiritual triumph along the road to peace, love and freedom'.....'
Much Love Mina Valentine xxxx

"Wow Mary this is a great accomplishment! I have thoroughly enjoyed reading about your Soul's journey so far. The knowledge, experiences and wisdom contained within these pages will open up the hearts of all that read them."
Tracey Barton

"Love, laughter and tears of sadness and joy, I am ever amazed at Mary's ongoing journey, from being a jumping goldfish to a rocking kingfisher! I knew 2 pages in, that I was in for a treat and I couldn't put this down. Mary takes you on a journey into her soul, her amazing and inspiring journey, dazzling you with her thought provoking observations, teaching us how we need to be living, in

order to follow our true spiritual path. I am privileged to have watched some of Mary's journey and this book just re-iterates what I have always known... What an amazing lady Mary is. Mary and this book, give you amazingly thought provoking and powerful messages. Giving you hope, that you too, can change your life and be rocking like the most beautiful Kingfisher I know!"
Sian Collins

" *Mary Curtis has truly jumped from her metaphorical goldfish bowl and spread her wings in this, her second book, she continues her remarkable journey proving that she is not only an inspiration to anyone who has ever felt that life was passing them by, but has developed into a gifted and progressive thinking spiritual and holistic therapist. Her unique style of writing is both warm and informative a must read for anyone who has ever wondered what lies beyond our perception.* "
Colin Clarke

"Mary shares some more of her fascinating journey with us. It's guaranteed to make your heart soar at the prospect of an expansion of all that life has to offer. I have the honour of calling Mary a friend and can testify that her simple presence and effervescence for life is a gift. This second book is a must read and reflects Mary's talents she shares with joy, freedom and love. As she would say – "just do it"!"
Tracy Breen

I really enjoyed this book! Mary gives an insight into her work as a psychic and healer and also into her own personal spiritual journey. With her friendly and down-to-earth style this lovely lady has created another book which is a real "page turner" and also contains information and encouragement for everyone on the spiritual path. I didn't want to finish the book and I'm looking forward to the next one!
Esme Grossman

ACKNOWLEDGEMENTS

I dedicate this book to those who have touched my life and helped me along my journey, towards finding my souls purpose.

My very special and dear thanks to my mother Katherine, my father Colin, my dear family; especially my four wonderful children, their partners and my very precious granddaughters.

For those who have encouraged and supported me with love, laughter, hugs and smiles at all times.

Special thanks to Diane for teaching me the precious gift of Reiki over a decade ago and allowing me to find ME.

To my most dear friends; Julie, Tracy, Tony Mirror, Chris, Phyllis, Colin, Becky, Gary, Rupe, Clare, Annette, Dawn, Joanna, Jo, Tony, Amy Christof, Roxy, Racheal, Dave, Andy, Dawn, Mark, Chloe, Little Mark, Steve, Karen, Georgina, Esme, Austin, Debbie, Katie, Will, Jennifer, Marion, Stella, Louise, Jason, Chris, Paul, Ashley, Peter, Andrew, Karen, Bryan, Brian, Katrine, Kevin, Jackie and Family, Iona, Sian, Suzanne, Jacqueline, Leah, Kelly, Greg, Izzy, Kahil, Mandy, Vicky, Adka, Leanne, Jana, Steph, Nataleen, all the staff at Lane Ends Dental Practise, Caroline and Bob McFarlane and so many others that have inspired this book into life.

A special thank you to Tony Johnson for just everything!

Emily Griffiths for the amazing artwork too. You're a truly amazing lady. And David Lynam for incorporating this artwork into and creating this amazing book cover.

Just to mention also Mark Rigby for the artwork for my first book.

My grateful thanks to you all forever.
Love, light, laughter, blessings and hugs to you all.

Mary x

From "The Voice of Silence"
by Oonagh Shanley - Toffolo;

"A strong woman works out every day to keep her body in shape...but a woman of strength builds relationships to keep her soul in shape.

A strong woman isn't afraid of anything...but a woman of strength shows courage in the midst of fear.

A strong woman won't let anyone get the better of her...but the woman of strength gives the best of herself to everyone.

A strong woman makes mistakes & avoids the same in the future....A woman of strength realizes life's mistakes can also be unexpected blessings, and capitalises on them.

A strong woman wears a look of confidence on her face....but a woman of strength wears grace.

A strong woman has faith that she is strong enough for the journey.....but the woman of strength has faith that it is in the journey that she will become strong".

(Anon).

"The good of the whole must begin with the good of the individual...you help the world when you help yourself. Remember, we are all one, all waves in the same ocean, and one man's consciousness of abundance and well-being with its outer manifestation releases more light into the race consciousness for the benefit of all. So start with yourself."

Jason Andrews

An extract from the "The Superbeings"

THE GOLDFISH FLIES

360 DEGREES TURNING POINT

"Far away there in the sunshine are my
Highest aspirations. I may not reach them,
But I can look up and see their beauty,
believe in them, and try to follow
where they lead"

Louise May Alcott

360 degrees. A complete cycle. A new beginning. 360 means so many things to so many different people. Life is ever changing with many bends in the river. Being spiritually aware, I knew it was the end on one era and the beginning of another for me. A re-birth and the thoughts of what that might bring allowing me to experience an excitement which filled my bones; actually it filled my whole being. In my soul, my knowing was showing me that it was to be a time of advancement in all things positive & it was about to unfold right here, right now. Little did I know at the time just what the implications of that 360 degree turn-around would be? Patience is a virtue! Little could I have imagined what was in store from that day?

My daughter, her husband and their family moved from their council house to a new home – a house which was so immensely significant in so many ways to me. The Universe had answered a request that I had sent on Christmas day of 2012. They had been living with noisy neighbours, dogs barking day and night and various misdemeanours which had all added up to leave them frazzled and desperately frustrated.

Christmas morning my son Matty and I were invited to share with them some precious family time. Avoiding the dog mess upon our returning to the car I said to my son how marvellous it would be to see them happily settled in another property. How often do we realise that thoughts are energy. The ever listening Universe combined with the wheels of life, were turning.

Within two or three days an opportunity arose for them to move to a private rented house and a moving date discussed. The house number was 360! It was the end of one year and the start of another. New beginnings and a new life was presenting itself. Of course they were all delighted and looking forward to a nights' sleep, peace from the neighbours, dogs, motorbikes and they recognised it was time to go forward. A new intention-that of a better life had been set and they were ready to embrace their time of going forward.

They were delighted, packing was a joy and within weeks they were laying down new roots.

For me it represented much more. The 360 degree cycle was a signal from the universe to me too. It was all about my beginnings as a young child, growing up in that same village and returning to it in later years to start my spiritual journey; leading to a completely new life and way of living.

Now my daughter and her family would embrace the changes as they awakened to their spiritual journey, allowing life to take them around a new bend in the river.

They were moving closer, literally just around the corner, to where I had lived & played as a child. My granddaughters were enrolled at the school I'd attended throughout my early and teenage years where I had learnt so very much over 35 years earlier.

It was certainly a good omen, life was on the up and we all knew it. The school was also where I had learnt T'ai Chi over ten years ago. That in itself was truly a masterpiece from The Universe as it was from there that I had begun my soul's journey. The T'ai Chi allowing massive shifts in my awareness and spiritual connections on so any levels.

My granddaughter moved schools before they moved house and so the New Year represented new beginnings for her. Her reading, writing and arithmetic; the 3R's improved dramatically. It was a very visible and tangible change within days.

Life has a wonderful way of playing its wonderful jokes on us in many ways and many times over, certainly such a card was about to be played. As I collected her from school as I usually do on a Tuesday afternoon, I realised there was something familiar about the lollypop lady; the voice, the hair and especially the LAUGHTER.

It was Dorothy, our dearest neighbour with whom I'd been very close as a youngster. She had lived in the same close and was still a dear family friend over forty years later. We laughed and chatted easily. We reminisced and smiled as she recalled helping me to get ready on my wedding day in 1986. The volume of our conversation increased when we both remembered how she had sprayed furniture polish into my hair that morning rather than hairspray!

We howled with laughter together like children, as others looked on at our silliness. Years after my marriage, her husband had taught me to drive and had thus added much to my independence over two decades previously. Funny that my driving assisted me greatly when I was getting divorced! Dorothy has a unique and very 'subtle as a brick' sense of humour. "I always said I'd end up on the streets" she joked, "Just didn't know it would be in this way"…more giggles and more laughter.

So, a 360 degree turn. A complete cycle or recycle? The school where I had grown up, the school where I had learnt T'ai Chi and the most important of all changes in my eyes was that it was here I'd learnt how to open my heart centre and listen and grow from my soul. My spiritual journey had begun in this place and was about to grow further too. I remember updating the book recently and my guides laughed even more when I re-read the introduction – 360 degrees….how many turnarounds have I indeed had already this year! All was about to be revealed….read on & you will understand the humour that spirit guides love to bring into our lives. Many believe that the spiritual beings are serious and stuffy – let me assure you that this could not be further from the truth. Yes, of course they can be serious though most of the time, they love nothing more than laughter and humour in many, many ways.

"If we wait for the moment when everything, absolutely everything is ready, we shall never begin." Ivan Turgenev

It was a truly wonderful rebirth and a beautiful new beginning. Now I was here, no longer a young girl, but a very proud grand-mother who recognised the changes I'd undergone in myself. It was indeed an invocation from the Universe that ALL is a cycle. As one door closes another opens and the Wheels Of Life continue to turn. This has been known and understood by the Sufis & Buddhists for centuries, ancient priceless wisdom which we have allowed ourselves to forget.

A new chapter had begun in their lives and a new chapter was definitely beginning in mine too. Little did I know then that actually many new chapters and avenues were about to unfold.

LOVING KINDNESS

"Loving compassion is like sunlight,
Awakening and bringing joy to beings. Its
Beauty is like a rainbow, lifting the hearts
Of all who see it"

Tarthang Tulku

My self-awareness had grown intensely in 2012.

The Mayans had said it would be the end of the world on 21-12-12. It was in fact the end of the material world as we know it, the beginning of another more spiritual time; from the Age Of Aquarius to the Golden Age. The reconnection was happening as new energies from our planetary system were entering the Earth's atmosphere and bringing changes with them.

This meant that we as a community were being assisted in becoming more spiritually aware; more conscious of our connection to Mother Earth and ALL things; earth, planets, stars, moon, the animal and plant kingdoms too. Sometimes we refer to it as the RE-Connection or RE-Remembering who we really are. Sometimes it is referred to as "The Collective Consciousness" as we as a population of humans all affect one another and therefore as more of us re-awaken, we in turn, re-awaken others. Like attracts like and the domino effect comes into play. The story of the "HUNDRED MONKEYS," really confirms this perfectly.

It didn't mean that we were all suddenly going to be transformed in to hippies though it would certainly mean we would be returning to basics and re-evaluating our learning, belief systems, patterns of behaviour, social and other conditioning, awareness of our appreciation and gratitude. Simply put we would be reconnecting to our **heart centres** which in turn would open and expand our soul...thus our consciousness. This raised state of awareness allows our DNA to hold more light, it then leads to an increase in our energies; mentally, spiritually, emotionally and physically. This increases our light quota; we are simply made of light, sound and energy after all. Thus in turn, the auras' energies increase which simply mean increasing our vibration. Our vibration is a reflection of how much light we can hold in our aura.

The more pure our thoughts, words, actions and deeds are, then in turn the more pure our light and the more abundance of it too. All spiritual gurus hold masses of light in their aura and this is what we feel or see when we are in their presence. Their light is pure and a reflection of Source/God/Ascended masters and the spiritual realms. They hold only unconditional love towards themselves and others.

This is simply what the light reflects; pure unconditional love. It is pure, free of judgement, criticism, malice and without any form of inappropriateness to be seen or felt. They are totally at peace within themselves and share that light so others can know that serenity and feel it tangibly. This power is strong enough to allow healing. This is how Christ healed simply through his presence. He trusted that light would pass through his body and automatically create an increased quota of light in the other. It's a process rather like osmosis. If you have two containers; one filled with ordinary water and the other with a high concentration of salt, then when you introduce a semi-permeable membrane between the two containers, the salt concentration will equalize in them both; a simple physical fact bringing balance.

Light is always and will always be much stronger than darkness. Think of the strength from the light from one single candle in a darkened cave. Our physical illnesses are only a result of where our light energy has got congested/stuck. Once that energy is moved, just as we would introduce fresh water through stagnant water to allow the stagnancy to recede and be cleared, then so too a higher and purer light concentration will affect a duller quality of light.

Thus our spiritual/soulful responsibility to ourselves is to hold more light. This is achieved by letting go and healing old wounds; grief, jealousy and generally ALL negative patterning, conditioning and yet at the same time taking the spiritual lessons too of experiences. Think of emotions in terms of lightness. We think of joy, bliss, happiness as light and heavy emotions such as sadness, depression, grief, hurt, blame and jealousy for example as heavy or darker colours.

The true journey of the soul is the understanding and learning of what it is on a deeper level that we are here to resolve and comprehend, it is a journey of letting go of all the emotions and thought patterns, conditioned patterns of behaviour – in fact anything which prevents us from holding pure light. This book is my gift to you in sharing my learnings, into how to hold more light and in turn spread that to others. Most of all, this book is a journey through pain and emotional roller-coasters that have enabled me to change my life from one of emotional pain, misunderstandings and grief, to one of peace and balance. I am much happier now than I ever have been and I hope that by sharing, I will inspire you to move through your emotional clutter and begin to live in a much more healthy way.

The reviews from my first book "The Goldfish That Jumped" were true testimony that I had inspired many towards improving their lives and I hope that here too I achieve even more of the same; maybe even more than that.

PERSONAL RESPONSIBILITY

*"The Time is always right to what
Is right."*

Martin Luther King Jr.

The Buddhist and Sufi concepts are vast and the wisdom is tremendous. One main concept is that we are all ONE. We are all inter-connected and inter-related on levels far beyond our human understanding. Some say that we all are connected as we all have DNA.

My spiritual journey had begun some 12 years earlier. I had become aware of the Law Of Attraction and within that I then became aware that I had created ALL that had been around me....albeit on a subconscious level.

This realisation and the full implications of MY total personal responsibility were amazing. Contrary to my previous beliefs, I WAS & DID have control over my life. This was something I could OWN and I could now admit responsibility for my thoughts, words, actions and deeds. I began for the first time to realize that I had created a life of negativity and a series of painful dramas. Indeed I had been ignorant of the influence & the potential of karma. In fact, as I began to go through my whole life it really was quite a revelation. I'd realised that indeed I had created my own reality and the world I lived in at that time. *Simply put, life sucked and I needed to change!*

Through the understanding of the concept of Law Of Attraction, I had changed many of the ways in which I reacted in certain situations. I was taking the first steps towards self-awareness and self-realisation. I was certainly becoming aware of my personal response-ability; the ways in which I responded in any given situation were *my responsibility*. Whether I reacted with wisdom, anger, tolerance, patience, etc., were now in my hands.

I became aware of the power of my mind and thus became more diligent of the thoughts I allowed myself to send to The Universe as prayers and affirmations. The process was indeed enlightening. It was also a very painful admission when I became aware of all that I had created along the journey, leading me up to the present understanding of now. It was almost tempting to go back to sleep to the ignorance I had previously experienced, though I knew there was by now no going back! Rather like taking the blue pill in "The Matrix" I had become aware of so much more than I had ever seen before.

There is a spiritual saying that "Religious people are afraid of hell, spiritual people have been to hell". It's usual that those of us who find our essence/Higher Self/Soul, do so from coming out of the dark night of the soul – that would be the painful darkness that WE have created for ourselves! Be it divorce, bereavement, family upset, or redundancy; our pain is often our growth curve.

These changes lead us into the unknown and our culture teaches us to be afraid of the unknown. F.E.A.R. is False Energy Appearing Real and it grips us. If we dare to allow ourselves to go into the fear we realise that there is absolutely nothing to fear.....we should simply accept change as the necessary part of life. Just like the changing of the seasons and move on, thus moving through the situation, rather than getting stuck in it.

This leads us to TRUST – Trust that The Universe/ God/ The Creator has a much bigger plan in the greater picture than we have any awareness of at the time.

When Christ healed the sick and said "Now pick up your bed and walk" that's what he meant... to pick up your personal responsibilities and look at yourself. It means to walk with them daily in our personal awareness.

Self-awareness is the journey into understanding our personal *response abilities*. How do we *respond* in any given situation? One thing is for sure. If we always do what we have always done, then we will indeed always get what we always got. If we always respond with anger, fear, pain, sadness, playing the victim, etc. then how can we possibly expect to bring positive change or changes into our lives? There is ALWAYS another way to respond to given situations. This is about remaining detached in situations and maybe seeing things from the other person's perspective. It may be about looking at how the situation came about in the first place. Did we cause it, or any part of it? Did we react appropriately? What could we have done better? What options have we got for change?

Self-awareness is being aware of those things that are important to us? Which things empower us and which do not as they take our energy and/or our power away from us? How much time do we spend being positive/negative? How much time do we really use wisely? Just how many times a day do we judge ourselves or others? How often do we criticize others? How often do we criticize ourselves? How often do we allow ourselves to be criticised and belittled without awareness for healthy barriers and boundaries?

Do we criticize our house or our home? Our health or our body image seem to be under the microscope constantly and we are in a society in which through a combination of social pressure, peer pressure, media, political and religious constraints, we allow our lives to be ruled.

We are taught how to think, walk, talk and behave. So many of my clients and patients have lived trying to please others and never even realised the dire consequences that this can bring to their own health and well-being. So few people follow their heart's desires and live their truth instead of just fitting into a box or being labelled as a teacher/social worker, etc. which then becomes their defining role in life. *It becomes the mask they wear to symbolize their status in the society that is in itself just one big mask!*

It becomes the way they are identified and accepted, or not, in society. To be honest I have always seen the aura so have always been aware of the amount of light or darkness that someone holds. The light represents their soul. The more light in the aura, the more empowered the soul. If I see someone, I honour their light and feel much more comfortable around people with light than without. Whether they wear a label of a VIP or a house-wife I really couldn't care less; without the light we have no true essence and thus I value a person by their light. This simply means that the more light they hold in their energy field the more I feel drawn towards them and feel their soul & connect more easily. I have compassion for those with lesser light. I am merely trying to explain here that I am more comfortable with those who are lighter beings. These are often those who are self-aware and take personal responsibility for their thoughts, words, actions and deeds. Please note here that there have been many times when I have held and embraced my own dark night of the soul too. I am human after all!

APPLYING QUANTUM PHYSICS TO THE MIX

"An extraordinary life is all about daily, continuous improvements in the areas that matter most."

Robin Sharma

The real question of importance is this; we know Law Of Attraction is at play – every moment of the day. Scientists can now prove that our very thoughts affect the world around us. When we have a thought and we choose to *feed* the thought, our DNA activates and as we are magnetic beings, we attract these things into our lives.

What are you attracting into your life? Is your life desirable to you or do you want change? The real question is perhaps HOW much do we want that change and are we actually willing to do what it takes to bring about that change? Do we have passion, determination, self-discipline, motivation? Can we indeed think for ourselves? Can we judge WHAT is right for us?

We are creators of that world and as such, how often do we think and value our soul or spirit and to what degree? Where are our daily thoughts? Are we in the past or the future? Do we allow the past to influence our future? Are we even aware that we do this? Are we repeating the same old dramas and experiences? What major changes have you experienced in your life?

What about being present, right here, right now? That's why it is called the Present. IT'S A PRESENT; A GIFT FROM THE UNIVERSE.

Personal accountability lies within each of us; to think clearly about what we desire and what we want the most. It is our choice to believe in ourselves and to have confidence and self-esteem or to choose doom and gloom. As a child we have innocence and over time that is masked over with constraints and societies so-called rules. The innocence is squeezed out of us as we learn to compare ourselves to others, rather than accept ourselves as perfect as we are and learn to grow in the perfection with which we were born.

We learn peer pressure and are taught that wealth, social status and materialism are valuable. We are encouraged to be academic achievers and taught that the arts and numerous crafts, such as art, needlework, sculpting are not as valued, if at all. Skills such as carpentry, wood carving, dancing, music, stone-masonry, even cooking are dying out. How can it be that we all fit into a compartment of academic protocol?

These are Victorian rules and regulations. Is it true that the 3R's and our ability to learn them will shape us for the rest of our lives? How can it be right that we are not taught how to communicate properly at school? Surely if we were taught to use and listen to our innate intuition this would empower us when making decisions. Instead we make decisions based on the thoughts and beliefs of society. I often ask my friends/clients and patients when they are faced with a dilemma – what FEELS RIGHT TO YOU IN THIS SITUATION? It seems bizarre to me that most have NEVER even considered themselves in their OWN decision making process.

Surely it would be better to teach practical things such as: team-building, listening skills, patience and tolerance, to name but few? Why does our society not allow our children to be children? How many parents do you know who actively encourage their children to play, enjoy nature, to colour and draw, invent stories and use the gifts of their vivid, powerful imagination?

So often parents compare their children to others so early in their lives, that children learn competition and feel loved only if they achieve high academic results... from the age of four or five. Children are like sponges and grow up to believe what they have been taught, especially when living in a culture that is without wisdom or at least lacking in encouraging that wisdom. Do or did you believe everything that you were taught, either in school, church or by your parents? Did you ever think for yourself? Wisdom & discernment – how do you understand these concepts and bring them into your daily life?

Do you ever think of what *"FEELS"* right for you?

When we look at children we can learn so much. A child awakens daily with a unique joy and a fresh feeling of excitement. They look at life as if it's an adventure. Every moment to them is a joy and is very precious. Whatever they are doing they are totally absorbed IN THAT MOMENT. Children are always present. They are totally in the moment. They are not thinking about the past, nor the future. They are not worrying about things over which they have no control. They do not even consider control or the implications of controlling their lives; ***they simply allow.***

Children are in the flow of life and they embrace it. They look forward to adventures and playfulness. They accept change and changes easily and beautifully with little or no resistance. This is how they adjust so quickly to new situations and circumstances. They squeeze every ounce of joy into each and every single day. Ever wondered why they never want to go to bed? Most adults crawl into bed shattered at the end of a long day, mostly because they have created their own stress throughout that day!

17

This was why I had moved from a life of pressure and stress, to a life of balance and harmony when I "Jumped Out Of The Goldfish Bowl." I made a conscious effort to change and to move forward to create a better life for myself and my children. I recognised it would take courage to undo all the old thought processes and conditioned patterns of behaviour I had succumbed to over the years.

I knew that if I wanted change then I had to be that change.

Learning to trust in myself and my judgements was quite a journey indeed! Simply by changing ME, by BEING ME and re-finding the REAL ME underneath all the conditioned patterns of belief systems, I began to change my life. From reading my first book, many of you know that the journey was a painful one though very rewarding too. Would I go back to my previous life? NO! Would I change my learnings? NO. Would I do it all again? If I needed to, absolutely YES. Have there been times when I would love to jump off the spiritual train? ABSOLUTELY!!! Who would really want to take personal responsibility for their actions every day of the week without being able to blame someone else? That's a decision only YOU can make….I made mine years ago because I had reached a point in my life where I simply could no longer carry on, carrying on.

"As within, as without", "As above, so below" This simply means whatever thoughts go on in our mind – above….so we create below on the earth. Law Of Attraction at play.

When I wrote "The Goldfish That Jumped" I had by then over ten years of consciously unpicking bad habits, conditioned behaviours and coping mechanisms which were no longer serving me. Most of us live in our heads. When we do this it is often draining and we are unhappy and depressed. The brain mind; or EGO mind as the

Buddhists call it, is predominantly giving us thoughts which are negative and belittling. It is a difficult transition for some as they come out of their mind or head into their heart.

The heart holds wisdom and deeper knowing so is actually more kindly and supportive of us living a successful and happy life. Living in the head is often just a way of masking our outdated patterns of behaviours and work is often used as a coping mechanism to avoid our true feelings. Healing is a great way of moving from the head to the heart, as is walking in nature, meditation and other techniques of connecting or RE-connecting to our souls.

I was listening to my soul and beginning to enhance its power further, using it wisely by listening and acting on my intuition, looking for coincidences and *feeling in my heart-centre what was right for me. When we listen and work with the heart our whole life can change as we become whole-hearted. I had certainly thrived since I had listened to mine. Friends and family were delighted at the changes in me. Some were bigger than others but nonetheless ALL the changes were significant.*

The Universe needs balance, give and take, Yin and Yang, night and day, water and fire, air and earth, male and female, to name but a few. I was learning balance from a life where there had been none or very little balance. I had worked full-time, managing my home and my four wonderful children but I was and had been running on empty for years. I hadn't dealt with issues from my childhood, my divorce or a million and one other personal issues. The answer lay in seeking BALANCE. This again comes back to self-awareness, or rather the lack of it in my case. My life wasn't balanced. It was a life filled with work, sleep, work, sleep, work, sleep. I was barely managing whilst coping with restoring my house, finding time for my precious four children, homework, housework, living on a low income, doing a job I was beginning to resent for many reasons – especially for taking me away from my precious family…… and I certainly wasn't listening to my soul. Hence the title "The Goldfish That Jumped" – I had spent too much time thumping into the sides of the goldfish bowl and crashing time and time again. This repeated crashing meant that I was often ill. Let's face it, I had been running on adrenaline and we all know there's only one way we can go from there!

I believed everything our society teaches us; "life is hard", "to get anywhere in life you must work hard", etc. To be honest my main problem was that *I was too hard on myself….*time and time again. I felt guilty for a million and one things. I must also mention that I felt *inadequate* and the amount of thoughts of "I could have done this", "I should have done that", etc., the regrets in my life were driving me crazy. Yet it was *me* that was allowing *my mind* to take control, to rule and to RUIN my life.

Peace of mind was something that I never had and to say I was a "stress-head" was probably quite appropriate! I was merely existing rather than living and life had to change, which meant that I had to change.

When I was forced through illness M.E. or C.F.S. (chronic fatigue syndrome) to slow down and was no longer able to work, changes were forced upon me. M.E. is all about ME! It was an illness created so I would be forced to learn and understand ME. WHO WAS I?

TAKING HOLD OF THE STEERING WHEEL OF LIFE.

"Wisdom knows what feelings are present
without being lost in them."

Jack Kornfield

At that time I certainly wasn't self-aware. I was actually totally unaware that my negative thinking had created all that was around me and actually present in my life. I had created this illness; or rather my body had done so to make me sit up and listen. I had had a wide variety of warning bells before being ill but had failed to recognise their significance. The body will NEVER LIE. Any illness is showing an imbalance. Listening to our bodies and becoming aware of the body wisdom connection can be quite revealing. It is also sometimes known as the body-mind link.

Personal responsibility is a huge part of the awareness that gathers when we actually slow down, breathe and simply make time to ask the body "What is it that you are trying to show me through manifesting this illness?" If only I had known then what I know now! Mind you, until we are ready to listen, very little will change.

Looking back, my body had given me numerous signals – all of which I had chosen to ignore. I had had Labyrinthitis about 18 months earlier; an illness which was causing me to lose my balance. This was showing me that my life was out of balance. The migraines were telling me to slow down too. I was constantly tired and run down. The tendonitis I had had in my right arm was about holding on too tightly to things in life over which, in reality we have NO CONTROL.

If only body wisdom was understood and acted upon. Just imagine if it were taught in schools? Hardly any wonder that the Royal Family and most famous people have their own Homeopathic consultants. One of the main subjects we are taught as Homeopaths is the body mind link and the wisdom which is behind whatsoever the body manifests. The questions are structured in such a way that the patients become more self-aware and making the link to illnesses and lifestyles is much more natural and makes perfect sense.

Did you know that most people who have a heart attack have no actual pathological reason such as high cholesterol or heart damage/disease? I find it fascinating that learning Reiki and Homeopathy has given me the understanding that many have a heart condition because they shut down their heart centres. They close off to their emotions due to broken relationships or lack of parental bonding. Slowly and surely over time through loss, disappointment and attachments, together with expectations of love and how to love others, the energy simply gets too dense and damages the energy of the heart; in turn affecting the physical heart. Most of us cannot love ourselves so how on earth can we really love others?

The heart chakra simply stops spinning or slows down so much that death is a natural reaction. How many of us truly know LOVE and feel it? Is it possible that we can feel loved WITHOUT being in a relationship or indeed needing to be in one? Is it really possible to connect to the LOVE WITHIN? Surely, if we do not truly love ourselves, then how can we really love another person?

The first thing we do when someone upsets us is to withdraw inwardly and often over time we place barriers over the heart centre to "keep us safe." Rather than keeping us safe, they just re-create the same problems because through Law Of Attraction (like attracting like principle; as we sow we reap), we will then attract a partner/relationship where the other person has also got lots of barriers and shields around the heart centre to keep them "safe."

The cycle spirals and rather than having a free & undamaged heart with which to love, we just damage each other by thinking that defending ourselves is our priority. In this way we often deny love, rather than opening our hearts to the possibility of love in its most full & absolute capacity.

No-one can harm us but ourselves. When we love with an open heart then we attract someone who will love us from their open heart too. Unconditional love is the key and until we love ourselves unconditionally the rest just pales into insignificance. Can you look in the mirror and truly feel that you love yourself? Can you honestly tell yourself whilst looking in the mirror that you are lovely, valued and appreciated? Could you honestly believe that, if someone told you?

LISTENING TO THE WHISPERS OF THE UNIVERSE

"We are all inventors, each sailing out
on a voyage of discovery, guided each
by a private chart, of which there is no
duplicate. The world is all gates,
all opportunities.

Ralph Waldo Emerson

NOTHING in The Universe is ever by chance. Prior to my illness I had attended T'ai Chi classes weekly and loved every moment. I had finally found something I thoroughly enjoyed and had ME time. Any busy mother or father will tell you how precious and valuable ME time is to them. I had made many new friends and was always welcomed into the group.

When I was ill it meant I was far too tired to attend and one of my friends who I had met there had enquired about my long-term absence. I was blessed as whilst I was ill, The Universe directed Sally to phone me and enquire about my well-being - or rather lack of it! Sally was then a trainee Homeopath. She was looking for patients to treat and I certainly had nothing to lose. At that time I knew nothing about Homeopathy and hadn't even heard of it. Homeopathy is known as T.E.E.T.H: Tried Everything Else Now Try Homeopathy. Yet the Queen, Royal Family and many film-stars use Homeopathy. The story was about to unfold.

The initial consultation was over two hours; dredging through my life story and listening to my sorry story from childhood, how I hadn't dealt with the issues surrounding my divorce or actually ANY of my outstanding emotional upsets which had brought me to this point! I was knackered, wiped-out and exhausted; no longer would my physical body play ball. The system had collapsed and in no uncertain terms had told me to sod the hell off and was refusing to continue being abused. My body would not comply until I learned to listen and respect it, to understand and to listen to what it had been trying to tell me for years.

The Homeopathic questioning greatly assisted my learning and understanding of me. It opened my doorway to self-discovery and awareness. It allowed me an understanding of my PATH which is rather appropriate as Homoe means balance and Path is direction. The questions are geared to source information about balance: mental, spiritual, physical and emotional. If one is out of balance the chances are that they all need work, as they too will be out of sync.

Sally treated me for shock, stress, my lack of vitality and over the coming months, for transition as I began to change and to blossom. She obviously did a great job and I am forever grateful. Many who find Homeopathy, love it and to date I have NEVER known anyone who comes into contact with holistic treatments to return to conventional medicine or that way of thinking. It's a fascinating journey through life and one which we either choose to embrace or to sink into discontent.

Homeopathy greatly assisted in my self-awareness and understanding of ME, eventually allowing me to know and to heal myself. In fact it inspired me so much that I went on to train as a Homeopath, which I now know was and is a huge part of my PATH. Thus it is hardly surprising that over 10% of the population have their own Homeopath. I love my work as a Homeopath now and have over 400 remedies for the treatment of shock, stress, grief, emotional trauma, transition and all the pathologies that the body creates as a result of closing down to our truth.

During the time I was ill – which was almost twelve months I had TIME to listen and learn as I was simply too tired to do anything else. I spent my days reading spiritual books and sleeping. Goodness knows how many books I read in those months, though it really was giving me the time to process all that I was learning. The Law Of Attraction was attracting to me all I needed at that time. I was finally ready and willing to learn, to grow and to change. Learning through a variety of nudges from my spirit guides to listen and listen well, was truly amazing.

The Law Of Attraction means that we attract what we need to learn at any one time, for the fastest and highest growth for the soul to flower. Everything we attract around us is there for us to learn from, whether we like it or not! For me previously I had just been asleep to this fact. Therefore now, I was learning to look for signs/coincidences/synchronicities along the way of life, for what was right for me. What felt right for me and learning to comprehend what did not feel right. Using my wisdom and discernment became part of daily life and has always remained with me throughout that process and time. They are now a natural part of daily life and living. Of course any spiritually aware person will tell you these are not coincidences at all – rather they are universal clues and nudges.

The habits which were no longer serving me were being brought into my awareness and thrown at me so I would sit up, take notice and change. It takes a tremendous amount of courage and effort to change. Taking personal responsibility for our lives sucks! The understanding that to one degree or another I had actually caused my own pain was indeed an unpleasant realisation.

Seeing life through my real eyes; the eyes of my heart & soul was a revelation. Some revelations came willingly and I saw my journey as an adventure. Some issues were incredibly painful; dealing with my own hurt, and the hurt that I had caused others too; especially any that I had caused my beloved children.

However, to be perfectly honest the main motivation was that now, I knew the alternative if I failed to continue listening & learning from my physical body and my soul. I certainly didn't want to ever be ill like that again. The thought of going back to how I had previously lived my life was certainly not pleasant; no peace of mind, no sense of calm, lack of time as I always kept busy rather than being able to sit and enjoy silence. How much silence do you have in your life? Sometimes it's worth getting up ten minutes earlier to enjoy the peace and maybe simply enjoying listening to the birds singing.

For the first time in my life I was beginning to experience balance. I actively sought balance daily and listened to my body when I was tired or craved fruit/veg, etc. whenever I felt I needed to be in the garden or go for a walk. Housework was less important and the real things in life such as quality time with my children were paramount.

I was beginning to live, to breathe in life and actually to enjoy life actively. Just like a child, every day became a source of joy. By conscientiously breaking the old thought patterns: "life is hard, that's how it is, we can't change anything, life happens to us regardless" etc. I was certainly changing how I lived, my attitude to life and circumstances surrounding me. I was loving this new journey and finally in love with the journey of life too. The results of my changed perspective began to bring positive changes too; new people, opportunities and situations were now featuring in my life for the first time. Things that had previously upset me, no longer held the amount of deep pain, if indeed any at all.

People who had caused me pain – at least in my eyes, I began to forgive and to recognize what I had learnt from them. I actually learnt to thank them for my new learnings & understandings. Some people show us how not to be and that is their gift to us. I certainly was seeing life through different eyes and beginning to understand what, who and why I was shaped the way I was then and am now. Recognizing these as blessings was truly fabulous, inspiring and thrilling as one revelation after another came to mind.

THE PASSING OF THE DIS-EASE TO PLEASE

"You can search the whole universe
and not find a single being
more worthy of love than yourself.
Since each and every person
is so precious to themselves,
let the self-respecting
harm no other being."

Buddha

My addiction to finding the perfect partner/relationship/marriage kept repeating itself until I faced my inner fears and demons that my lack of self-love and regard/self-respect meant that I looked to another to fulfil that in me. Some call it "The Disease To Please". It seems crazy when I look back!

Why had I tried so hard to please and fix others when it was now so obvious that the only person who needed fixing was me! My previous belief was that "I'll fix you if you love me and fix me in return." I now know that this was an expectation and attachment to an outcome in those relationships. No wonder the Buddhists and Sufis advocate living free from attachments, expectations and conditions.

Fixing me would have been an impossible task for anybody. The only person who could fix me was ME! The only person denying that fact was.....ME!!!

Looking back at the person I was and who I am now, there seems little comparison. This is why self-awareness/self-realization is so very important. What makes us tick, what floats our boat, where are our passions and creative abilities? Self-awareness allows us to honour who we truly are and honour our qualities. I was stressed, tired, and in a total state of wipe out prior to this time. I'm now calm, balanced and centred (most of the time at least)! I had been living a life of obligation – living by what others thought of me or what I thought they thought of me! Crazy or what!!! I had allowed myself to be controlled and/or manipulated by others and was playing out drama karma daily.

BE HAPPY WITH YOUR POTENTIAL

"Our deepest fear is not that we are inadequate.
Our deepest fear is that we are powerful beyond measure.
It is our light, not our darkness that most frightens us.
Your playing small does not serve the world.
There is nothing enlightened about shrinking
so that people won't feel insecure around you.
We are all meant to shine, as children do.
It's not just in some of us; it's in everyone.
And as we let our own light shine,
we unconsciously give other people
permission to do the same.
As we are liberated from our own fear,
our presence automatically liberates others."

Marianne Williamson.

Most of the Ascended Masters such as Christ say "You know not what you are capable of… ". We only use 10-15% of our brains. Over eons of time we have simply forgotten how to use the rest. Many of the ancient peoples still use these parts. Think of the Aboriginal who can track a man, understand and move the weather, tune into animals, etc. Their intuition is far superior to ours. We are all capable of re-learning these skills. We have simply lost our connection to Source/The Divine/The Great Spirit. This is where we re-remember who we truly are and connect to our personal truth and our inner knowing. It begins by understanding, listening to and trusting ourselves.

We all have intuition, it may be that I have it and have always had it to a greater degree but we do all possess that ability. Most of us can run, swim, jump, yet athletes have it to a much greater degree too. They're classed as normal individuals....just exceptionally talented in their field. There is nothing weird about having intuition to a greater degree, rather there is certainly something very odd about a society that suppresses our natural abilities. Throughout history the leaders of the country, the Kings and Queens have had a magician or sorcerer in their court. I believe the latest term is "intuitive aid".

Some say that the term 'sorcerer' comes from being more connected to Source.

For example, ask yourself, what makes gold or silver more valuable than other metals, why do people want these? Nowadays they are used for show, but in ancient times crowns were often mere circlets of gold, with a few crystals added to enhance the Monarch's powers of intuition and intellect, so that when they were acting as judge they would be able to see through the lies or stories of the two people who were in dispute, and connect to their inner wisdom, and find the most just solution.

In what we now call pagan times, this knowledge was known, at least by those in power and also by the 'wise women', herbalists or 'cunning men'. Each village would have these in the days before doctors, which in any case no one could afford.

The Kings and Queens would have their own court magician, although they may have been called court Astrologer, or court Astronomer. At one time it was against the law in England to cast an astrological chart for the reigning monarch, because it might be possible to find out weaknesses that could be used to attack the king or queen!

For example, Queen Elizabeth 1's court magician was Doctor John Dee. He straddled the world of magic and science, just as the two were separating into different branches of study. It is also said he was Elizabeth's spymaster, using both conventional and magic means to spy on her enemies. He was a renowned mathematician, as well as studying alchemy, divination and Hermetic philosophy (that is, Egyptian magic).

Legend has it that it was Dee who created the storm that wrecked the Spanish Armada far more than anything the English fleet did.

You may just wish to check out "The Queens Conjuror: The Life and Magic Of John Dee" by B Woolley.

Knowledge is power after all.

I AM THAT I AM

*"In the end, when we look at our life,
the questions will be simple:*

Did I live fully?

Did I love well?"

Humility is the key in all of who I am. I am that I am. Which simply means I am all that I possibly can be, to the best of my ability with the influence of a Higher Consciousness. That Higher Consciousness we may call God/Source/Divine Spirit/Master. The question is does it actually matter? We all agree that there is a force or power far greater than anything we can ever comprehend. A force far greater than we will probably ever be able to even comprehend!

Knowing this with humility and trusting this force allows us to be confident with humility and grace. The Master or wise guru has nothing to prove to anyone – his peaceful presence is a tangible feeling for all to feel and be touched by. His vibration, an acceptance of his grace and awareness is wonderful to behold. He is totally present, totally in the moment, totally self-aware, totally mindful and aware of his connection to ALL things in Divine Order.

It begins and ends with us... mastering ourselves through self-awareness. By feeling that connection and maintaining that connection in all our aspects; body, mind and soul we respect ourselves and others. By listening and continuing to search for balance, by understanding the things which remove us from our place of balance and harmony, and actively working towards understanding the lack of balance, then we can aim for a far better quality of life and living.

There are so many books on spirituality which simply means soulfulness. To be aware of our soul – to be present – in the moment, right here, right now. There are also so many books on Law Of Attraction and manifesting, the Holy Grail, which ones to choose and which routes to follow. Wisdom and discernment are your keys. You are only reading/acting out someone else's truth, yet using wisdom & discernment you must **seek to find your own truth.**

Some people say there is a quick fix. I do not agree. It is a journey we choose to take as an individual. It is personal to us and is not a race. It simply takes as long as it takes, teaching us to be patient, kindly to ourselves and allowing our personal nurturing and growth.

What is the point of being aware of the Law Of Attraction and working towards manifesting a new Porsche/mansion then realising that we don't really deserve it through lack of self-love/esteem/regard? It begins and ends with us looking at ourselves and beginning our Inner Journey, being present in the NOW. "The Power of Now" is a great book by Eckhart Tolle.

How can we manifest if we are not mindfully present and aware in THE NOW?

Most of the time I was unaware of my thoughts; we each have approximately 60,000 of them daily!

This is why meditation is an absolute key to mindfulness. When we can control our thoughts, we then learn to control our actions and deeds. This in turn will obviously benefit our lives. If we often think negative thoughts then this is what we will indeed create. How can we manifest if we are coming from the past and playing out old dramas? This will obviously result in repeating our stories and reliving old hurts. This is certainly not the way forwards; backwards yes, absolutely!

Are you living in your past or future? The future none of us knows; even for me as a psychic, I can only feel whatever is in your auric field at that time as to the most likely outcome. Therefore if we are stuck in a drama – "Oh my ex-husband cheated on me" and we keep telling our friends and family then guess what we will attract in a new relationship? It's really simple; it is certainly not rocket science! We carry the hurt like a bad smell and the anger too so guess what we attract? More situations of anger and hurt of course, we will just be in an ever increasing circle of destruction and destructive behaviour.

So when we look at Law Of Attraction this is what we manifest; wherever the greater percentage of our thoughts go, is the given law to what we will attract. It is simply a conscious choice. The laws of physics tell us that like will always attract like. In the Bible texts: "Reap what you sow. As above so below".

Just as gravity is a law in physics, so is the law that LIKE ATTRACTS LIKE. The Law Of Attraction is simple. Wherever you place your focus that is what you will create. If your thoughts are focused & balanced then your life will be focused and balanced. If your thoughts are all over the place and unbalanced then your life will also be all over the place and without balance too. If you focus on negative things then your life will indeed reflect that back to you. If you moan about others then they in turn will moan about you. If you gossip about others then you will attract others who gossip but also they too will gossip about you.

If there are 60k thoughts daily my advice is to use them wisely; each and every single one of them. Visualise placing money in the bank of life, having loving friends and family. If you have a dragon for a mother in law then visualise her being nice to you. Stay with that thought and even if you struggle at times then return to the positivity as soon as you can. Distract yourself from the negativity whenever you need to, by going for a walk, a swim, a dance. Do what you love doing and enjoy it more. If you are unsure as to what it is that you love doing then you must take the time to find out. Otherwise the writing is on the wall and you too will be crashing into the goldfish bowl through illness or some other life crisis until The Universe gets the message across to you to listen and to LIVE. Is your life full and rewarding or miserable and challenging?

If you have an awkward teenager and you keep thinking and replaying over and over in your mind how you perceive them to be hard work, guess what you will create? That is *your judgement* of them anyway. Do you make time to listen to their point of view or even visualise them being happier around you? Do you treat them with loving kindness? Or even yourself?

LOA is a very simple universal law and it cannot be changed. This is why if you want change in your life YOU have to create that change and YOU have to become more personally responsible. Yet throughout our lives we listen to people saying that it's someone else's fault or the Governments fault or that of our society.

There are so many cultural and political misunderstandings, not to mention the religious misguidance. My golden rule is that if you have checked in to your heart and your soul and if something feels absolutely right then do it. If not then take more time to think about it or if it is definitely wrong then you must move on. One thing in life is for sure; as one door closes then another always opens. The Universe is in constant flow and will never stop, just like the cycles of nature. Flow is guaranteed, now and always.

The first time you realise that life is really in your control, then life will change for you and others will indeed notice in a beautiful way. Some think it is so hard to think out of the box, to actually stand tall and say that I actually had a hand in having created all that is around me. However walking the walk and talking the talk can really make such a massive difference to our daily lives.

The Universe forced the changes upon me; as it does with many others too. Joe Vitale is another example and I can name many more who are personal friends and those whom I have had the privilege to teach and share life experiences with over the years. You as the reader may just be thinking...ummm...I wonder if I really can change things for the better.

ABSOLUTELY YOU CAN AND NOW IS THE BEST TIME TO START.

After having studied the Law Of Attraction (LOA) for so long and having read many books on the subject, I can honestly say that the very best by far is "The Power Of Your Subconscious Mind" By Joseph Murphy. That book changed my life in 2013 and really allowed me to deepen my understanding of LOA.

FLEXIBLE MIND = FLEXIBLE BODY.

"Shoot For The Moon. Even If You Miss It You Will Land Among The Stars."

Les Brown

One of the key principles in Homeopathy is that like will treat like. Using Apis, which is potentized (diluted) bee sting, will assist in the healing of a wound which is red and swollen. Using willow which is a flexible and moveable tree will assist in the healing of stiffness and joint problems. It can also help with fixed ideals in the mind too. My dear friend Dave recently said that the more flexible the body, so the correlation with, the more flexible the mind too. Of course knowing and understanding body wisdom does in fact make perfect sense. These are just two examples of common-sense energy medicine in motion.

Our physical bodies are made of light, sound and energy. Balance the energy and you bring balance to the body, mind and soul. How much balance is there in your daily life? Are you lacking in vitality, motivation, energy, positivity? Any holistic form of medicine will be looking to restore balance in ALL ways. If you are not in balance, maybe it may be worth you looking for a Homeopath or reflexologist or Reiki practitioner? It's certainly worth a thought and it's worth experiencing holistic medicine for future reference rather than conventional medicine when you wish to restore full health for the remainder of your years. What have you got to lose?

COMMON SENSE; THE SCIENCE OF THE BLEEDING OBVIOUS

"Love surrounds us,
but only one who loves
can direct its current".

Our physical bodies are made up of light, sound and energy. As such our bodies are electro-magnetic; specifically our DNA which just so happens to be in every single cell of our bodies. The chakras; which are energy vortexes located at various points on the body, allow us to experience life through feelings and emotions. The chakras allow us to receive and to transmit energies. If we think of emotions as energies then light emotions such as joy, bliss, love would lift our vibrations, allowing us to experience feeling light, happy and fulfilled.

Obviously the opposite is true of heavy emotions such as doubt, guilt and fear. Hence they slow down our vibration and our energies, this then means that we feel tired, run down and exhausted. This is why it's essential to clear our cluttered inappropriate emotions.

Logic tells us that if we don't clear them out, then the old patterning will result in our LOA meaning that we attract more of the same. Do you feel stuck or stagnant? Do you feel that you cannot move on? Maybe it's time for an emotional de-cluttering? An example of this is a child who has been belittled. Often they will grow up to believe that they are inadequate, thus attracting others around them who feel inadequate. It is like running a computer programme with the only information in there to say inadequacy. As that programme runs then we attract more of the same. Once we are re-programmed to think differently then things change.

Our relationships as adults will result in those inadequacies being destructive and until we awaken and realise that our behaviours are not serving us then we will carry on, carrying on. If you always do what you have always done then you will indeed get what you have always got. Changing is a CHOICE. Have you ever wondered how many conscious choices you make daily? How many you made yesterday and how many you made the day before? How many tomorrow? Think of the power of NOW.

Conscious choices, conscious living, conscious love for life.

Thinking consciously will result in a fully awakened and thoroughly enjoyable lifestyle. How many constructive habits do you have? How many are no longer serving you? Do you really want to put the effort in to bring about change? Or do you want to carry on, carrying on? How much courage do you have to make those changes?

Think of your life in a year's time, six months, three month's time.....even next week. What positive changes and new habits can you introduce into your life?

In Reiki we often say healing is about peeling back the layers of negative influences that we have accumulated over the years; just like peeling an onion of its many layers. Healing the hurt will place a different perception on our Law Of Attraction magnets (DNA). They are electro-magnetic instruments attracting ALL of your experiences to you. Scientists can prove this and imagine if this knowledge was taught in schools? The question is therefore WHY is it NOT taught in schools? We are all aware that knowledge is power. Maybe that is the answer...food for thought certainly. Our DNA can be changed with unconditional love, healing, meditation and self-awareness, T'ai Chi, Chi Kung and most holistic therapies play a vital role in this.

So as you heal and peel and begin your life-changing process then guess what you will attract? Other people and situations to enhance your journey and show you how much progress you have made and how far down the road you are. You'll begin to attract people who are like-minded and beginning to take personal responsibility in their lives too. Then by sharing stories we begin to share our experiences and learn from one another too. In fact our DNA upgrades as we let go of old wounds and thought patterns – we actually re-programme it and in turn this means that we hold more light in our being and obviously our energy field.

What makes us human? What holds us back from our potential?

"*GOOD BYE EGO*"

The Ego is the part of us
that continues to worry,
lives in doubt,
is afraid,
judges other people,
is afraid to trust,
needs proof,
believes only when it is convenient,
fails to follow up,
refuses to practice what it preaches,
needs to be rescued,
wants to be a victim,
beats up on "self",
needs to be right all of the time, and
continues to hold on to what does not work.
You are now put on notice that…….
YOUR DAYS ARE NUMBERED!!!

An extract from "One Day My Soul Just Opened Up".
By Iyanla Vanzant
A beautiful description of the ego.

Is it life, karma, our relationships, family, friendships, our circumstances, work and/or our past? It is US! Pure and simple, it is our responsibility to change and to go forward. All of the above will influence us certainly though I guarantee it is our **F.E.A.R.S. False Energy Appearing Real** which will hold us back.

Our fears limit us and hold us from so many possible achievements, challenges and opportunities. They keep us locked down and stuck. How many people do you know who are stuck in an empty relationship and too afraid to move on in life, simply because it means moving through & into the unknown? People are often fearful of being alone. My personal opinion is that being alone and feeling lonely in a relationship is far worse than being single.

Fear creates stagnant energy and stagnant energy is fatal for the soul. Just as you wouldn't wish to drink stagnant water so why would you want stagnant energy in your physical vessel and clogging up your chakras? Ever felt stuck? Stagnant? This is the reason why. It really is simple energy awareness and often just by creating that ONE change in our lives then the dominos begin to drop and so we create another change leading us to other changes that can be welcomed into our lives.

Our intuition is the absolute key to our living to fulfil our potential. When we are completely locked down by fear our intuition is closed.

NO INTUITION, NO SOUL, NO TRUST, NO MOVEMENT, NO LIFE AND NO LIVING.

This is the most basic simple truth to the true art of living.

That same energy will lead to physical pain; think of the word *disease*…an unease of energy; a dis- ease.

That same energy also causes stagnant thoughts. "I can't do that, it's always like that, I can't change…" Stagnant thoughts will lead to stagnant thought patterns & also frustrations, oh and definitely lead to stagnant living.

BRITISH BULLDOG SYNDROME

"The Language Of Conscience is sweet & good.
The language of blame is devilish."

Very few of us know how to deal with our frustrations. It's our British culture…. "Oh Darling, we don't talk or deal with anger, stiff British upper lip and all that." Many patients I see have either very little or NO awareness of their anger. Many say that they never get angry and yet as a Homeopath we know that unresolved anger leads to the body manifesting symptoms such as headaches, lack of decision-making, digestive issues, gall stones, joint problems, sleep problems, stress just to mention a few! Try punching a cushion, or the air or start to go to a boxing club; I guarantee you'll feel better. (Don't practice on your husband or wife by the way….or your boss, sibling, or teacher)!

Anger creates lock down and stagnant energy in the chakras. The most obvious symptom is lack of vitality, poor sleep patterns, feeling de-motivated and stuck. Often people say they feel stagnant/stuck/can't go forward/can't see a way out of their current situation. Anger locks us down.

Other emotions such as grief, depression, jealousy, sadness; they are heavy and weighted. We transmit and receive information through the chakras so imagine a vortex of light energy which is weighted with heavy emotions. Rather than spinning at the correct speed and allowing natural life-force energy to flow, the weight of the negative emotions causes the chakras to slow down and thus we feel tired and this in turn will reduce our ability to embrace life and have the energy to move through challenges and gather opportunities.

This is why many conventional doctors cannot diagnose an illness/energy imbalance. Do you feel any heaviness in your body? Just close your eyes and go inwards. Tune into the body and ask it what it is trying to show you. Do you do any physical activities such as yoga, T'ai Chi, hiking, swimming, etc? If you don't exercise then of course you will indeed feel stuck. All energy needs to move such as water, wind, etc. Think of the smell of a musty room; if the air is then circulated the smell will be removed….think of your thought patterns, are they musty too? Does your physical/mental exercise routine need to be reassessed?

Our homes represent our way of living. Do you have a cluttered house? Does your mind feel cluttered? Do people say that they feel comfortable in your home? Do people stay for long periods in your house or can't wait to leave? Are you comfy in your own home? Is your personal space comfortable or are you uncomfortable in your own skin? Even a desk at work can be made into your sacred space by adding a few nice photos and or maybe some crystals.

Years ago I met a delightful client with advanced pancreatic cancer who decided to opt for chemo and radiotherapy. She was a really lovely soul and had been warned that she would be in hospital in an isolation bubble for the duration of the treatment. She had a daughter of two years old and obviously had been told that her daughter would not be allowed to visit for approximately a month whilst treatment was given, due to the treatments reducing her auto-immune system. I advised her that the isolation bubble needed to become her inner sanctum or sacred space whilst she was ill.

It would be a fabulous idea if she should take her favourite clothes, photos, teddies and books whilst in there to keep her spirits up which would obviously assist her recovery. "That's a great idea" she said…."I certainly will gather up my most precious things whilst I'm there".

Often, we talk of having an altar or sacred space in our house, maybe even a small space on a bedside cabinet. To be honest, my whole house is my sanctuary and my garden too. Our homes and living spaces really do reflect who we are and we can really use that space wisely or perhaps more wisely. Take a few moments to visualise what you could do to change and improve your space.

Understanding energy is simple, like attracts like and it's a "YES" Universe means that simple quantum physics is at play continuously, thus our thoughts are listened to, acknowledged and acted upon by The Universe constantly. There is no escape or days off when The Universe is asleep or on holiday! Thus, as we follow simple rules relating to energies then we should really keep it simple and as such, keep our lives as simple as possible too. Often they are filled with so many distractions and coping mechanisms.

Coping mechanisms are those things which distract us from fear, fear of silence, fear of feelings, fear of a million and one other things in life, often just the fear of moving on and through a situation; so a huge system of coping mechanisms are to blame. By blaming our parents or anyone else for that matter *in any situation* then the blame will distract us from who we really are and our experiences.

Other coping mechanisms include many things such as TV, radio, obsessive compulsive behaviour, picking our skin or nails, routines and regimental behaviours, basically anything that is preventing us from using our time wisely to do what we really want to do, or at least creating a clear space to move forward and through life in positivity. Taking the time to write down our coping mechanisms can be quite revealing indeed and merely witnessing and being aware of them can be life-changing. By becoming aware of the distractions in life we can than change them and the related inappropriate habits.

If you feel a situation which causes you emotional pain and you are still blaming someone then just have the courage to take an honest look with your heart and combine that with compassion for the person or people involved and also, perhaps more importantly, *have compassion for yourself too*.

Usually you will find that you bear some of the responsibility too. The realisation of this alone and allowing yourself that time to honestly reflect on the past will indeed enhance your future for the better and thus personal responsibility is key to all wisdom and understanding. How we choose to react in ANY situation is our choice and making conscious choices is often life changing.

Slowing down the mind, maybe through meditation – mindfulness is truly remarkable when often we have been unaware of the often unhealthy thought patterns we have had in the past; *one simple new positive thought can affect the whole of our future* and lead us towards positive thinking and a positive life.

This is why self-awareness is so important; it is an awareness of ALL we do, all we say, how we think and how we feel, it also encompasses how we react and how clearly we communicate. It is being aware of our energy levels; do we feel tired or energised? What time of day do we peak or feel tired? Do we listen to our bodies and sleep when we are tired or just stay up for the sake of watching TV or for some other reason?

Do we live by obligation or from the heart and the soul? What are our principles in life and our belief systems? When do we feel our way through life rather than just stumbling and bumbling from one disaster, to another disaster?

A step towards self-awareness can be the most important step you will ever take.

As we become aware, the energy gathers momentum and then more momentum, just as a stone gathers moss. The Law Of Attraction at its best, like energy attracts like energy so the more self-aware you become, the more you will attract other people who are self-aware too. One step towards self-awareness will attract another one and so on and so forth.

Self-realization and self-actualization are all terms which mean the same thing on a deeper level. By understanding that we are all like a computer, programmed to our backgrounds and our parents' backgrounds, cultural, social, religious and political influences.

"Our DNA can be recoded, although the scientists believe that only 4% of DNA is important, this simply is not true. In 1990 Dr Pjotr Garjajev put together a group of scientists from many different disciplines in order to examine DNA more closely. They found that human DNA has characteristics that enable the string to be reprogrammed. This can be done through speech.

DNA is also very sensitive to the frequency of the heart & love, 528 Hertz, otherwise known as the Solfeggio. Therefore by frequently repeating affirmations whilst playing this sound will increase the individuals' abilities for manifestation.

Through the voice, emotions and intentions we can create coherency and are able to reprogram our DNA. This is certainly living prove that PMA and LOA have their place. Love, joy, bliss and positive emotions will get you anywhere that you wish to go. Fear feeds discordance to our DNA and stimulates incoherency in the whole biosphere of the human form".

Christof Melchizedek   Mind/ Body/Soul LIMITLESS.

LIFE INTO LIVING

"The Universe Is Infinitely intelligent,
and it is for human intelligence to recognize
just how intelligent".

Most people are totally unaware of how they live their lives and react to new information and they cannot cope with another person's point of view if it contradicts their own belief system. Yet experience of life and those GOLDEN OPPORTUNITIES for change can indeed create changes within ourselves which can assist us to change ourselves & others. Tony Robbins is an amazing guy who changed his life through self-belief and is now one of the top motivational speakers in the world. There are many more which include Joe Vitale, Dan Millman, Jim Rohn, Dr John Martini and Bob Proctor. These people are living proof that changes can be made.

The chakra energy often becomes compromised due to painful emotions, being in unhealthy situations, around people who perhaps take our energy in some way; psychic or energy vampires, recreational drugs and too much alcohol, conventional drugs; especially vaccinations, anaesthetics, etc, **and particularly by denying our creative abilities.** By denying our abilities and qualities, we actually deny the soul, thus denying who we really are.

If we always do what we have always done, then we will always get what we always got! How much flow is there in your life? Do you live by routines or are you spontaneous and aware of what **feels right?** Do you listen to your intuition? Do you have a positive attitude to life or believe that nothing can change?

What do you think your DNA is emitting right now?

Often when the energy is so full of weighted emotions, such as pain, grief, sadness, disappointment, unrequited love, etc. especially if the heart chakra is affected it may cause us to manifest a heart attack. Over half of patients who have had a heart attack have no physical problems with cholesterol, stress or any physical reason for their illness. This is quite a revelation and although the emotional process of de-cluttering and letting go of old hurts is painful, what is the alternative? To hold onto anger and hurt isn't going to help in any way. Sore feet can represent feelings of "stuckness in life." Any digestive issues relate to how we do or rather do not digest life. Headaches often relate to congested energy around the head because we think too much and fail to listen to our intuition. There are many more examples and one of the very best books to read is "Heal Your Life" by Louise Hay and/or "The BodyMind Workbook" by Debbie Shapiro.

When we are told as children "Little girls/boys should be seen and not heard" and generally not taught to listen nor to communicate clearly, then we often have a blocked throat centre leading to pathology such as tonsillitis, pharyngitis, thyroid problems. It may also extend to our hearing capabilities; we may become deaf, have hearing difficulties, balance problems and vertigo for example.

Another example of a chakra that spins slower than it should do normally, would be the base chakra; (which represents security) when perhaps our security has or is being threatened. Think of a woman whose husband has always paid the bills, she has never worked, nor has she needed to. He suddenly drops dead and she has no idea about how to pay the bills nor of how to take care of household practicalities. She may also suffer sore hips as she cannot stand in her own power, on her own two feet. Backache and sciatica are other common ailments associated with this too.

I often treat patients and clients for anger. Often the situation has gone on for years if not decades and that anger has been festering away for such a long time that they may not have realised that the other person either has no awareness that they caused it in the first place. The only person we hurt when we hold anger is **ourselves!** That realisation is so freeing as an emotional release that it's amazing.

It's so rewarding when as a therapist we allow our clients and patients that understanding that it feels like a miracle has been uncovered. The emotional release is massive and beautiful to witness. Are you still holding anger towards someone or something? Do you honestly feel that it is benefitting you in any way? ***Sit with it and really feel it***. Decide how you want to deal with it appropriately and whether you ***really are willing to let go and move on in life.***

www.heartmath.org is a wonderful website and there is a free PDF download explaining the workings of the heart. How lovely it is to live with a beautiful unblemished heart and one that is free of inappropriate emotions. To live a whole-hearted life and a fulfilled one is much more important to me that to live a life of anger, resentment and bitterness.

Just because we do not all see energies, ***we all feel them***. We can all relate to someone who is stagnant and fearful. Someone who constantly goes over and over old hurts and their regrets, someone who talks about nothing else is very definitely going to miss opportunities in life to go forward and move on by letting go. A person who is a constant worrier is the same, as the same old thoughts go round and round constantly.

Stagnant thoughts, stagnant energy and stagnant patterns of behaviour equal STAGNANT LIFE!

Hence the title – "The Goldfish That Jumped." If we always do what we have always done, then it's a certainty that NOTHING will change. Are you going around and around the goldfish bowl? Do you keep thumping into the sides? Are you feeling trapped or stuck? Maybe it's time to take a look at your life for habits and patterns which are or certainly are not serving you. Some people like to have the same meals on the same days of the week at the same time. These are all control mechanisms and one thing is for certain; none of us have control over anything in life at all – apart from our personal thoughts. Thoughts lead to actions and behavioural patterns.

Change your thoughts and change your life through your actions.

We can all relate to a teacher at school who was miserable and depressed. Their aura would be grey, brown or black. Yet a teacher who displays loving, kindly & patient qualities would have lighter colours in their energy field. This is very basic energy awareness and we all leave energy trails behind us wherever we go-just as slugs leave a silver trail. We have a conscious choice to leave a lovely shiny, sparkly trail or a miserable cold, uncomfortable trail. Ever heard someone say "There's a bad smell in here" and yet it's odourless?

We have all walked into a room and it is obvious two people have just had a row or there is an uncomfortable atmosphere. Similarly how many people say when they have been house-hunting that they "Just knew it was right" as soon as they walked into the property? Equally sometimes you know there are negative or unbalanced energies in a house/building/work place. We all have intuition; I recognize that I have it to the extreme degree though we all have a choice to listen with wisdom and discernment on a practical, grounded daily basis, or to ignore. I often find successful people will honestly state that they listen to nudges, hunches, etc.

We each feel energies constantly, be they peaceful, flowing or of an emotional nature. Surely if we were taught and actively encouraged to understand them then we would make wiser choices? If you are in a room of loving, happy folk, how do you feel? If you are amongst miserable people then how does that change? Think about how it then impacts on your loved ones, on your families when we arrive home. If we constantly hold anger or hostile thoughts towards someone throughout the day, think how that affects our aura too. How do you think they feel?

Children especially, are little sponges and if they grow in a loving, balanced healthy atmosphere then of course they will grow up to be the same. If they are surrounded by arguments and negativity then they will learn this behaviour and think it's quite normal. Just imagine if we were all encouraged to be positive more frequently and thus we encouraged others to do the same? Would we need a Government and armed forces if we all took *personal responsibility* for our thoughts, words and deeds?

A society controlled by fear is far easier to control that one full of love and cooperation, peace, harmony and balance.

GRATITUDE

"Gratitude is better than that gift"

Gratitude and appreciation are some of the most powerful emotions besides unconditional love, joy and bliss. When we radiate these to the world then miracles can and do happen frequently. The DNA is then highly charged when we are in a state of intense appreciation. Thus we will attract more situations in which we experience and re-experience intense gratitude.

Think of a time when you have felt like this or when someone you know has shown these qualities to you.

An attitude of gratitude will in fact get you everywhere.

When we are appreciated we will do anything for the other person/people. Think of a time when you have appreciated someone and you too have been appreciated. Have you ever been told that you are loved and appreciated simply because you are YOU? If not it is probably because you don't appreciate yourself. Are you your own best friend? Letting go of the old patterns of behaviours which led to this negative state can be painful at times. It is always so worthwhile though, as anyone will indeed tell you who has found freedom from releasing their emotional pain. Many continue to react to pain with pain. The writing is then on the wall. If we always do what we always did...guess what will happen?

For me when I see an aura of gratitude it is a delight. The person glows like a light house or a beacon. Think of all that wonderful energy being received into The Universe! It is a state of bliss and joy

– something which we can all choose to embrace on a regular basis. Once again it is all about choice.

When we know what we actually want in life, what floats our boat, where our passions are, then imagine how powerfully our DNA glows. The passion is such a powerful emotion and that's why we then have so much more energy to manifest our desired outcome(s). This is why those that have found their niche in life will tell you that they don't work – whatever career they follow is just fun! I haven't worked for over a decade!

THE IMPORTANCE OF SILENCE

"In The attitude of silence the soul finds the path in a clearer light, and what is elusive and deceptive resolves itself into crystal clearness."

Mahatma Gandhi

One of the greatest keys to finding this is SILENCE. Quietly sitting and observing how your body really feels. It is vital that you listen, and, indeed, listen well. Where do you feel the tiredness? On a scale of 0-10 how tired are you? Where exactly in the body is it? It can be all over, though very often it's just in one knee or an elbow – often that's where you will find many symptoms – such as tennis elbow or a painful knee. Once you start the listening process your whole life will change.

Making time to listen in life is essential.

We ideally need time for ourselves, loved ones, families and especially our children. When was the last time you listened to the sound of the waves crashing on the beach? Do you ever listen to the birds in the morning, or the nothingness, in the silent early hours of a new day?

We can all say we don't have **TIME. TIME** is your greatest asset. You cannot buy it, nor make it bigger. How well do you use your time? How much time is wasted in a day? Do you NEED to have noise all the time, maybe from the radio, TV, etc.? How well do you cope with silence? Some people hate it. Guess what? Do you think they are going to make healthy life changes without some periods of silent reflection? If we really have between 60-90k thoughts a day then surely the more time we have while in a positive state then the more we can create positivity in our lives.

The only thing that ever holds us back is US! We all have emotions, situations and daily challenges to overcome. We each know that we have some days which are much better than others. We know that certain situations and people affect us adversely. Maybe it's time to take a greater look at things such as self-awareness; this is the key to undoing ALL which no longer serves you in your daily life. This usually means breaking habits and out dated conditioned behaviours.

By creating change around you, you will in fact create change in your life. As you begin to embrace new opportunities such as joining a dance group or book club you will meet new people and your thoughts will be filled with more positive aspects and probably friendships too. You will then be more likely to feel, acknowledge and embrace that you are in the driving seat of YOUR LIFE.

By starting with baby steps at first, you really can begin to make huge changes. *Remember to be your own best friend and be patient with yourself* just as you would be willing to be patient with anyone else. Do you know anyone who learnt to ride a bicycle the first time they rode it? Or indeed anyone who learnt to drive a car in a day? Patience is the key to allowing and embracing change. When do you ever show patience to yourself and others? How tolerant are you? When were you last kind to yourself?

THE EGO MIND

"EGO is the fuel of Hell."

The Buddhist philosophy mentions the "ego" mind or the "Monkey Mind" as we term it. It is that part of us that tends to fuel us with stress, through belittlement and grief – our self-destruct button? As spiritual beings it is for us to overcome and move through until we reach an understanding of the ego mind.

"The ego, aka subconscious mind, aka inner child, is your personal book of truths. Inside you, there is a younger you, a totally innocent you, who didn't have to carry all the should's and should not's, the ought's and ought not's, of others as you grew up.

Over time, these take us away from our true innocent self, as if we become wrapped in layers of bubble wrap. Our biggest fear is rejection, and, by taking on our parents or guardians beliefs & values as truths, the ego keeps us in line and keeps us safe from said rejection.

Our innocence tries to fight through the layers of bubble wrap, but it can't, as years of programming push it deeper away. As our ego protects us from rejection, criticism, hurt and abandonment by holding onto the beliefs of others, as if they were our own, and this is where we have the conflicts, the blockages in our life.

On the spiritual path one aim should be to love our ego, or the inner child, as that way we catch more bees with honey."

(PS I added the greatest bit as a smile, Chris Gelder).

As children we are taught that to fit into society we must behave in a certain way. Children are so powerful and so aware of their surroundings. They listen to EVERYTHING and they are like computers in that they store that information readily.

Imagine a child is dancing freely in the kitchen and a parent says "Oh, you can't do that, someone will laugh at you". The little child stops dancing and is then frightened to dance in the future whenever someone is around as fear has now spoilt the experience. A child will naturally believe its parents when they explain behavioural patterns. Why wouldn't it?

A child has come into the world full of trust and has trust for its elders. They have wonderful, colourful, vivid and very powerful imaginations too. Yet how often are these actually actively encouraged? Many times the little child will be told not to do something such a sing, dance, paint; just generally doing what children do! A child may have painted a fabulous picture and in their minds eye they know exactly what they have created. Yet a teacher/parent may ask what it is by saying that they can't see it or rebuke the child. The child is confused and then obviously that confusion spreads to other areas of their lives. When the Law Of Attraction is added to the mix then of course confusion will attract more situations of.... beginning to see a pattern?

Little by little, piece by piece the natural abilities and talents of the child get suppressed and repression results. When we tell a child not to be so soft or not to cry they learn more suppression as they lock away their natural feelings. Eventually, over years and years, of learning a wide variety of conditioning behaviours, they stop recognizing their emotions. Then we have an unemotional being; who is living in denial. A child that then grows to ignore their passions and often their needs too.

Ever wondered why you don't know what it is you really want in life? Not exactly rocket science is it? We then learn coping mechanisms to cope and to distract us from our original pain. We then wear masks to take our attention to other things in order to hide our lack of confidence, perhaps by becoming a body builder, or pushing ourselves to be the best at something that we actually don't want to do though we are trying to please others and looking for acceptance too. I truly love the character Aubrey in "Pitch Perfect 1."

How many masks do you wear?

Do you wear different ones for work?

Family? Relationships?

That's why in healing we use the term *"Heal and Peel"* as healing allows us to remove the layers of patterned behaviours leading us to suppression, repression and lack of understanding for ourselves. Is it really any wonder that through peer pressure youngsters feel that they don't fit in? Generally peer pressure in the school system means that unless they are tall, slim, fit, good-looking, sporty and/or academically successful and have wealthy parents that they are not good enough, at least in some way, shape or form, to a more or lesser degree.

I have so many clients with confidence issues on some level or another. It is very painful to look at our wounded inner child. I often think that our society has indeed so much to answer to for, in the way that children are lacking in confidence, social awareness and communication skills. Many of them now spend hours alone on the computer or in their bedroom on games, etc.

Please note that I am making a huge generalisation here to make the point. Of course I do see many conscientious parents who are mindful of how much time and how often their child/children is/are allowed to spend on the computer, how often they spend doing homework, attend social events and learn dance, art, sport, etc.

The Rudolf Steiner employs the Waldorf education principles in their schools and as such offer so much more than an academic school of learning. The principles are based on a philosophy of a humanistic approach to learning.

The pedagogy emphasizes the role of imagination in learning, striving to integrate holistically the intellectual, practical and artistic development of pupils.

The division of a child's development is in three major stages – hands on activities, creative play and elementary education which focus on developing artistic expression and social capacities; and to secondary education – critical, reasoning and empathetic understanding. The overarching goal is to develop FREE, morally responsible and integrated individuals equipped with a high degree of social competence.

The first Waldorf school opened in 1919 in Stuttgart, Germany. At present there are over a thousand independent Waldorf schools, approximately 2,000 kindergartens and 646 centres for special education located in 60 countries. (Source: Wikipedia).

READY TO GET READY

*"Everyone has great ideas
but those who are great
have acted on them."*

Mansukh Patel

Wisdom and common sense seem to be lacking in our society. How arrogant we are to believe that in so many ways our society has progressed! I ask the question...progressed in what way? Many people have confidence issues, **most have no idea how to resolve conflicts within relationships. S**o many people are on medication for depression. Progress? Not in my eyes. How many people do you know who really stand in their true power? Who **know** what they want in life and are TRULY happy? How many people do you know who are truly living with their integrity? Do you live in yours?

Is it any wonder why many who have gone through this system have no awareness of their life purpose? Surely our whole aim in life is to share that unique gift that only WE can offer to the world due to our uniqueness? Every artist paints a different picture or sculpts slightly differently to another.........isn't this how it should be? That our individualism should indeed be respected?

Our society has lost its sense of community. Yet, many ancient cultures had the wisdom to recognise the need to share. In the evenings they would gather together and sing, dance and share their daily experiences. The Essenes, Sufis and many Buddhist cultures believe sharing is key to harmony. Attending an evening of folk music, dancing and singing is truly uplifting to the body, the mind and ***most definitely the soul.*** What feeds your soul? What causes your heart to expand?

We are a human being having a spiritual experience. Our existence should be treasured and we should all live each and every day as if it's our last. By squeezing every ounce of joy into a day and enjoying lunch or a coffee with a friend or doing things that we want to do; ***rather than what we think we ought to do***. No-one on the planet knows how long we have. There are choices to make and decisions daily; to eat healthy or otherwise, to wash, brush our teeth, etc. How many of your choices are serving you? How many CONSCIOUS choices do you make daily?

What do you enjoy doing the most in a day? How do you start the day? Do you feel positive? Do you just go through a list of jobs in your mind? Do you dread getting out of bed? How we choose to start the day is so important and sets up the whole day and often the whole week too. What are your first thoughts as you start the day?

These are very simple awarenesses & thoughts and these simple steps can lead us to making much better choices and a feeling of well-being, balance and ultimately leading us to a much better life.

How much time do you think about your spiritual growth? Do you ever reflect upon your day? Could you have chosen a better way to share something with someone? Perhaps delivering constructive criticism with kindness, loving kindness and heart-centeredness, rather than seeming to be destructive and cold? Do we ever think about what we have learnt throughout our lives so far? More importantly, what have we chosen to do about it? If we always do what we always did then we will always get what we always got!

Do we ever consider what life-lessons we may be learning currently and those we may have already learnt? Do we ever think of how we have understood these lessons, etc.? What have we learnt to date? Do we even consider our personal awareness and self-empowerment?

Many people when I ask about their passion, what it is and how it makes them feel, have to ask me what I mean. So many of us get lost in the jungle of trying to fit into society's box of *supposed perfection* that they miss the point of life and living that life entirely.

We live with the disease to please and often put ourselves last on the list when it comes to taking care of ourselves and doing things which make us FEEL happy and contented. Instead we do things that we THINK will make others happy rather than what we FEEL will make others happy and certainly what makes us FEEL happy. In fact many of us have forgotten HOW TO FEEL because we have spent a lifetime suppressing those self same feelings.

Our culture teaches us to believe that to make time for ourselves is wrong. That it is selfish and unkind. Yet, by actually making *quality time* for ourselves we function much better because we are not exhausted and tired, often resentful and frustrated. Our energies become balanced as we maintain our harmonic state and of course LOA means that our balance will spread and influence others. The more we seek to achieve balance then the more we will indeed maintain that balance too. LOA at its best.

As a Homeopath I am trained to look at the body wisdom and how the body manifests anger. Symptoms might include joint pain, gall stones, gall bladder problems and digestive problems to name but few. So often I ask my patients how they deal with anger. "I don't do anger, I never get angry" Yet their pathology shows their body is doing it for them. This can be through gall stones/gall bladder problems/water infections/headaches/backache/digestive issues/high blood pressure to name but few.....If I had a £1 for every patient I have questioned who has said "My skin makes me feel angry"......!!! "My tummy always plays up when I'm around my mother, she makes me feel angry and my tummy is angry". Listening to the body provides us with so many answers and will ALWAYS TELL US THE TRUTH.

"Every exaggeration has its effect in the human body" Walt Whitman

This is why the **body wisdom** is amazing and by understanding that then we can begin to move forward towards a balanced, happier and more fulfilling life. How many people find their soul through or following a period of illness? They are then forced to rest and forced to listen to their bodies. The healing process will then commence and they will often completely change their lives.

I have seen it so many times when people begin their souls' journey and remove themselves from toxic relationships, inappropriate careers and **stagnant living**. They begin to flower, often becoming more creative and frequently find new friendships/relationships, careers, etc. They begin to communicate and relate to others in a much more appropriate way too, namely because they **actually listen and learn to communicate with themselves**. Basically their resolve is to live better and more healthily than they were doing previously by **actively making positive changes.**

If you want to get fitter you have to make an effort to improve fitness. The fitter that you want to be then the more effort you will indeed have to put into this project. This means making TIME and putting in effort to go forward. Daily routines have to include physical fitness regimes. Self-discipline is paramount and although this is important, we MUST CHANGE OUR DAILY ROUTINES AND HABITS. Without changing these, then guess what, there will be NO improvement to physical fitness.

In the same way, if you want to find your purpose, you must change your life to include some silence. Do you honestly think that you'll find it amongst the noise and chaos of normal life? Watching TV or just drinking to drown life out? How much TIME do you use wisely and productively?

There are 24 hours in a day, 7 days in a week and 365 days in most years. Are you happy having maybe one or two weeks holiday a year? Is that your quality time? Why not imagine that you are actively PRESENT from the moment you awaken to the moment you go to bed and rest your head? *Being aware of your thoughts, actions, words and deeds is truly life changing. What is the alternative?*

Honesty is a great place to start. When were you last honest with yourself about your life, goals and happiness? How many hours a week do you work? How much quiet time is there in your life? What do you do for yourself? What do you enjoy doing? When did you last have a REAL CONVERSATION that was both meaningful and touching? When was the last time you were actually really listened to or even when did you ever really listen openly to another, with sincerity and without judgement?

Watching the blossoming processes in my clients/patients and friends is truly wonderful to me. By sharing and empowering others

I truly increase the celebrations in my life daily now. I give thoughts and thanks of gratitude as I lay down to sleep at night and I awaken wondering what miracles the day will bring. It has taken me years of fine tuning this I agree. Would I swap my life now and go back to my old life? Not in a million years!

FEEDING THE SOUL

"If we don't know our own value,
Even though we may know the value of everything else,
we have failed in the most essential of knowledge."

I recently spoke to a client who was tired and lethargic. He is a lovely guy, hard-working and has a beautiful relationship with his wife. I asked a few simple questions as to the quality of his diet; he was eating a lot of convenience foods. I then asked what quality of sleep he was getting and how much, this too was poor. I continued to enquire about his working life and how much time he spent at work – knowing he does love his work although 70 hours is far too much for any one of us. I then asked how he felt about himself. On a scale of 0-10 where was his rating for confidence, ten being the most? "Between 2 – 3" he stated. If he would have had more self-awareness and confidence then he would have had better health. This question gives me so many clues as to a persons' well-being.

Self-confidence relates to our self-respect, self-awareness and self-regard. Often this question alone will show why the patient may have sleep or digestive problems. It really is that simple. I then asked what he enjoyed doing and how often he did it. He replied "I walk in the mountains once a month." My reply was spoken with loving kindness as I said *"So, once a month you take time out to feed your soul."*

The sound of the pennies dropping at the other end of the telephone was music to my ears. I forwarded some confidence remedies and remedies to detox the liver from the anti-depressants he was taking. I also sent a great deal of healing to him and his wife too, as no doubt she was struggling to witness his lack of vitality and the state of his well-being, or lack of it.

I have checked up on him recently several times and he is feeling amazing. Taking personal responsibility for our lives is indeed very enlightening. Many simple changes will lead to other changes which will in turn lead to more self-awareness.

He had not previously been self-aware enough to listen to his heart and soul and feed them. Once he increased the soul feeding life changed instantly.....What feeds your soul? Dancing? Singing? Walking? Swimming? Spending quality time with friends and relatives? Spending time alone in nature? Painting? Sculpting?

If you really don't know what feeds your soul, I would suggest that you close your eyes, turn off any nearby electrical equipment and place your hands on your heart centre. Quietly ask your soul/heart what it would like to show you and listen with an open heart and mind. The answer may very well surprise you.

CLEAR THINKING?

..."Your beliefs become your thoughts,
Your thoughts become your words
Your words become your actions
Your actions become your habits
Your habits become your values
Your values become your destiny"

Mahatma Gandhi

Many of us know the power of water to clean. Think of the power of a jet washer, a storm or heavy rain fall to wash away the dust from a pathway. Yet when we think of water how many of us think about water to clear our minds? Are our daily thoughts clean and clear? Every process in the body uses water; expiration, digestion, excretion; in fact we cannot sustain life without water for long.

If you could look inside your brain at the thoughts you have, is your brain clean? I find that by drinking plenty of water it keeps my thinking clearer and refreshes my thoughts. How much water do you drink daily? *Water will clean and clear the DNA of negative energy and as water holds memories it will enhance your déjà vu.* It improves our connection to Source and clears out old emotions and memories that no longer serve us. If you feel stuck or stagnant it may be time to drink more water daily. I guarantee you'll feel better. That feeling will spread to *all aspects of your life;* work/working relationships/family/siblings/relationships generally; both with yourself and others too.

Our gardens need weeding regularly, our teeth need brushing at least twice a day, our bodies need washing and our clothing/bedding needs to be washed regularly too. There are daily housework/domestic chores, house repairs, etc. There are consequences when these are not dealt with...untidy house, houses that need extensive repairs, smelly bodies, dirty laundry, teeth that are in need of repair or halitosis, etc.

Ever thought that the thoughts you think today will be those you think tomorrow unless you change the way in which you think? Water helps with this process too as water clears emotions away and washes out the old. By changing our thoughts we then change our behaviours, our actions and our deeds too. This in turn will lead to good habits and self-awareness.

Yet how often do we think about the value of cleaning our minds? This is why the ancients have used and advised us as to different meditation techniques. Just like learning a new job or learning to ride a bike, some will find meditation easier than others. We all need to be our own best friend and being patient with ourselves is the first step towards that.

Meditation starts with our being aware of our breath and breathing consciously. When did you last think about breathing? Simply sit and breathe in four deep breaths – slowly and consciously. Listen to your body and as you do this and you'll automatically find that your mind will slow down too.

Five or ten minutes a day can and will produce amazing results.

"The ancients taught that to understand one's self was to understand God, and through the process of meditating one could release the divine energy from within and transmute discord into harmony, ignorance into wisdom, fear into love and lack into abundance. The Initiate was trained to conceive the highest and noblest ideas as a vision for manifestation, and then to identify the symbols of the vision with the Master spirit within – The Source of all."

There are so many different meditation techniques and looking through YouTube you can find many for beginners. My personal view is that, like anything else, be patient with yourself. Build it up slowly and be sensible. Do what you find comfortable and also my absolute favourites are Sound Healing Meditations. During these sessions the therapist plays a wide variety of instruments which will bring a sense of balance and de-clutter to the chakras. I have loved each and every one that I have experienced.

FEELING THE VIBRATION.

*"Developing our presence, our inner being,
is developing that which is most essentially
and characteristically human."*

We all remember that feeling of being "in love". We all know that look on someone's face when they're in love too. We feel nice when we are around a positive person or someone who is extra happy. Their positivity spreads to us and that's always a fabulous experience.

Our aura/energy field can also become clogged up with negative energies too. Just imagine that you are having a fabulous day and then you get a call from the hospital to say a relative is in the accident and emergency department. As you walk in the hospital people are worried, some are sick, some are very sick, the staff are probably tired and maybe stressed out.

Have you ever even thought that we are all made up of energy so by the simple process of osmosis we are exchanging energy continuously? So, that being the case, how do you think your energy field now looks if it was nice, lovely and sparkly when you walked in? A little tarnished, maybe dusty or dirty? Over time how do you think it would look if you were to visit this place daily for a fortnight?

Your aura is your body armour and is a protective layer against negativity. By keeping it in great shape it will STAY in great shape. Positive mental attitude is the key, as is a healthy diet and a balanced lifestyle in ALL aspects.

We all have times of feeling low, lacking vitality and feeling life is weighing us down. Just suppose that we are in control of our lives and we can change things for the better ourselves? How powerful that thought would be if it were true! Guess what? It is true!

The Emerald Tablets are ancient sacred teachings which have been written out of the Bible to disempower us as a society. Quite a thought when we as a society are surrounded by doom, gloom, repression and suppression. Ever wondered why the news contains doom and gloom, rather than happiness and stories of peoples positive achievements?   There is a reason behind what is communicated to us. Just imagine how different it could be if we were bombarded with positivity daily and inspiring stories on the news. Imagine if the news were true depictions of daily life rather than dramas and gossip? I wonder now if you would still want to watch the news? Would you still read the newspapers and allow your soul to be compromised? Food for thought, I'll leave you to figure out the rest.

Many ancient teachings of Christ are held in the Vatican. You may be interested to look on YouTube at Josh Reeves Emerald Tablets, Sacred Science or Secrets In Plain View. These are teachings about LOA, positive mental attitude, karma and how it affects us and a healthy awareness of ALL things.

Knowledge is power, it's a fact.

"In the Nag Hammadi texts discovered in Egypt in 1945, considered older than the New Testament gospels we have a literal library of Gnostic writings. In A.D. 180 Irenaeus, Bishop Of Lyons, attacked independent thinking and all teaching relating to the Oneness of God and man. He believed that a spiritual consciousness and a

personal union with God would undermine the authority of the priests thus directed his wrath upon Gnosticism. A fixed dogma resulted and the shift in mind direction from within to without began – Emperor Theodosius made Christianity the sole and official religion in 395, the Institution assumed complete control over individual minds and humanity entered the thousand year period referred to as the Dark Ages.

The keys to spiritual enlightenment were held by the church leaders. Extreme penalties were enforced on those who interpreted the doctrines freely.

Ralph Waldo Emerson, Madame Blavatsky, Henry Olcott, Mary Baker Eddy, Alice Bailey, Edgar Cayce and Paramahansa Yogananda were main contributors to the New Age of spiritual unfoldment.

After more than 2,000 years of censoring, editing and translating the Golden Light Of The Fathers Assurance remains".

John Randolph Price.

Maybe if we could understand about positive and negative energies we could become more aware, and work towards improving our lives? Powerful thinking; that maybe, just maybe, by both accepting AND understanding that particular life lesson we could make life easier for ourselves rather than seeming to swim upriver. What life lessons have you learnt? Or are still learning? It is certainly true that our fears will indeed hold us back from our real souls' abilities and its wisdom.

We can consciously choose whether or not to bite into the drama of a situation or perhaps play the victim or be manipulated by one? Do you want to change? How much do you want to change?

"Who's Pulling Your Strings" By Harriet b. Braiker, Ph.D. and "The Game" By Neil Strauss are excellent reads.

NO effort then NO change. No change without pain. No pain then NO gain.

Changes take place on a daily basis. Moment to moment changes take place. Rome was not built in a day. If you want to continue playing the victim and thinking that you have NO control of your life then I'm afraid it's too late. This book is so full of positive healing energy and you have picked it up for a reason. That positive energy is certainly strong enough for you to use, to at least begin the process of positive change. It is now time for you to at least awaken to the possibility that's it's now out with the old and in with the new. Onwards and upwards, as each door closes and another opens, you may need to be ready to grab at the opportunities ahead, for just as sure as night follows day, as once that door is closed, new opportunities can & will come in very fast indeed. Get ready to "Rock & Roll"

Have you ever had *brain fog?* Felt like you just can't think straight? Some areas like busy cities have dense energies as they are filled with people with heavy thoughts of rushing around, pressures, strains and "Dog Eat Dog" mentality. I often walk up hillsides or mountains and feel lighter the higher I go. The reason is because the dense energy that is made up of peoples thoughts collects and weighs heavy in the earth's atmosphere. Thus, the higher you go the lighter the thought waves. That's why you often get clarity of thought when you stand on top of a mountain. Another excuse for me to go walking and hiking!

A local visit to the countryside can have quite an impact on us because the areas are rural so the thought patterns are clear and most people welcome you into the community. There is usually NO vandalism and gardens **are** clean and tidy. Heavy thought processes of inner cities do not serve humanity, nor do they serve the planet. Things are certainly changing for the better as more and more people are reconnecting and moving away from *fear based living. How much fear is in your life?*

Over time the numbers of those reconnecting will multiply more and more. This in turn will reduce the heavy vibrations/heavy energies and heavy thought patterns which will continue to thin the veil to which many of us are exposed and to which many are still blind. This cycle to thin the veil has started and cannot be stopped. There are planetary influences which are also affecting this thinning it is essential as our planet affects others in our galaxy.

The saying that "We Are All One" has far reaching consequences indeed.

THE INVITATION.

It doesn't interest me what you do for a living.

I want to know what you ache for,

and if you dare to dream of meeting your heart's longing.

It doesn't interest me how old you are.

I want to know if you will risk looking like a fool for love,

for your dream, for the adventure of being alive.

It doesn't interest me what planets are squaring your moon.

I want to know if you have touched the centre of your own sorrow;

*if you have been opened by life's betrayals or have become
shrivelled and closed from fear of further pain.*

I want to know if you can sit with pain, mine or your own,

without moving to hide it or fade it or fix it.

I want to know if you can be with joy, mine or your own,

*if you can dance with wildness and let the ecstasy fill you to the
tips of your fingers and toes without cautioning us to be careful,*

to be realistic, to remember the limitations of being human.

It doesn't interest me if the story you are telling me is true.

*I want to know if you can disappoint another to be true to
yourself;*

*if you can bear the accusation of betrayal and not betray your own
soul;*

if you can be faithless and therefore trustworthy.

*I want to know if you can see beauty, even when it's not pretty,
every day,*

and if you can source your own life from its presence.

I want to know if you can live with failure, yours and mine,

and still stand on the edge of the lake and shout to the silver of the full moon, "Yes!".

It doesn't interest me to know where you live or how much money you have.

I want to know if you can get up, after the night of grief and despair,

weary and bruised to the bone, and do what needs to be done to feed the children.

It doesn't interest me who you know or how you came to be here.

I want to know if you will stand in the centre of the fire with me and not shrink back.

It doesn't interest me where or what or with whom you have studied.

I want to know what sustains you, from the inside, when all else falls away.

I want to know if you can be alone with yourself

and if you truly like the company you keep in the empty moments.

Oriah Mountain Dreamer. "The Invitation."

A FOOL KEEPS TALKING WHILST THE WISE MAN IS QUIET.

"We need to find God, and he cannot be found in noise and restlessness.

God is the friend of silence. See how nature – trees, flowers, grass – grows in silence;

see the stars, the moon and the sun, how they move in silence….

we need silence to be able to touch souls."

Mother Theresa

I see this time and time again in my work. When a patient or client comes for any number of the therapies I offer in some way shape or form, they will always receive healing from me as well. In fact the house itself is full of magical healing energy so people feel relaxed straight away. This healing is simply a case of putting positive energy in and removing negative. Negative emotions and negative energy are removed or certainly begin to loosen. We can receive negative energies from being in a place where the energy is of a negative vibration.

My suggestion to you is to become more aware of how you feel in places; workplaces, public places, home environments, etc. If you are not comfortable there and perhaps others feel the same – they usually do, then that negative energy will affect your well-being on one or more levels. We are beings made up of light, sound and energy after all, so are obviously affected by the light(s), sounds and energies around us. Putting positive energy in the physical body when doing Reiki or any form of healing will of course move out the negative, similar to forcing a boil and then releasing the pus.

Recently I had a lady who not only looked younger throughout the session but who actually looked really different by the time I had finished the healing session. She had carried so many heavy emotions for years; she had worked without having a holiday for three years solid and was exhausted to the core. Not making time for herself had left her shattered and when she first walked in my treatment room her aura was dark and heavy. Needless to say, she was not just lighter and brighter by the time I had finished but she looked younger too! I forgot to mention that she felt amazing of course and has since gone on to change her life. New career and a new man in her life are her new beginnings as a result of letting go.

Old energies and old patterns of behaviour weigh us down, healing removes these and then, to be honest, absolutely anything can happen. Heal and peel the layers back and you certainly will find the sparkling *diamond* underneath. Its takes courage to look at our layers of trauma and pain accumulated over the years but the benefits far outweigh the fear. Always remember that fear is False Energy Appearing Real. To face and honour that fear acknowledge it and then it can be removed. Once removed you can and will live a completely different life.

When we watch children we learn so much from them. They are totally in the moment, happy and playful all the time until they are distracted or disturbed from whatever they are doing. I love watching my granddaughters and listening to their playfulness, telling stories and laughing to themselves. Through a variety of peer pressure, social and political pressures and belief systems such as religions; which instil fear into our beings then is it any wonder that we end up messed up? Often we lose sight of what is actually right and wrong for us, we forget to laugh and smile and look at life lightly with a sense of humour in all we do.

I meet many people who say that the amount of people that they know who are no longer having "real" conversations, instead they are talking about the weather, the political climate etc. How about conversations regarding how you really feel, honesty and integrity, conversations that flow easily instead of just chatting mindlessly and unnecessarily? People often feel they have to chat just for the sake of it. How comfortable are you with silence in your life? How much silence is there in your day to day life?

I actually love silence throughout the day and that to me is very important. I struggle when I go to another home where the TV/radio/computer is/are blasting away continuously. I have a friend who has a TV in each and every room of her house so that she feels she has company. Do you think she has a happy, contented and fulfilling life? More importantly, the question to you is this. How much silence is in your life? Are you comfortable and happy in your own skin and your own company? If not then what can you change? If you're not happy then how do you think other people feel around you whilst they are in your company?

Do you enjoy silence and can you actually be happy in that space? When did you last go into nature and just BE? When did you last just go into nature and merely listen to the trees, the birds and just watch the clouds in the sky? Is it any wonder that so many people are on anti-depressants and medications? It beggars belief to me that we often assume we are so far advanced as a society and that the ancient peoples were so backward, that technology has improved our lives.

TIME is your greatest asset; you can't buy it, make it longer nor get it back. When it's gone, it's gone for sure. It certainly is the most precious of commodities. Please think about how wisely you use your time. It is worth considering how much time you use wisely in a day, how much time you perhaps waste watching soaps, DVDs, programmes just for the sake of a distraction from your day. Coping mechanisms; such as OCD; obsessive compulsive disorder, cleaning, playing with your hair, picking skin, hair, nails, outdated habits etc. are merely distractions from reality.

Are you really aware of how many you have and how many you call upon each and every day? The question is this; are they serving you and now that you are aware of them are you ready and willing to change? You may wish to Google "Coping mechanisms"...most revealing.

Children live completely in the moment and neither in the past or the future. They are not thinking about anything other than that what they are doing at the time. They may be absorbed in colouring/painting/playing/running/dancing/etc. In our society, we then introduce peer pressure and advertising. They are led to believe that they must fit into a box at school. They must behave in certain ways and have to be thin, blonde, blue-eyed, etc. Yet we are all born as individuals and have our own identities.

We are not clones and not ONE of us is any better or worse than anyone else. Yet again, our society has its hierarchy. Lawyers are respected as are priests, doctors more so than nurses, managers are more respected than ordinary office staff for example. Yet common-sense shows that there are good and bad managers, doctors, arrogant consultants, etc. What matters to me, is the soul; nothing more and nothing less.

THE WAY OF TRUTH

"The intuitive mind is a sacred gift and the rational mind is a faithful servant.

We have created a society that honours the servant and has forgotten the gift."

Albert Einstein

It may seem very simple indeed but just imagine if we all thought for ourselves and that we all respected and treated each other with equal respect. How would our society change? Imagine if we encouraged mutual respect and it was earned in a beautiful, whole-hearted way. Imagine if we disregarded peer pressure in society as we know it.

Since my spiritual journey began, it's been truly amazing when I recall the lovely genuine people I have encountered along my path. My dear friend Dave Binder runs a spiritual meeting group called "Synchronicity". The first meeting I attended in Manchester was awesome and although I knew many people there, those I hadn't known previously just welcomed me with open arms. No-one asks what you do, neither are you judged or asked what car you drive, how big your house is etc. the simple reason is that no-one cares.

Real spiritual people want to get to know your soul, your essence and your vibration. They want to know what makes you tick, floats your boat, your passions and your well-being; in all aspects; body, mind and spirit. By asking you how you maintain that well-being, they share and we all learn maintenance of happiness from each other.

Usually the questions begin "With how did you get into this?" maybe a book, a friend, Reiki or illness, bereavements are common and then the conversation will flow naturally and getting to know someone with their soulfulness in mind is really breath taking and precious indeed. The end of mindless conversations!

Mark Abadi also founded a spiritual awareness group in South Manchester called "Holistic Manchester".

LIFE'S JOURNEY

"This is a great moment, when you see, however distant, the goal of your wandering.

The thing which has been living in your imagination suddenly becomes a part of the tangible world."

Freya Stark

"Life is a school of love,
and love is the only lesson
to be learned in this life."

We learn so very much from our relationships; relationships with others and with ourselves too: self-awareness. Relationships with friends, family and also our partners, all manner of relationships are reflections back to us. They lead us to more self-awareness and awakenings, which allow us to clear what is not serving us; if we choose to journey into the soul.

A big question is where do I choose to put my focus today, tomorrow and for my future?

I had had a life-coaching session almost two years ago. The first question I was asked was what is the most important thing in your life? My answer was forthcoming very quickly and said with a deliberation. It was unquestionably my soul. In my soul, lay all of what made me ME; my passions, my integrity, my joys, my memories, my being-ness and my one-ness, all whole heartedness and my LIFE.

My soul's journey had brought me self-awareness. All my past experiences have made me who I am today, the good, the bad and the ugly bits of me. Every day was and is a school day. We learn either willingly or not. That is a choice, either conscious or otherwise.

In my previous book "The Goldfish That Jumped" it's very clear that for years I had made my journey hard and painful. Self-awareness teaches us that through conscious choice and using wisdom and discernment daily, we can make the right decisions for us and those around us.

Each and every day, I make a conscious choice to honour and respect who I am. I can control no-one but myself. By leading through example and kindness I can allow others, if they wish to, to hopefully flower and grow. I feel I am here to encourage and empower others; in life, love and being-ness. In order to do this we need to be balanced, mentally, physically, spiritually and emotionally too.

If we live and respect ourselves then we respect others who in turn respect us. If we live with integrity then we too attract others who have integrity. By showing consideration to ourselves and others then we too are shown consideration. We need healthy barriers and boundaries to make this possible and to secure them for our future too.

Reiki allows us to do that and will show up all the cracks in your mirror which need attention in order that you can indeed arrive at your destination. By showing your imbalances you learn about balance. Reiki is really all about establishing balance; mentally, physically and spiritually.

Since my spiritual journey really began and I was trained in Reiki I have recognised that it is MY RESPONSIBILITY to take care of myself, my life and heal that which needs healing. I look at my reactions in each and every situation, taking self-awareness into account too. This usually means listening to *my* body and "Feeling" what is right for me at any given moment. LOA has taught me to look for Universal clues and follow up on whatsoever feels right, accepting that sometimes patience and tolerance are needed.

The more that I have healed myself and my life, family and relationship issues, the more I have cleared my emotional baggage as such. I am still a work in progress though I know my energy field is much clearer than that of most people.

Quantum physics means that the more I de-clutter my emotional stuff which adheres in the chakras, then, in turn obviously the more they are cleaned and the lighter they become. This affects my physical body which in turn feels lighter too and I then often look different and feel younger too. Obviously I have very few illnesses now although as you read on you will see that understanding the body leads to amazing results and a much better lifestyle too.

In this very simple way then the more I clean myself, my chakras and my aura become cleaner too. Healing is about putting positive energy into any given situation or being able to hold positive energy when healing another. The less emotional dross then of course, the more light energy I can hold which makes me a stronger and more capable healer and therapist too.

It's not always an easy journey and like anything else, taking personal responsibility for EVERYTHING in my life means that I am walking the walk and talking the talk. Some days are harder than others and yes if I'm really honest some days I would just love to live on a dessert island and be left alone. Don't we all? It may take me an hour, two or three hours, a day or two to come back from this dark place but…..just like an elastic band I spring back; eventually!

Learning to recognise what The Universe is showing me, what feels right has of course developed and deepened over the years. Self-awareness means that I know my body and I know when things are working and when they are simply out of balance. When this happens I have learnt through experience that if I do listen, I can have greater wisdom and understanding. On the other hand, if I do not, then the writing is on the wall, as the situation will fester and just as I was brought to a complete halt in 2002 with M.E/C.F.S, then it really is a "non-brainer." We all have choices and through mindfulness I am definitely more aware of each and every choice I make.

No-one will ever get it right all the time.

We only have the abilities to make the choices as we go along in life and rather than playing the victim, we should recognise the learning(s) from each and every situation.

My life, my work and my healing journey has brought many miracles to me in many ways. The publication of my first book "The Goldfish That Jumped" is true testimony to that fact. There are many more. If I had Mr Zuckerberg to thank for meeting Gary through Facebook, for the completion and publication of "The Goldfish That Jumped" then I owed my whole life to Mr Google. So many wonderful people have found me through the power of the web.

One such instance stands out above many others. Dave was a desperate father concerned for the welfare of his daughter, following the death of his wife. His daughter had not been coping well and he wondered if healing could help. The appointment was scheduled for the weekend and I was delighted to meet them both. She was such a bright and charming creature. We instantly connected and the bond I felt was very, very strong indeed. The healing energy surged through my hands, the heat was amazing. I felt so much sadness and grief from this little lady.

Healing transcends negative/imbalanced energies, changing them to positive instantly. She explained what she had been feeling and within minutes she was smiling and relaxed in my company. I was delighted as she relaxed more and more deeply through the session. We continued to chat easily; it felt as if we had known one another for years. I felt a powerful closeness with this young teenager. Her aura began to change and lighten, she was soon laughing too. The healing was definitely working its magic. There was quite a difference from the weary, tired, fraught & frightened child who had entered my room only minutes previously.

Following the beautiful healing, I reunited father and daughter. The change was incredibly noticeable and he smiled with relief. He asked my advice upon how frequently she should receive treatments. I explained, under the circumstances that I would like to see her weekly, at least for the time being and that we would reassess her progress after each treatment. She was duly booked in for a healing the following week. I was secretly delighted as I knew I would see both of them again soon.

As I watched them both walk down the garden path, the closeness between them was apparent. A loving father and his precious daughter: special memories that are still with me as I write now. I was privileged to watch as they chatted easily, walked closer to one another now that magical healing restoration threads were weaving a beautiful tapestry of family bonding. I love my work and experience great joy.

This was truly a very special moment indeed, one which I will treasure forever in both my heart and soul. I have learnt so much from these special people over the years and this has brought me my own understanding and healing process too.

This is just one of many examples of my healing work. I have had two patients with liver cancer and with the healing, their pain eased greatly and they both managed to pass peacefully at home rather than needing to be admitted to hospital in their final days. Both managed without morphine until their last 48 hours which was incredible. I remember crying when I heard of each of their deaths though I was honoured to be a part of their dying process.

Many more spring to mind and having looked through my notes whilst writing I feel overwhelmed. Sarah felt particularly lost as besides running a business and managing two young children she was tired and stressed. Family hurts had added to her pain and with just one healing she was transformed. Her batteries were recharged and she kept in touch, letting me know that she was beginning to heal her family relationships, enjoying quality time with her husband and changed her business which then became more profitable.

I use a combination of healing and hypnotherapy, besides Homeopathy wherever I need to do so. One such occasion springs to mind as a patient with a severe chest condition reported that her sputum load had reduced by half its usual amount after a session with me.

Groin pain and deep emotional hurt were causing Alfred to feel like life was really not worth living. His distress was painful to witness although obviously I maintain my professionalism. Seeing a young man at his wits end with life and all its ups and downs and watching him cry was testing indeed. After one session he felt amazing, he was pain free & began to look forward. He attended a workshop I was running and as his motivation grew he managed to get a job he loved and to make new friends. He has since become a great friend and watching him flower has been an honour.

Mac was stressed over some business decisions which had been hanging over him like lead weights. It was affecting his vitality, sleep, stress levels and in many other ways too. Following his healing he felt amazing and learnt to trust more in his intuition which impacted throughout his private and professional life to bring about many positive changes. He is now much more balanced and is more than happy to enjoy quality time with his family.

Elizabeth called to explain that she had a brain tumour and would I be able to help in any way. I was delighted to see her and felt the healing energy pulse very quickly through my hands. She was due to have surgery and explained that prior to her having the tumour; she took life and her family for granted. She actually said that she had learn so much from it that she had asked the surgeon to leave some in her head just so she would remain grateful for the lessons it had given her. She felt much calmer, balanced and centred upon leaving and her coordination had improved too.

Obviously some people stand out more than others and Isabel was a really happy Scouse lady who attended one of my workshops. She couldn't believe how much she learnt about herself after meeting me and was delighted to be in the presence of like-minded people. She really was a wonderful lady and touched my heart. In fact she was so inspired following that one workshop that she has since learnt Reiki with me and has progressed onto other holistic practices too.

She's had several miracles herself along the way and I'm delighted that she has now also become a dear friend. Watching her progress and certainly blossom and flower has been a great gift for me to witness. In the last year she moved house after her divorce was finalised, she moved careers too and is now engaged to her true soul companion.

Through the Reiki and her own journey of self-discovery she has learnt so much and in turn now inspires others with her story. No-one can argue that she is a changed woman who now stands in her own power and strength. I am blessed to know her and to share her life. I am looking forward to getting my hat on for the wedding too – you know who you are and you know I'll be there!

Sue had been introduced to me several years before she learnt Reiki when she had come for a reading with me. The Reiki training day was awesome and she shared the day with some other truly fabulous student healers. Throughout the day besides learning about Reiki, which is essentially about listening to the heart rather than the head, they are also taught about the aura, chakras, karma, karmic contracts and advanced Reiki besides many other teachings and they also have a group healing treatment too.

As she lay on the plinth we began the healing and she could feel the heat and the re-balancing taking place. It was amazing and a lovely experience too. Once we were healing her legs we all felt a very cold energy as though the energy was stuck. It took four of us 45 minutes to get that stuck energy to move but throughout the process she felt amazing. By the time she was healed she looked 15 years younger. She and each one of us were amazed and delighted too. She and her husband had wanted to move to their dream house for years. They always felt that something was holding them back. Within weeks of the healing, they moved and have been incredibly happy there ever since.

Another such miracle day was when Julie came for her Reiki training day on crutches as she had damaged her tendons. By lunchtime she walked unaided though limping through the day. She left late afternoon, without her crutches and had to come back to collect them later after her husband had picked her up. Needless to say the limp had disappeared and she certainly looked ten years younger.

I love these miracles and another immediately springs to mind when I treated a lady who had had an awful life of abuse from her husband. The pain and suffering was very evident and coping with the intense emotions over the years had left her with severe digestive disorders, sleep problems and several other symptoms. Her progress was amazing as she began to understand herself more and her health issues disappeared, she moved house and began to sort out her emotional issues now that she has found the courage to tackle long-outstanding problems.

She and her family are very close friends indeed now and I have treated many friends of theirs too, all with fabulous results. One such lady stands out. Gemma had a new baby who just seemed unsettled most of the time. He didn't sleep and she was concerned for his welfare. Following one healing he slept through the night and his grumpiness disappeared. I was delighted for the whole family as they were all upset by his sad nature at such a young age. He is now a delightful little boy and a very happy one too.

Elizabeth was an older lady who had family issues and was most definitely being affected by karma. She hadn't seen her grandchildren and was obviously upset at life's ups and downs. Within weeks of receiving a healing from me they were reconciled. I have had several situations like this and it would be impossible to list them all. Reiki seems to assist in resolving and letting go of karma and to be honest most people do begin to get on better with their friends and families, living more enriched, fulfilling lives.

Alison was in a marriage where her husband worked about 70 hours a week. When he was at home at the weekend he often wanted to be out with the boys playing golf and despite her having explained *that she wanted and in fact needed quality time with him*, nothing ever changed. She became depressed and was greatly saddened by his lack of response to her. Following Reiki she found the courage as the marriage deteriorated to move out of the marital home and make a new life for herself. She is now happier than ever before and again watching her blossom has been a huge honour. She has flourished in her new life and I think of her often on her new journey.

Sue was a burnt out nurse, tired and frazzled. She had only known conventional medicine but following her friends' suggestion made an appointment to see me, though of course was quite sceptical. As I began the healing she couldn't believe the heat from my hands, her features softened and she felt uplifted and relaxed. She has kept in touch to say that she still feels amazing & has come off her antidepressants. Needless to say I was thoroughly delighted.

Anita too was a burnt out nurse. She had been married for years and was stuck in a rut. Following a recommendation she called to ask if I would teach her Reiki. She too is now a dear friend and reconnected to her artistic aspects. She has painted some beautiful pictures and is thriving. Her children and husband now also get the benefit of her happiness and EVERYONE has noticed the difference in her.

I see her on a regular basis and the more I have empowered her, so the more in turn she has empowered me too. We often share our spiritual experiences and as one reaches for the phone to call the other, the other has already started dialling! Some friendships are meant to last lifetimes and we both KNOW that this is one of them. Recently she treated me to a spiritual day out at Gorton Monastery in Manchester as a birthday treat. This story will be uncovered later although for now let's just say that I am forever grateful to her and for her kindness.

Chronic fatigue syndrome is very restricting and having had it I can sympathise with anyone who explains their frustrations and upset at the illness. Sophie had suffered for years and came on recommendation. She was ready to try anything as all else had failed. Soon she was converted and laughing and smiling too from ear to ear. It was a delight to see the difference and using both healing and Homeopathy she can now FULLY embrace life again.

Isabel called me to enquire about my skills as she was covered from head to toe in eczema. Her pain was intense and she was fed up and listless. Through the healing the redness began to fade and she couldn't believe it as her pain eased. She was so impressed she too learnt Reiki and now works with others spreading the word.

Bernie was a beautiful lady who had lived her life pleasing others. She was tired and worn-out having divorced her controlling husband. After receiving healing and attending a workshop her confidence and self-awareness grew. She was a changed woman and began to understand the processes and conditioning from childhood which had led to destructive patterns of behaviour within her current life. She is now finding the courage to change and embrace life.

Craig was tired and worn out with life. He worked long, hard hours for little reward and felt unappreciated. His family life was suffering and he was desperate to find a solution. Through the healing we chatted easily and discussed possible changes he could make for the better. He kept in touch for months after re-affirming that the progress was definitely onwards and upwards. He is a definite example of the power of our own choices and willingness to make them in a positive, wholehearted manner. I'm so glad to have helped him on his journey.

I often see people who are burnt out and frazzled. They often say that they don't cry nor show emotion. This is a natural part of life and crying a natural outlet for suppressed emotions. Indeed, in Homeopathy one of the important questions we ask is that how do patients feel about crying. Often a patient will reply they never cry, yet, looking at their pathology and symptoms it really is obvious that they are holding on to many emotions.

Frequently those who say they never cry begin to let go of the tears whilst they are with me. It's an honour and I know the benefit to them. Their whole bodies begin to relax as the physical vessel lets go and is given expression and a voice. Many come to mind as I am writing this and it really does make such a difference to people when they allow their emotion to surface.

One such lady comes to mind and as she began to cry she explained that her husband was controlling her with belittling and critical comments. Her story was indeed a very sad one and I was deeply moved. She began to cry for the first time in years and the tears flowed easily as she knew she was in a safe space to share. She stated that she had no idea about holistic medicine and how important it was to look at emotional, spiritual, mental and physical well-being together.

The difference in her is remarkable to this day and when I explained to her gently that *she* was allowing her husband to talk to her inappropriately and that until *she stood in her ground* he would continue. I asked if she would allow anyone else to behave like this with her. The look of realisation on her face was truly fabulous and quite "a light-bulb moment" as she clearly and assertively said "NO". At the same time she did recognise the love they shared and would concentrate on that whilst resolutions were found.

Katie was riddled with rheumatoid arthritis and pain. She too had had a troubled marriage and a controlling husband. As I started the healing she relaxed and stated the pain had lessened and in some areas disappeared. She was truly amazed. She came for healing a fortnight later and again the results were impressive. Within weeks she found the courage to separate from her husband and is now a completely different woman. She is learning about herself and enjoying "BE –ing". She is much happier now and lives a whole-hearted life. Despite losing family members through death following the Reiki and my teachings, she has come to understand death as merely a transition. The soul goes on; it just changes its form.

ROCKING WITH THE DIAMOND

With real awareness we can make our lives into something."

Mansukh Patel

The next part of the book is about my learnings and growth over the years since my first baby: "The Goldfish That Jumped" came into the world. I hope that once again, the book inspires you, just as did number one and I hope that it brings both laughter and a light-ness to your life too.

- THE DIAMOND

"The diamond is a symbol of purity. Its pure white light can help you to bring your life into a cohesive whole. It bonds relationships, bringing love and clarity into a partnership. It is seen as a sign of commitment and fidelity. Diamond has been a symbol of wealth for thousands of years and is one of the stones of manifestation, attracting abundance. The larger the diamond then more abundance there is. A large diamond is also excellent for blocking geopathic or electro-magnetic stress and protection against cell phones.

Diamond is an amplifier for energy. It is one of the few stones that never needs recharging. It increases the energy of whatever it comes into contact with and is very effective when used with other crystals for healing as it enhances their power. However it can increase negative energy as well as positive.

On a subtle level it fills holes in the aura, re-energising it. Psychologically the qualities that diamond imparts include fearlessness, invincibility and fortitude. However the merciless light of diamond will pinpoint anything that is negative and requires transformation. Diamond clears emotional and mental pain, reduces fear and brings about new beginnings. It is a highly creative stone stimulating imagination and inventiveness. Mentally diamond provides a link between the intellect and the Higher mind. It brings clarity of mind and aids enlightenment at a spiritual level. Diamond cleanses the aura of anything shrouding the person of inner light, allowing the soul light to shine out. It reminds you of your souls' aspirations and aids spiritual evolution. It activates the crown chakra, linking it to divine light".

Judy Hall "The Crystal Bible".

106

THE DIAMOND HOUSE

"Humility is our awareness of
Our dependence on a vast Intelligence"

My first encounter with the diamond came at the beginning of June 2012. I received a phone call from a lady who requested an appointment with me. Instinctively, I knew her voice and felt like I knew her very well, although, as with many people previously, I knew that I had not known her in this lifetime. As we chatted, I explained that I felt I knew her and she agreed that she felt the same. My intuition was confirmed; we definitely knew one another from a previous life.

I asked her where & how she had come across my number. "Ahh well that's another story," she said. "I was on a train from London and the girl in the other compartment was saying how she'd had a reading with you and was reading your book. I just **KNEW** I had to see you!"

Her need to see me was urgent, although I was due to travel to Germany within the coming days, so, we scheduled our meeting for the 8th June. I was excited to my core to meet her and although I was certainly looking forward to visiting Germany, I kept thinking of this lady and knew that when we actually psychically met it would be amazing!

The seminar in Germany was superb and I had loved each and every minute. Arriving back in the UK I had something else to look forward to now. She was booked in to see me that afternoon and I felt like a child in a favourite sweetie shop! My soul was on fire and excitement ran through each and every cell in my body.

She arrived in perfect time and what a reunion it was. We had definitely known one another and standing in my hallway, we both knew without a doubt. I have met many people on this spiritual journey who, like me are so powerfully aware of their origins/past lives/ soul aspects. On many occasions we have not needed to speak – rather we spoke through the heart and soul. This meeting was certainly incredibly powerful.

The reading was amazing and she confirmed most of my "knowings." I saw a beautiful, detached house with a pool by a lakeside which I knew to be Lake Geneva in Switzerland. Despite having an Australian accent she had lived in many locations across the world. In the reading I could also see myself staying with her and knew that it would be that summer! She knew the house as it belonged to a friend of hers. My guides advised me to call the house **"The Diamond House."** Bizarre indeed although the story would unfold and reveal itself.

We chatted for three hours that day! Just like old friends who had known one another forever. My soul was on fire and we promised to keep in touch. The following few weeks were difficult for me on a personal level and she supported me through a huge transition. My soul, body and mind were exhausted and I needed a break from life. The Universe once again came up trumps.

The friend who owned "The Diamond House" was selling it. Beth had been asked to stay there whilst it was sold as the owner worked away. She called me to ask if I would like to stay there with her and come over to Switzerland for a short break? Of course I did!!! I had already packed my case in my mind before I got off the phone. At the time, another very dear friend had split from her husband and she asked if she too could come along.

My guides told me clearly that I needed to be there between the 5-10th of August and it was ESSENTIAL that I be there on the 8th. A dear friend called one day quite by chance, as I had not seen him for about two years. He needed a healing and as we caught up on one another's lives, I explained that I was off to Geneva the following day. I told him that my guides had advised that I needed to be there on the 8th. "Do you know why?" he asked. "Nope, you know me; I just go with the flow and do as requested." "It's the Lion Gateway" he replied and explained that many planetary influences would be bringing energies to the Earth in order that more and more people would re-connect and re-awaken. As we had worked together previously doing much earth healing, he knew my abilities and confirmed that my reason for going was indeed to anchor these energies into the planet. "Good excuse for a holiday to Switzerland then" I replied!

We boarded the plane and were incredibly excited. Beth collected us from the airport and arrived in an open topped sports car as we drove like "Thelma, Louise and A.N.Other" across Geneva and then into France. We were not at this point staying in "The Diamond House" although we were due to visit there later in the week. In fact, we realised soon enough, that we actually got an even better deal!

Her dear friend had gone on holiday and asked her to house sit the pets. As we drove through the countryside and began to ascend into the mountains the views were truly breath-taking. WOW. I was definitely meant to be here. The house where we were staying looked like a few terraced houses stuck together. Very picturesque and in fact it had once been a restaurant.

Once inside I was utterly speechless. The close attention to detail and quality of the interior design were truly outstanding. However, we were only on the ground floor. The views from the rear of the house opened onto Lake Geneva itself and I actually cried with sheer delight. There was a huge garden and the whole area was so stunning. Mont Blanc was directly across and I could feel its power. To the right I could see the famous fountain in the lake too.

As we went upstairs I was shown to the Master bedroom. I needed to take a breath and pinch myself. A huge king-size bed, en-suite bathroom to die for and.....not only that, patio doors that opened onto my own veranda and an even better view over the said lake and mountains. There was no artificial lighting up here, so I knew the views in the evening would be well and truly out of this world.

The feeling that I had died and gone to heaven does this NO justice at all. Absolute joy, bliss and ecstasy come close....! We unpacked and Beth suggested that we travel to the next town for food and supplies. Once again this magical place inspired my soul and was recharging my weary body. We were pet sitting half a zoo and I opted to care for the dog "Tango." He was an amazing golden Labrador that I had already fallen in love with and connected to on a very deep spiritual level. There was obviously a bond between us and thus it was my job to walk him twice a day.

Being in the Swiss mountains was truly even more beautiful than any holiday brochure can ever justify. As an earth healer and so sensitive to energies I was in my element. The energy here was of such a high vibration indeed. As usual I just followed my nose and had come across a lovely footpath which opened out into the Alps. Tango was happy and I was overcome with peace and a deep feeling of harmony. I loved this place and had felt so settled immediately that I just knew it was right.

Over the coming days, we travelled to various places. One such place was a chapel in the middle of nowhere. The energies there were particularly outstanding; as I felt the healing surge through me, wherever we walked, despite the fact that there was no wind, the trees moved in our presence. There were people looking on in amazement, so we just smiled across at them and carried on healing the whole area. This was just one of many miracles that week.

We were all conscious of the importance of the 8th which was looming fast. We had all intuited that we should travel by the lake, if not on it, via a cruiser. We had fallen in love with The Freddie Mercury statue and the town of Montreux, so that seemed an ideal place to visit that day. From there you can see a huge distance along the Lake so it would be a great vantage point to deliver and rebalance any healing energies.

The night before I struggled to sleep as I was so excited, wondering what the following day would bring. As I lay there looking out at the stars and the mountain tops, I sent invisible prayers to my beloved family. I wished they were here to share this awesomeness. I prayed that I would fulfil my task(s) the following day too. As I drifted off to sleep, a deep peace came upon me and I slept deeply and soundly under the stars which shone through the patio windows. It's been years since I have drawn curtains/blinds at night. I love the open evening sky and the Universal connection when looking above.

Train travel seemed easiest the next day and we were all happy to just BE. Arriving in Montreux we were ready for some lunch and as usual in my crappy French accent I ordered a "chocolate cat" rather than a hot chocolate! As the poor waiter looked dumbfounded Beth came to my rescue!

After lunch we found a most delightful and spectacular crystal shop. I purchased a clear quartz Merkaba and although I was delighted with it, there was a huge crystal Merkaba which held a price tag of over £3,000 that I was desperate to hold!!!

The energies could certainly be felt that day and I was keeping in touch with healers in the UK who were assisting too. We knew we had to be on a boat and travelled across to Lausanne that afternoon. As we pulled into the open water, the merkaba vibrated so violently in my hand I was scared I might lose it.

It was an altogether memorable day for many reasons and those memories are close to my heart now as I write. Switzerland holds incredible knowledge and wisdom, power and majesty. It's a place that feels like a part of my being. I would return: of that I was sure. For now though, we had just one full day left before our return to the UK. Mixed emotions fell over all three of us, although we all knew that our friendship was cemented forever.

MIRACLES

"Service is a sign of our active connection to Life"

Over the last few years I have received many patients and client recommendations from Oscar, a guy whom I had never met, that also worked locally in Penwortham. Despite not having met me, he had heard of my reputation and recommended a vast number of people with a wide variety of pathologies and complaints to see me.

I am very aware of my well-earned reputation and had NEVER recommended him to anyone as I hadn't met him and was not therefore sure of his quality of workmanship. I guard my reputation fiercely, as it has only been earned through hard work and integrity. My logic is that I will only recommend the Crème de La Crème, as someone may receive a less than satisfactory service from someone else and thus it may rub off on me!

One such recommendation stands out for many reasons. James had been suffering with M.E./C.F.S for over eight years and despite having tried every therapy and therapist in the area, had found either NO relief, or very little.

One day whilst receiving a treatment from Oscar he remembers clearly that Oscar mentioned he ought to come and see me for a professional consultation. He duly made the appointment and after just ONE treatment huge improvements were noted. He was amazed and duly re-booked. In fact, over the coming weeks he was so inspired that he trained as a Reiki healer with me. He had since been treated by Oscar and he honestly could not recall recommending me!

Unbeknown to me, James had purchased "The Goldfish That Jumped" from WHSmiths and had started to recommend the book to many people. One such person, one of his closest friends being Peter Sanderson who had ordered his copy and was reading it in Switzerland! Once more the miracles would unfold further. Peter was so impressed with the book and the difference in James that he contacted me via email. He was English and had actually grown up in Preston before moving over to live in Switzerland.

The communication was so positive and over the following weeks he explained that he would love to meet me whilst in sunny Lancashire! I was so stunned. Not only did he want to meet me, he wanted to train as a Reiki healer! I was so excited; not only to meet him, but also to teach and inspire him in a way that would no doubt change his life as it had done with hundreds of others too.

The day he walked down the path to my home, I will remember fondly forever. Once again we knew that we knew one another. The day passed incredibly quickly and he made it clear that he wanted to do Reiki Two ASAP. He was a brilliant and very motivated student and I was in no doubt that he would use this magic gift regularly.

Indeed, over the coming weeks and months our friendship deepened as we shared our spiritual experiences. In fact, he too recommended me to numerous people; one in particular stands out amongst the rest. Dawn came for a reading and healing just over two years ago and we instantly connected or rather re-connected. What a truly beautiful soul indeed. Our friendship grew and grew and she too trained in Reiki and the recommendations kept on coming.

During this time I still hadn't met Oscar.....that would unfold later. I have so much to thank him for. As the story unfolded the recommendations kept flooding in.

My Swiss miracles kept unfolding, as I was invited to work with a family several months later in November 2012. It was amazing and I was ready for more adventure too; and, this time actually getting paid for being in Heaven too! The villa I was staying in was just outside Montreux itself and I was experiencing even more magic daily.

My love of Switzerland was growing more and more and again in November 2013, Peter asked if I would like to travel over there and promised that he would organise my clients and appointments. He would also pay for my ticket too! "Non-brainer, count me in" I agreed as tears of joy streamed down my face. Once again the whole experience was truly fabulous and I had yet another five days of bliss and being in a position to help and assist others, whilst developing and expanding friendships.

The miracles were to unfold and several stand out more than others, although each and every day was a marvel. The first full day after I arrived, Peter and Beth had organised lunch for us right by the side of the lake in a fabulous restaurant with many other healers. There were approximately 10 of us in total and it was a day that I will never forget.

Being introduced to so many and being welcomed with open arms was truly humbling too. One lady I was introduced to had one of the largest and most clear energy fields that I have ever seen, Carolina invited us to her group meditation, which was to take place a couple of days later. It would be held on the floating platform on the lake itself and I "knew" Peter and I had to be there.

We arrived early and met up with some friends. Just before the main group gathered a French chap approached me. He began to chat in French and although my French is okay, it was certainly lacking as he continued...it was obvious that he "knew," he "knew" me, or certainly knew my energy signature. Peter's French is obviously much better than mine, although he too struggled. Language can be a good and bad thing.....we were all mutually aware that there was a huge knowing between us and we merely accepted that fact and, as all great healers do, we had a group hug!

The healing circle gathered and there were approximately 40 of us sending healing to Mother Earth. We had notified other groups across the world and we were all allowing our energies to mingle to share and spread a lighter vibration across the planet and to those in positions of power. It was so amazing to be a part of all this! Then the best part happened...Carolina who had organised the event called me over and asked me to run half of the meditation with her too! What an opportunity indeed! Peter was on the other side of the circle looking over in bewilderment at me as she announced in French what her plans were and then explained it in English. She had promised to translate for me when my turn came!

It was amazing and touching; people from all over the world, many different nationalities and all backgrounds with a common theme of health and well-being for the planet. I was truly blessed and touched. To be honest, it was bloody freezing on the open platform and we were all cold after having been sat around for almost an hour. When my turn came I was inspired to send a healing prayer and asked everyone to stand as I knew it would warm us. I also asked her to translate my words, as I suggested that we sing "Shima, Shima," which simply means love and is a Native American Indian chant. I began to sing and Peters face from across the platform was a really picture indeed! (Deva Premal and Miten have a most beautiful version of this. It really is an absolute favourite of mine).

As the time approached for the meditation to close, we all stood in silence for a minute before we said our goodbyes. The French chap approached me and hugged me tightly, and, despite the language barrier, it was obvious that he had loved each and every minute, as had many of the others.

Peter eventually managed to locate me and said "Bloody Hell, not only are you a great healer, psychic and many other things, but blimey you've certainly got an amazing voice for singing too. You kept that one close to your chest didn't you!"

So, as you can see I have an awful lot to thank Oscar for!

"To make profound changes in your life, you need either inspiration or desperation."

Anthony Robbins.

MOVING TO NEW DIMENSIONS

"Desperation is the raw material of drastic change.
Only those who can leave behind everything they have believed in,
can hope to escape."

William S. Burroughs.

From my very first encounter with spirituality, especially having learnt Reiki, I continued to work on my inner self, releasing old hurts and conditioned patterns of behaviour which no longer served me. I was determined to become more soulful, as I let go of frustrations, hurts and anger, old belief systems, conditioned patterns of behaviours and took a very deep look at ALL the things that created a disharmony in my life.

These create blocks and/or barriers to our being-ness. They are held in all or some of the chakras and as the chakras hold light and energy, then these negative feelings cause the chakras to slow down and become weighted with *heavy emotions*. I recognised those that were no longer serving me and that needed to be released, no matter how painful that release might be when I would look deeper; through either regression/hypnotherapy or meditation.

This is ABSOLUTE personal responsibility and it takes a great deal of courage and commitment to stay on the spiritual path. For me the fact that I am a therapist and spiritual teacher, mean that I have NO right whatsoever to teach and heal, if I do not practice what I preach and walk on that path.

There are always aspects of ourselves from which we can learn by looking at our anger and unresolved emotions. This may well cause us pain, as we uncover that maybe we too had something to do with an unfortunate situation such as a divorce. Nothing is ever just one person's fault, even if we have been battered or harmed emotionally in a marriage/long-term relationship, the responsibility is ours, we had allowed it in the first place through lack of confidence, self-esteem, barriers and boundaries, etc.

Often it is from these dark nights of the soul, that we learn to find ourselves again. Looking back at your painful experiences, it may just be worth getting a sheet of paper and writing down the person's name and or the situation at the top and then focusing on the learnings.

What did you learn from the breakdown/situation? What responsibilities did you have in the situations? What would you certainly do differently if you had your time over? Can you forgive them? Can you forgive yourself?

We might learn **how not to be** in a given situation, we learn **what we don't want** for the next relationship too. We might actually learn what we do want and also *learn **assertion**.* This is a brilliant exercise to do if we still blame our parents for their roles in our lives. I see patients and clients in their 50's and 60's, who have not forgiven & thus haven't moved on and are stuck in the past. They even sound like a stuck record when they tell me their stories.

The question is this. **Do you have a story?** If so, is it serving you? How long have you been stuck in that story? Perhaps the bigger question is this. How much longer do you want to be stuck there? How do you propose to come away from that story? Reiki,

Homeopathy, reflexology and so many such therapies will certainly help and assist you in many more ways than you think.

I've had so many patients and clients leave my home after a session looking ten years younger. Heavy emotions weigh us down as they weigh down the chakras. Maybe it's time for you to let go? Imagine how that would feel? Are you ready to take the plunge and take personal responsibility for your life?

HEAD TO HEART

"The more we fall in love with truth
the more our intelligence increases"

My mission was to clear my inner space, get out of my head space into my heart space, therefore allowing my soul to blossom. This, in turn, would allow the rose petals of the heart to unfold and as the rose opened, it would then allow the light and the love of life direct from Our Creator to flow in. Inside the rose, the stamens hold the colourful pollen; the sweetness of life and that which the butterflies taste when they approach. This is the true Sufi teaching of pure heart-centred living.

Throughout all the years that I have been in business I have always had a rose on my business literature. Now it is very clear why that has always been uppermost in their design.

I was beginning to understand that I held the sweetness of life in myself and it was my responsibility to find it – no-one else's. We find love inside ourselves by de-cluttering all the things that have deadened our inner child, our laughter and our innocence.

There is a spiritual school of thought that for all the decisions we make daily, we need to consider the aspect of the inner child, the adult we are today and also the aspect of us that is the wise crone/sage/elder. How different would the world be if we all considered these aspects of ourselves daily?

Life is full of synchronicities. I am a very determined lady and when I set my mind to something I usually achieve the target. Being self-aware I knew that despite aiming for abundance, I was still just managing financially and I desperately wanted this to change in order that I would have more time and more energy without squandering it worrying about my bank balance and paying bills. I was between a rock and a hard place as I felt I was chasing my tail. I was much happier within myself and my work; though felt that financial freedom was a goal which I would set for myself.

I always ask The Universe for help and meditated to seek the answers. A dear friend from my days as a student of Homeopathy came to mind, so I contacted her whilst focusing on abundance. We duly agreed to meet and she suggested that we rendezvous in Southport. A friend of hers, whom she wanted me to meet, had a shop there and many of his customers were interested in Law Of Attraction. So she suggested it would be a great idea for me to discuss business ideas and moving forward towards wealth and prosperity with like-minded souls.

It was almost the end of the year and at Christmas things can be tight financially so I really wanted to get this situation nailed; once and for all. Many of us who have worked on personal development know that once we wish to move forward and begin to set intentions and goals, we must follow the trail of breadcrumbs....my trail was about to take a huge leap forward!

The people I met that day really inspired me and we are all great friends to this day. Many were part of a Law Of Attraction meet up group who attended regular meetings in Manchester. Yet another Manchester link was about to be added to the chain. It certainly felt right for me to attend with them and I had agreed to do the driving – as long as they directed me as, at that time, my knowledge of driving through central Manchester was not existent.

I felt an excitement in my soul and was really looking forward to meeting yet more like-minded people. Sitting amongst them was blissful and talking about energies made me feel really at home within the group. I was keen to listen rather than partake as Ben introduced himself and explained how and when he had come across Law Of Attraction and indeed how it had changed his life.

As he told his very personal story, it was music to my ears and invited lots of others to explain their stories too. He later played a recording from Jerry and Esther Hicks which I loved.

Looking around the room I recognised a guy whom I had met several years earlier whilst I had run a workshop with a dear friend. Paul Ryder had offered me a place on his life-coaching course three years earlier although at the time I had turned it down...mainly as I did not know what it was!

Paul told his story and we chatted briefly about how we were doing, etc. The Universe works in mysterious ways and we agreed to catch up sooner rather than later; especially as we are members of similar spiritual groups.

Over the years my fear of Manchester has eased. You may recall from reading book one that Julie Silver introduced me to many spiritual people in the city which assisted this greatly; especially when I gained such a huge client base that I was travelling regularly across the area. However, I never felt comfortable travelling here alone nor on the train. I feared many things, getting lost, the Unknown and the Greater Unknown? To be honest there was NO reason I could place to explain these unreasonable feelings and emotions. It was simply that I had an incredible fear of the place.

Thus, although many friends had mentioned the Manchester Christmas markets and I had so wanted to attend for over two years, I had no courage to take the leap of faith and travel alone to seek them out. I had asked friends and up to this time, had never managed to visit them. Imagine my surprise when we left the Quaker House building to find that they were directly across from us outside the Town Hall. I was so pleased I felt that I could cry. None of us were in a rush to get home and so we all opted to take a look around. I was like a child in a Sweetie shop. The lights, the music, the smells, the hustle and bustle, not to mention the coconut macaroons filled me with glee!

As we fought our way through the crowds I was so pleased and delighted that I felt I could pop. We laughed, danced and sang until early evening. I had truly had an amazing evening with friends and succeeded in achieving another goal, which I hadn't even expected.

The story was about to unfold further. Over the coming weeks and a few more meetings I became very friendly with Ben who asked me on to his Radio show. He had just written his book and asked my advice, we simply knew, we knew one another. Ben and I conversed through Facebook and text messages frequently and a lovely friendship developed. He was moving home and asked me to come along. I duly agreed of course as it felt so right. I arrived and his lovely family were there along with some of the people I had met at his meetings. We all chatted easily and I was delighted that he was so settled here.

I had travelled over an hour so explained that I wouldn't be staying long and that I had a busy day the following day with granddaughters, etc. More and more folks arrived and the flat was getting cramped. I turned to use the bathroom when who should be there but Paul Ryder! I had seen him talk several weeks earlier and, as we passed in the hall way my spirit guides told me quite sternly to make an appointment to visit him on a professional level.

I chatted to Paul briefly and explained I would like to see him on a professional level. He suggested that I message him through Facebook and we would take it from there. As I said my goodbyes and wished everyone well, I was filled with a sense of knowing that something was about to unfold in the not too distant future. That warm feeling of knowing I was moving on was with me all that evening and throughout the weekend.

HIDDEN TREASURES

"The sign of the faithless is that he is lost
in the horizons.

The sign of the one with faith
is that the horizons are lost within him."

Muhammad Iqbal

I remember very clearly that first appointment with Paul. Driving to Manchester alone, in and of itself was a huge step for me and managing to find a nearby car park. I had set off early, so that I would have adequate time should traffic be heavy etc. It was a very smooth run thanks to Mr Sat Nav and I arrived early enough to find a wonderful café. It was right on the next corner to Paul's office, so I was delighted that I had somewhere cosy to sit and JUST BE, whilst I waited for my appointment time. It just so happens that this café served the most amazing hot chocolate....just confirming that I was absolutely meant to be here.

Sitting across from Paul several minutes later he asked why I was here. "Oh, its very simple really" I explained, "My guides told me to make an appointment with you and we kept meeting so often, that I know you have, in some way, shape or form, the ability to help me through the rest of my life." Please note that at this time I had NO idea what life-coaching was about in any way, shape or form!

Paul's face was a picture. "So basically you're unsure why you're here." "Yes indeed" I added. "Okay, then so really you don't know why you're here?" he quizzed me. I agreed and he just smiled saying "Okay let's just run with this then and see where it takes us."

I was happy with that and when he asked me to explain my life story I told him that as a light-worker I was constantly healing and peeling my issues away and letting them go. I understood them more and became more self-aware of who I was, how certain situations had influenced me and by using Law Of Attraction just what I wanted to achieve. I continued to explain that I was happily single, loved my life, family, friendships, work though would love abundance in order to gain financial freedom and travel across the world and maybe find a soul companion.

As I continued, I also explained that though single and still learning about me and self-love, I would also love to have a long-term loving and fulfilling relationship too. I had recently met someone and we were texting on a regular basis, although there was very little spoken word. We had met a few times and I was really taken with this chap, who was a healer and we had both known when we met, that we both knew one another from previous times. The connection was strong, although I was becoming frustrated that he had made many promises to come over to Preston and spend quality time with me and my family. I was becoming disillusioned with it all and fed up with empty promises.

Paul asked me to go through my relationship history and childhood too. I relayed a very quick summary and within a few minutes he just stated "ummm, so lots of power and control then in all your previous relationships and certainly plenty with the present texts?"

I was completely taken aback, as the volume and weight of what he had just said hit me like a ten ton truck! My illusions that this potential "relationship" was going anywhere faded into the misty depths of a vast ocean of nothingness! Bloody Hell I thought as I realised another red herring was playing out his tricks in my life. Would I ever find a soul companion?

Paul just held my space whilst I blubbed and the realisations sank in to my awareness. I was saddened by this and as we chatted, he asked me to imagine that said chap was sat in the chair across from me and I could tell him how inappropriate he had been towards me in his actions and empty promises. Expectations, attachments and conditions!

I poured out my frustrations at the empty chair and felt marvellous afterwards! Paul and I devised a plan to allow natural closure to the texts. I booked in for another session, upbeat about moving on in my life, and letting go of the past by understanding it more thoroughly than I had done previously.

The following day more promises were made to meet and this time I failed to reply and fuel his controlling issues. After three unanswered texts he asked if I was ok to which I replied "NO" by text of course. Now that I could see through the illusion, it was as if my rose coloured glasses were well and truly off! He suggested we chat rather than text the following morning and although I doubted he would call at all, agreed.

The following day the weather was quite lovely and my guides told me to walk in the local country park where I had had my very first experience of déjà vu several years earlier. They told me that I would see a kingfisher and that it would indeed be a sign that all was well. I was a little surprised although I knew through experience that they are always right. Who was I to argue anyways?

Amazingly he called! I spoke my truth coolly and calmly and explained that he was leading me up the garden path. The conversation was simple and I asked him *not* to contact me again. He was obviously surprised by my response, although he could tell by my tonality that I was not prepared to be challenged. Amazing. Simply amazing.

I was upset and to be honest shed some tears, although luckily very few folks were around as it was early morning. I just wandered around and wondered whether or not I would actually see a kingfisher since I had never seen one here before, nor had I ever heard my friends mention that they had ever seen one here either. I continued to walk down towards the river and something just made me glance to my left. There it was.....just sitting in the tree. It stayed there for several minutes which is extremely unusual for them, as usually they are so fast in their task to fish and return to their homes. Tears rolled down my face as I stood there in awe and wonder. It wasn't just the sight of this beauty but also the confirmation from The Universe that all was indeed well.

Over the coming months, which would roll into years, Paul was not just my life-coach; he was a dear friend & dependable rock. Lifting off so many of the emotional layers meant that I was now in fact in my Pandora's Box; lifting off the deepest, painful and most horrible of the emotional blockages which were blocking me from embracing my deepest desires for love, freedom, peace and success.

Throughout the previous two years I trained as a life-coach with him and was noticing many miracles unfolding in my life.

MIRACLES AND LEARNINGS

"Life is like a boomerang and you always get back exactly what you throw out."

Paul Chek

I was still training as a life-coach, now training in the advanced life-coaching. I spoke to Paul about my over-whelming feelings of fear of being in the public eye, not knowing where they had originated. It was strange because I really loved doing the presentations and yet although I felt ready for change, I also felt a terror in some level. The Universe loves a void and thus, the more I released old hurts, behaviours and emotions the more I created space for the new. The story was about to unfold.....

Since my early childhood, without realising that I was a healer then and without training, I have had an *inner knowing* about how to clear spirits/souls back to Source. They have missed their first opportunity, so I merely offer them another opportunity to return to Source or Heaven. Often they fail to realize that they are dead and when the initial white light comes for them to carry them up to heaven/source, they are so afraid they fail to move into the light. They can be stuck on the earth plane for years, decades and even centuries.

I have cleared many battlefields; the soldiers not understanding they are dead, believe the light is probably a bomb or from a shot. This simple understanding of death should be taught in schools, to prevent soul fragmentation and loss.

If we are taught to fear death then surely we fear living too?

131

Teaching both the fear of God and death, whilst concentrating on this fear in particular often means that many deceased people think that even when the light comes they are unworthy. This is why they remain earth bound and restricted. In my work to free them, besides the intense reassurance, I also create a vortex of light for them to be received back from whence they originated. It's very moving work and I have done it naturally since being a toddler.

I was recently advised to watch a YouTube clip about DMT by Sacred Science about healing in the jungle by the shamans. It was wonderful I have to say, although one particular part of the documentary really touched my soul and was incredibly thought-provoking. The shamans were treating Western people with serious illnesses, some close to death. Many had decided that the conventional medicine was just not worth the trouble such as chemotherapy or radiotherapy. Their fear of death itself, was tangible.

I have been aware of the process of death, as far back as I can recall and I certainly have no fear around death itself. I truly know in my whole being, that when my time comes I am going to be in the soul only. I am going to be welcomed to Heaven with the most beautiful light which is filled with loving kindness. My physical body will be no more and that it is going to be a truly blessed experience indeed. I expect that my loved ones, such as my dearest grandparents will be there and also my cousin too.

Just as the shamans accept and feel spirits all around I too have felt the spirits of the dead around from an early age. Thus, when the documentary was coming to a close, they were filming a shaman as he canoed down the river through the jungle and his words went something like this. "You Western people are very strange people, you have been taught to fear death and *that death means only fear.* Because of this, you then fail to live life, allowing the fear to cloud and *influence everything you do whilst you are supposed to be alive".* As I listened to this wisdom I was deeply touched by this man's honestly and simplicity. I began to see how others really are affected by this fear and to see life through the eyes of normal people. To be honest I was quite shocked.

Often I get phone calls as people have unwanted guests in their homes. Otherwise known as ghosts or spirits, they are, in very simple terms, people who have passed over and been so unaware and fearful of death, that they just do not know that they have passed.

Several years earlier one such phone call relating to unwanted guests had my full attention. A local couple had visitors of the spiritual kind in their home and also many unbalanced energies (geopathic stress). There were several reasons for this; for example there can be a portal or a vortex of stuck energy. Even whilst listening throughout the telephone conversation, I was re-balancing and tuning into the energies, which were incredibly disharmonious. It was hardly surprising then to know this couple were desperate to have the energies rebalanced, as it was affecting their sleep and they were unable to relax whilst in their own home environment.

I knew that despite not yet physically having met them, they were going to have a huge impact into my life. How they were going to do this, I had no idea at the time, I just knew I had to be there to assist them, knowing that we would be friends for many years; if not a whole life-time. There was no expectation on my part, just a decision to listen to my heart and soul and follow my inner guidance.

I made the appointment to see them the following day and duly balanced and cleansed the house's energies. They were a lovely couple very much in love and their unbalanced home was causing them unnecessary distress. They could feel the difference as soon as I arrived and were so delighted that they recommended my services to many other friends and relatives. My reputation grew massively and I was delighted to receive so much support and many opportunities to help and to meet other lovely people across Lancashire.

Over the coming months I got to know many of their friends and relatives and cleared many of their homes from negative energy too. It was truly a blessed time for me and I loved every minute of getting to know them. Sara's husband owned a TV studio and he asked me to clear the energies there too. I had never been in a TV studio before and it was actually quite exciting.

The various studios where different sets were laid out for filming was quite a surprise, as I had always thought TV studios were glamorous, but, seeing behind the scenes I began to realise that there was much hard work involved and much time and effort needed, changing sets and scenery.

The control room where whatever was being filmed came up on multiple screens, was a hub of activity and the noise of the fans cooling the computers was fabulous too, it just added to the mix. It was a technical experience indeed, a dream in fact for others maybe. In the control room are several TV screens showing whatever is going out live at the time through the Sky channel and whatever is being recorded in another studio. The guys in there obviously knew their roles and the whole thing seemed to flow smoothly. So many things to experience all in one day! My inner child was mesmerized.

Over the next three years I got to know many of the staff and from my initial meeting with Sara and Harry a whole network had built up. I loved each and every minute I spent with them, either at her office, the studio or their beautiful home. Sharing samosas or curries and getting to know them over the years was truly a blessing to me.

FAITH, HOPE & TRUST

"Faith is to believe what you do not see; the reward of this is to see what you believe".

St Augustine

We kept in touch for several years and then as time passed we had drifted and allowed several months to go by without communicating. Whilst I was training as a life-coach Sara contacted me out of the blue, as she had concerns that the new premises where she now worked were out of balance and required my opinion. As I drove across Lancashire I was excited and looking forward to meeting her. I tuned in to her and the building where she was now located, though I felt nothing inappropriate.

However, as I approached I was drawn to another building very close to her offices and was taken aback by heavy, negative energies, which I immediately worked on to reset and restore balance. Some energies are easier to re-balance than others and, even for me; this is what I term as heavy duty! I usually find energy work easy. In this instance I really had to work. Once sorted I travelled on to Sara's workplace and looked forward to seeing her & catching up.

As I pulled into the car park I telephoned her to let her know that I had arrived. The excitement was obvious in her voice. I scouted the surrounding area; though felt nothing was wrong with the energies. As she met me, it was obvious that we had much to catch up on and we were both delighted to see one another. The new offices were wonderful, modern and very tasteful, and, as she showed me around, I was reassuring her that all was indeed well. Her relief was evident, though I explained that I had had to work on the other building nearby.

Sometimes one building's energy can certainly affect another. Imbalanced energy is often referred to as geopathic stress or earth stress. Mother Earth has ley/energy lines and often these can get out of balance or compromised for many reasons. All was now well. I reassured her and confirmed her thoughts.

We chatted easily and she explained how life was treating her and that she had been meaning to call me for weeks. She asked me where I was up to and what I was doing work-wise. I explained that my friend Amanda had asked me to do a talk on health and well-being at a local hospice, as she couldn't attend and had been asked to run a workshop for the staff as part of their pamper day. I continued to explain that I duly booked the date in my diary and was excited yet unsure as to what I should expect. *I knew I had to be there* and had cancelled my other appointments. It was to become obvious that this would in fact be a life-changing day for me on many levels.

Little did I know at the time though just how life-changing it was to become.

I continued on to explain that when I was asked to take Amanda's place, I was delighted and said "Yes" immediately; though I had no idea about how many attendees there would be, neither did I know their background or for how long I was talking. Sometimes you just have to go with the flow and **trust that you are in the right place at the right time!** I knew this was right and have always got such a buzz from delivering a talk or seminar to people who may have previously been asleep to holistic medicine and the simple concepts of well-being.

I remember that day so clearly, pulling into the car park, not really being aware of where I should park or which entrance to use. I was nervous yet filled with excitement at the same time. Sara could see my delight as I continued with my story. I was introduced to the staff and told that I had been booked for the whole afternoon. Three and a half hours with a short break in between and there would be a demonstration of T'ai Chi, which I was welcome to attend. The day was getting better and better! I continued to relay the story to her as she sat listening intently. It was a beautiful sunny afternoon, so we would be out in the open air on the grass.

For those of you who have read my first book, you will recall my fear of worms which had prevented me walking on the grass bare footed. Now I was actually going to do T'ai Chi outdoors in the sun without footwear! This was fast becoming my pamper day too!

The staff working at the hospice had much need for a team-building day. Working with terminally ill children and their families is a very tough job indeed. I was filled with admiration for these precious and most valued ladies. Most were nurses though some physiotherapists and other therapists too.

Whatever our backgrounds or occupation, we all like being pampered and we all need to live a balanced, healthy life. Respecting our time and being aware of making time for work, rest and play are vital for our mental, spiritual and physical well-being. By maintaining balance, being aware of our energy levels and being conscious of what our bodies are telling us we really can make massive changes for the better, to our quality of life and our life-style.

One simple change can start other very beautiful changes because as we change, we embrace other changes in both ourselves and others around us. The more positivity we feel and experience so the more we will attract to us. LOA at its best. Like energy attracting more like energy. Explaining to people that we can all make positive changes indeed brings so much more to our lives. We all have the ability to change and all it takes is a little courage.

When I deliver a talk I begin to *feel my way through conversations* and as I listen to the questions being asked I begin to know my audience. I feel my way through to the next level of learning so that they can understand and use my teachings in their daily lives. It truly makes my heart and soul sing to inspire and motivate people, to bring about their own changes and bring them to incredible realizations of self-awareness. Getting to know people along their journey and watching them flower is truly the most wonderful part of my work.

She could *clearly see and feel the passion,* as I recounted the story where I arrived to find myself talking to almost thirty health workers and would be here for three hours. It was part of a well-being day for the staff and a treat for them to be able to learn and experience holistic medicine first hand.

Holistic medicine is very different to conventional and so I wasn't sure what my welcome would be like. Upon my arrival I was soon completely at ease and looking at the ladies auras I knew this was meant to be. They were all bright, light & glowing. No grumpy ladies present – all was well.

I continued to relay the story to her as she listened with great intent. "I love listening to you, I could listen to you all day" she said, as I explained that I had taught them about healing, Homeopathy and how our spiritual well-being affects our mental state, affecting both physical and emotional well-being too. I was delighted as more and more light-bulbs moments sparked through the audience and they all began to understand further, as I explained the body-mind link/body wisdom and gave many practical examples.

I showed them some simple healing techniques for restoring the balance to the aura and healed those who requested it. I was buzzing and felt even more fulfilled than I do in my everyday work, purely because I love being and inspiring many people at once.

Meditations can help with relaxation, not to mention pain relief and other things. Introducing all these things to the staff was such a delight for me. In fact, they were so inspired that many have since trained as Reiki healers with me. They have now become great friends too.

As I recalled the scene to Sara my passion became so evident that she said "right, you can do a session with my staff right now". "Just let me catch my breath for ten minutes" was my swift reply. Luckily I was already booked to do a talk that evening and so I had my aura & chakra pictures and much of my other teaching literature in the car. I took several deep breathes as I walked to collect my briefcase from the car. Wow I thought, this is it...I'm doing what I love to do best!

As she introduced me to her staff & then left the room, I remember thinking "well this is it! A room full of strangers and I've got the opportunity to make a difference or miss a golden opportunity". I usually start by asking people what they do for themselves, as it is a good way for me to get a feel of their levels of spiritual awareness.

Spiritual awareness is self-awareness which comes from the heart-mind, closely linked to the soul. Most people are completely asleep to their soul and the needs of the soul. We are after all a spiritual being having a human experience and as a spiritual being we are here on the planet to enjoy and embrace life daily. We should find joy in everything we do – just as the ancients did, living outdoors, appreciating everything they had, the trees, the miracles of nature and the understanding that **EVERYTHING IS LINKED TO EVERYTHING**.

 Each tree is in harmony and balance with other trees, every flower has its place, every animal its qualities. Each of us should be in harmony with ourselves and others around us. We should be aware of our needs and those of others with respect and integrity. Thus, just as in nature, as a team in an office we all affect one another and we each need to work in balance with one another and maintain that balance.

Just as we need to respect one another's qualities so the ancients knew the power of each of the animal's qualities and would call for their assistance when required. The wisdom of the eagle is to fly over the valley and take in all the view as a whole. It's a great ability when we need to assess the whole of a situation or to help us with the understanding of another's point of view. That is why the ancients carved the totem poles shaped into animal form to ask and request these particular qualities. For example you could request the assistance of the dove for peace, the lion for courage, the butterfly for times of transition in life.

As I asked the staff what did they do for themselves they didn't even know what I meant and asked me to explain further. I asked the question again and a few slowly answered that they had hobbies, whilst other's lives revolved solely around work and sleep. I explained in detail the importance of having a life filled with things that we enjoy doing and which allow us to embrace life to the full. To engage with the soul and live life rather than existing is the greatest of all gifts.

The light bulbs began to brighten, as I gave example after example of stories and healings I had done, when clients were in a state of exhaustion, simply because they hadn't listened nor understood their well-being as a whole concept; mentally, physically, emotionally and probably most of all spiritually. Needless to say, they all loved the presentation and gained much insight. To me when we ignore the soul and its longings, then we may as well be dead because we are merely existing rather than living and by doing that, the writing is already on the wall for health problems in a huge variety of ways.

Just as I had done with the precious souls at the local hospice some weeks earlier, I explained about the aura, chakras, how positive and negative energies affect our well-being, how healthy eating has a huge role to play, as does drinking a healthy amount of water throughout the day.

Water in the spiritual sense allows us to wash away memories and old emotions, that's why tears are so important. Please note that I always advocate a water filter too as tap water is treated with approximately 350 chemicals that I certainly wouldn't recommend drinking it. The heavy metals alone are harmful enough. Just smell some freshly poured tap water and see for yourself – or rather **smell** for yourself

By letting go, then of course we are making room for positive change. By drinking more water we can wash out more of the old emotional baggage. Many of my clients do not drink enough water. I have found from experience that when they change this simple habit, then they really begin to change their lives.

I have done a lot of research into water and there is much evidence relating to the memories that water will hold. Indeed, as a qualified Homeopath, I am very aware that the more diluted a remedy the more powerful it becomes. In 1988, Jacques Benveniste published an article in "Nature." Other studies are those of Masaru Emoto; a true legend in this field.

I continued to explain that there is a beautiful fountain cascading at The Chalice Well gardens in Glastonbury. The particular way it is shaped allows the water to be cleared of its memories.

Explaining how both positive and negative energies affect us really gets the audience thinking. Asking them if they work in a healthy environment where they feel comfortable or do they feel uncomfortable. Explaining how that can affect the chakras and clog up the energy system, explaining how to move energy often using very simple T'ai Chi movements and a variety of energy techniques can really set them on fire. Even as I write this I'm on fire myself sharing these simple motions.

If someone has upset you how do you think your energy field looks? Will it be beautiful and glowing? Hardly! So, what happens when these people have grumpy clients on the telephone or for interview? How do they deal with that situation successfully? When we are self-aware we know where our energies are before, during and after these instances, this will allow us to know our own state of well-being. This means we can find our balance more easily and more effectively maintain that balance when we are challenged.

I use the 0-10 scale, 0 being feeling low and 10 feeling lots of vitality and a happy contentment. Thus the question I ask the group is "How do you feel at this moment and do you need or would you wish to change anything?

Teaching people to shake off unwanted energies is fabulous and making sense of the unseen world – or at least what is unseen to most. I see energies and chakras naturally, so therefore I see the interaction we have with one another's energy fields. I certainly see when someone is taking another's life-force or causing it to shrivel up. It is both fascinating and very painful at times, especially when you see one person take energy from another or watch bullying in action.

Explaining about diet and nutrition is essential as we certainly are what we eat to a bigger or lesser degree. We all know that if we eat rubbish then we often feel rubbish. Eating foods with a high Glycaemic Index is far healthier than eating foods with low GI such as crisps, white bread, processed foods, cakes and biscuits. The GI foods release sugar into the blood at a much slower rate and a rate that is fairly constant, so that our blood sugar levels remain reasonable level rather than yo-yoing, as they do with processed foods.

This peaking and lowering of the blood sugar can ultimately result in diabetes, not to mention obesity, as we feel hungry very soon after we have eaten. The more sugary foods we eat, the more we desire and a whole addictive cycle continues, until we learn the need for change; often the hard way too!

Candida; which is found in many foods, bread, mushrooms and especially wine can be a huge cause of many health disturbances, such as lack of vitality, poor decision making, poor sleep, self-discipline, digestive problems, to mention only a few. It is worth doing some research as there are suggestions now that many cancerous lumps are actually made up of candida which has perforated through the gut wall (which is only one cell thick) and then once through the intestinal wall can escape into the bloodstream and travel anywhere in the body. The holes which will obviously get bigger over time, will allow partially digested food particles to pass through too. It is officially called "Leaky Gut Syndrome."

These particles, once through, will of course be recognised by the body as foreign bodies as they should be in the gut still needing to be broken down further. However, as foreign bodies they are attacked by the white blood cells, setting up a reaction as the body's auto-immune system kicks into action. Have you ever wondered why you suddenly develop an allergy to something which you have eaten throughout your life?

DRAMA KARMA

"Letting go of our suffering is the hardest work we will ever do.
It is also the most fruitful.
To heal, means to meet ourselves
in a new way –
in the newness of each moment
where all is possible and
nothing is limited to the old."

Stephen Levine

"Healing Into Life & Death"

Dependent upon the awareness of the audience and their receptivity to different concepts I often explain the laws of karma and then advise them not to bite into what I call "Drama Karma." We all have a story or drama of our life *as we see it.* The question is, how do we deal with that and does it rule our lives, causing ripples and more negative patterning, or, do we choose to take the learnings from the drama karma and let it go. Being aware of whether or not our story is serving us can indeed be very insightful. It all leads to improved self-awareness. "Are you stuck in your story?" is a common question I ask an audience.

Letting go of old habits and/or stories is sometimes just a matter of becoming aware of the need for change. Sometimes by simply getting up ten minutes earlier and stretching our bodies or meditating, we start on that journey towards changing life for the better. It may mean just listening to your body when you start to get tired, rather than waiting until you become absolutely exhausted. I refer to it as "The Elastic Band Theory" – The choice is ours in any given situation, whether we allow the elastic band to get very, very stretched, a little stretched, or whether it becomes so stretched that it breaks.

That simple awareness will hopefully then allow room for at least one positive change into our lives, which will then lead to another change and, as that gathers momentum, it will lead to another as LOA plays its part. Like energy attracting like energy. It's a simple law of physics. If you focus on positivity you will attract more to be positive about. I had 15 precious minutes in which to explain and influence these people. Watching their faces and feeling the energies from this audience, I knew I had brought food for thought to them - and to their personal and working lives.

I always teach healing in practical, common-sense ways so that listeners can go home and make these practical and often incredibly simplistic changes whilst gaining great results.

So within those precious few minutes I had introduced health & well-being, diet, the importance of drinking water – filtered, of course, energy clearing and perhaps the ALL important need to balance body, mind and soul; to stay balanced and aware emotionally, mentally, physically and spiritually. These were basic self-awareness techniques and foundations to our personal responsibility.

Note; In many of my talks I will also explain about past lives and how they can and do influence our lives. However, in these formal events it was inappropriate. Certainly whilst giving a talk to a spiritual group, I will expand upon these, as most spiritual people really do understand the power of what I term "Drama Karma."

For your information the very best book I have read on the subject is by Brian Weiss "Many Lives, Many Masters." To be honest I have read all his books and would recommend any of them as a great insightful read, especially as he was originally a complete sceptic on all spiritual issues!

MOVING ON

*"Destiny is not a matter of chance, it is a
matter of choice;
it is not a thing to be waited for, it is a thing to be achieved."*

William Jennings Bryant

Sara is a dynamic woman and very much a lady who puts her all into whatsoever she is doing. I have a great deal of respect for her and always have had. Following the talk, her staff were leaving the presentation room and feeding back to her how much they felt uplifted and enlightened. They immediately began to use the energy techniques I had suggested to clear negative thoughts and feelings; they labelled it the "Shaky Wakey" exercise and they especially loved to use it in the morning.

She was delighted as they would come into work happier and much more upbeat. She noticed very quickly that they no longer suffered the morning slump and were much less stressed in their day to day working lives. Thus they were more productive and the whole atmosphere in the workplace lightened. The fact that they were clearly taking personal responsibility for themselves and respecting those around them meant that they were all certainly feeling the benefits.

Sara was delighted and gave me a "kindly kick up the back-side" as she explained that I should do more of these presentations and I needed to get my finger out. I agreed and over the following weeks we had numerous business meetings. She took the time to inspire and motivate me further.

To be honest I love my work and that's where my passion lies. Sales and business isn't really something that comes easily to me so I searched inside myself for the answers. I asked for my guides' assistance and was guided to read the book "The Power Of Your Subconscious Mind" by Joseph Murphy. After researching Law Of Attraction for over twelve years, I have to say that this is definitely THE BEST AND MOST MOTIVATING.

The book inspired my whole being into action and gave lots of examples to assist us in daily life. I allowed the words "Success, love, peace & freedom" to fill my thoughts as I drifted off to sleep every night and upon my awakening first thing in the morning too, I could feel the effects.

The difference was amazing and by using Law Of Attraction principles, I visualized myself talking at seminars and travelling across the world. I asked The Universe for assistance daily and listened to the clues I was receiving. I made a point to watch YouTube clips of Tony Robbins, who is surely one of the most wonderful motivational speakers, of our time to inspire and motivate me daily.

Every day I would imagine what it would feel like to work in the same way he does. I also watched YouTube clips on public speaking and whatever came to mind to fuel my passion. I was sending a clear signal to The Universe and knew I was actively changing my life for the better. I visualised targeting many people and inspiring them to move forward in life.

My plan was to inspire thousands and to make a difference in their lives through giving them the awareness of positive mental attitude, consistency, courage and determination, using LOA to bring positive changes to their lives. I was still working closely with Paul and healing and peeling whatever came up although by this time I was needing fewer and fewer appointments, as life got easier and easier.

The story was about to unfold. Little did I know what was around the corner! Sara had been the instrument of change in me and for that I am forever grateful. A new chapter in my life was unfolding and I could feel the change, though I had absolutely no idea where it would lead, nor had I any idea as to what the change would be; *I just knew change was coming.*

As my motivation and momentum grew I decided to post on Facebook that besides doing what I was already doing I would be including Motivational and Inspirational speaking. The response I received was awesome and most encouraging. It was fabulous to receive the support of friends, family and clients, allowing me to grow further and increase my momentum. My dear friend Colin asked if I would consider doing a team-building day for his staff. I duly agreed and was delighted to be given a golden opportunity. The Universe was indeed giving me its support. He explained that it would be after the festive season of Christmas and that he would be in touch further to discuss details. Another chapter was about to unfold....

Meanwhile Sara was so impressed that she recommended me to other companies and encouraged me to attend meetings with her. It was certainly all happening and I felt over-whelmed if I'm honest. It was like jumping from one pond to another, rather than a small goldfish bowl and even positive change is stressful. IT WAS PUSHING ME WELL OUT OF MY COMFORT ZONE!

Although Sara had recommended me to several other companies to do well-being presentations and team-building, as yet nothing had come about after several months. She had lined the dominos up for me though none had dropped. It was very strange indeed. Despite knowing that it was right for me to follow this path and that it was in complete alignment with my soul, I felt that something was missing. It felt as if something was blocking me or indeed in some way, shape or form, I was *in fact blocking myself*. It certainly didn't make sense so Paul and I guessed that the answer would probably lie in the subconscious mind.

Through light hypnosis we then looked into my subconscious patterning. Both the subconscious and superconscious minds are incredibly powerful at creating blocks and diversions for us to avoid pain and upset. Eventually we uncovered, after much digging, many tears and much upset, that I was playing out a pattern of behaviour where my inner child was sabotaging the playing arena.

I had had no previous idea of this little girl; *Little Louise* who felt abandoned and unheard. It was an unbelievable revelation indeed. Something which I had been completely unaware of for my whole adult life was about to be revealed. As we finally managed to convince the inner child to communicate with us, the inner child's story unfolded. I was truly shocked at the revelations. In the meditation I listened to her, maybe as a three/four year old, as she told me her feelings; those which I had long ignored and shut out. I could see her clearly in my mind's eye, as she relayed her feelings and the long felt grief. Especially of being unheard and feeling that she had been ignored for decades. (During the session under light hypnosis, she also showed me a *diamond,* though at the time, I failed to understand its significance).

She explained her feelings and the story unfolded. My real father had left the marital home when I was a toddler. As far as I have always been concerned, my step-father *is my dad* and I've always called him "Dad". He has been one of my greatest teachers in many ways. His support through my teenage years and helping with exams, etc. was truly fabulous. My adult self has always loved him & despite our differences over the years, I love him more dearly now, than I ever have and thus I hadn't even realised that my inner child longed for her natural father.

I watched as she had a huge tantrum *"I want my daddy".* What a revelation, I was gob-smacked and astounded, that I could reconnect to this little two/three year old who had felt abandoned, unloved and that she wasn't good enough and just maybe that his leaving had, in some way at least, been down to her. Children have an incredible memory for hurt and she was well and truly hurting. I felt her pain as she explained and I continued to feel her feelings of guilt; that maybe she had done something to make him leave?

She felt guilty through lack of emotional understanding, emotional intelligence and a deeper wisdom. Indeed, she had held on to that feeling for over 40 years. She was bereft; feeling lost as her daddy had completely disappeared – in her eyes at least! All those years she had festered and simmered under the surface and had tried repeatedly to be heard. Listening to her and actually feeling the emotions that she felt really were incredible and so enlightening. She really did miss her daddy and failed to comprehend why he had left, thinking he didn't love her. How could she, as a small child contact him or tell him how she felt?

By giving her the opportunity to speak and be heard, my understanding of **why** I didn't always trust people and found it very difficult at times of separation from others, began to compute. **What a revelation indeed.** Suddenly, as an adult I could understand my failed relationships and actually change my patterns of behaviour.

A really significant revelation which would finally allow me to move on in life; this had been a major block. She had never been heard and as such, had blocked me from being heard in public too.

The subconscious really is amazing and as these memories filtered into my parasympathetic nervous system, I began to feel incredibly spaced out indeed. Coming back into consciousness was like hitting the floor after a thousand foot drop. I couldn't even write the cheque for Paul after the session. I really was dazed by it all. A space cadet certainly had nothing on me in that particular moment!

Paul had known what the block was for some time and was experienced enough to know that the best thing for me was to take a walk in the local park, to ground myself back in my body, whilst my physical being recalibrated itself. My whole being was in shock. The chakras were clearing out and I felt so different. Finally the pennies were dropping and release was such a profound a feeling.

In my spacey state, I recall feeling like a zombie and I probably looked like one too! I certainly was in no fit state to drive at that time. Slowly, but surely, I came back into enough awareness and thought a hot chocolate at "The Slug & Lettuce" would help. It certainly did and I became aware that as my whole body was re-balancing I felt completely different, just as if a huge weight had been lifted from me. I felt like I was glowing and could feel a huge radiance around me. I knew my energy field had expanded considerably and was amazed that every staff member and the other customers kept looking over at me; their eyes in wonder.

Since that day I can honestly say that I have never felt the same. Every day has been amazing and though some are obviously better than others, I feel free. That feeling of intense **FREEDOM** is most welcome. Through the years since I became aware of Reiki and I began my inner journey of self-realization, I had discovered my inner freedom but this new feeling took it to a completely different level. I truly felt amazing.

For years I felt something was overhanging me, though I never knew or could not even have guessed that it was my little girl. She was frightened and scared, under so many layers of misunderstandings and a variety of confused emotions.

In energetic terms, I had carried that painful emotion of grief for decades and it had weighed me down. This is what happens when we suffer the feelings of negative emotions, they enter the chakras, weigh heavy and prevent the chakra from spinning at its optimum speed; thus releasing these said emotions releases the weight, therefore allowing the chakra to spin at a higher frequency, because the chakra is now lighter.

"Little Louise" as we named her plays a huge part in my day now. In respect I changed my name on Facebook to include Louise. If I ever awaken and feel out of sorts I ask her what she wants and often it may just be a walk in the park or to sing. The feelings then lift and I feel much happier in myself. Having granddaughters is truly a blessing and I love allowing *"Little Louise"* to play and to interact with them. She and I are one and being child-like in the day is essential. This may mean dancing in the kitchen or finding that

child-like, innocent way of looking at life. I have certainly benefitted from learning to listen to her and she's always been and always will be a part of me. Think about children, their innocence and love of life.....perhaps you need to find yours?

There is a spiritual school of thought that believes for all the decisions we make daily we need to consider the aspect of the inner child, the adult we are today and also the aspect of us that is the wise crone/sage/elder. How different would the world be if we all considered these aspects of ourselves daily?

"Children Learn"

If a child lives with criticism,
He learns to condemn,
If a child lives with hostility,
He learns to fight,
If a child lives with ridicule,
He learns to be shy,
If a child lives with shame,
He learns to feel guilty,
If a child lives with tolerance,
He learns to be patient,
If a child lives with encouragement,
He learns confidence,
If a child lives with praise,
He learns to appreciate,
If a child lives with fairness,
He learns justice,
If a child lives with security,
He learns to have faith,
If a child lives with approval,
He learns to like himself,
If a child lives with acceptance and friendship,
he learns to find love in the world.

Dorothy Law Holbe

LETTING GO

"Let us observe how we fill ourselves
And learn to be more empty."

As Paul coached me, I connected more and more with my dark painful sides, allowing communication between Little Louise and myself. One day he suggested we look at anger. He told me to come dressed in loose clothes and with an open mind. He explained that he had done quite a lot of boxing and that we would have a session connecting to my anger, through boxing – that I would box him!

I was certainly less than happy with that thought, despite his reassurances. However, I had known him long enough by now and had learnt to trust him too. He put on his boxing gloves, got me to put mine on and told me to hit him! I just simply could not do it! Despite repeating the need for me to do this I refused….his only option was to keep hitting me in the face to get me to feel and listen to my inner anger and that of Little Louise.

Eventually, after much protesting, I caved in and he promised that he was experienced enough that I wouldn't stand a chance of hitting him at all. I offered that if I did I would knock him out! After all, my ex-husband was a boxer, his father before and Chris had taught me how to fight. Needless, to say Paul avoided every blow and we had a great boxing session.

Throughout the boxing session I was just swearing at nothing-ness and Paul too as if he was someone else, which was indeed very therapeutic. Those people from long ago, who in my eyes at least had let me down, broken promises, expectations and attachments, frustrations and anger, which has **so limited me so many times.** And to think that I thought I'd dealt with SO much prior to this outburst! Good job the building was empty. I ranted like a demon!

We are so perfect as Brits! "Oh Darling, do put those emotions under the carpet, we don't deal with those." The problem is that the carpet gets full and the energy it takes to keep it hidden eventually becomes all consuming. Feel the fear and do it anyway! The courage it had taken me to keep cleaning, cleaning, cleaning over the years was finally worthwhile and very, very evident.

The following is an extract from my journal from that day! "I feel Fuc*** amazing, after my boxing session with Paul. I feel achy though great. Isn't life amazing? I'm sat in "The Slug & Lettuce" in Manchester. I couldn't even have put a foot through the door prior to my clearing the worm and slug phobia. Now I can eat and be comfortable in here too! At this moment in time I actually feel that the fears have gone. I feel okay just to BE in Manchester after seeing Paul. I've just enjoyed a hot chocolate and a flatbread – the waiter couldn't take his eyes off me! I can feel my aura expanding as I sit here.

Paul said I looked ten years younger after the boxing session....can't wait to see what my loved ones have to say! I can certainly feel myself shape-shifting. I feel like another new ME. It's wonderful".

The learnings with Paul, has been amazing and has been one of the best and most influential courses I have ever undertaken. It has allowed me to feel and embrace my anger which has been ignored for years & buried for decades.

I had actually had a phobia of Manchester for years; no particular reason, just an intense dislike and fear. Maybe the fear was because Manchester was to be the place where my soul would eventually find its opening place and I could BE? Maybe there was more to unfold?

Paul had said that I would soon enter into the most vulnerable period of my life. Another 360 degree link in the chain, was this yet another chain I was breaking free from? The main thing is I felt FREE. Where will I go from here? Who knows?"

UNFOLDING THE PETALS

"And you would accept the seasons of your heart,
even as you have always accepted
the seasons
that pass over your fields"

Kahlil Gibran

My determination to become a profession motivational speaker was gathering pace. The way in which, becoming more soulfully aware had changed my life for the better, a thousand fold, was my motive for sharing this wisdom. Moving from living a totally unbalanced life to one of more balance was an amazing shift for me, I wanted to use that momentum, to inspire and enthuse others to do the same.

I had by this point in my professional life managed to assist many hundreds of people to change their lives and was thoroughly delighted to have had the privilege of sharing and watching their process. However, my bank balance was in decline and although I had a healthy overdraft facility, I was, after a quiet Christmas period in 2013, beginning to become concerned about my financial security.

Moving to my beautiful home and living my passion were indeed my dream, but a huge mortgage, house repairs and various renovation works needed to be taken care of too. I had total TRUST in The Universe that things would come good and had been going to see Sara's husband and his business partner, Steve and Harry regularly at the studio for help and advice as to how I could bring this dream into reality. I was still learning a lesson in wealth and abundance,

161

which I recognised. I was willing to do whatever it took to clear the karma and the seeming lack of wealth and prosperity.

I have known for years that motivational speaking is my soul's purpose; I just needed to get from A to B as quickly as possible. Financially Sara had explained to me that I was such an inspiration to her and her team that I should indeed continue on this path. She had made me aware of the abundance available to motivational speakers. It would indeed be a dream come true to be able to have financial freedom and to do the things that I wanted to do, such as travel. It would also mean freedom of time; my most precious asset. I would have more time to spend with my beloved granddaughters.

Financial freedom would also mean that I would have more time with friends and family, not to mention getting my home completely refurbished and the external repairs completed. I had achieved so much already in my life that this would surely be the icing on the cake. It all pointed towards **COMPLETION.**

I was still allowing the words *"Success, love, freedom and peace"* into my subconscious mind first thing in the morning upon awakening and last thing at night too.

Harry and Steve both successful businessmen helped me a great deal in my business from late 2013. Towards Christmas they suggested we leave things due to the festive season break and resume in the New Year. I was happy with that though still felt weighed down with financial concerns.

In January the following year, as we sat in the office, Harry just glibly suggested that *I have my own show on the channel.* You can imagine my surprise! I just sat there, looked across at Steve than back to Harry and then in my gobsmacked state just asked if I had misheard him? I was well and truly blown away at the suggestion. I had never worked on TV before and despite being on the radio frequently, the two are completely different mediums for communication. We briefly discussed possible titles and when we should start.

The year had indeed opened up in an amazing way with my being invited to have my own TV show. I kept the offer close to my chest for the next 48 hours as I was so excited, fearful, anxious, nervous, and a whole range of differing emotions....right up to terror!

Suppose I failed and messed it up?

Harry and Steve left me to it.....I had to plan the shows, the guests and sort out everything myself. It was quite a challenge! Where would I start? I had a wealth of spiritual friends and had been given free reign to do what I wanted, as long as I was teaching spiritual wisdom, they were happy with that.

We needed a name for the show and after bouncing around a few possible suggestions, we came up with *"Living A Dynamic Life."* It seemed a natural choice, as prior to my spiritual/soulful wake-up I certainly lived a very mundane, un-fulfilling life in many ways.

They had certainly known me long enough and knew the calibre of my work and my integrity, therefore knew if I was given a task it would certainly be done to the highest of my abilities!

A few days later after coming down from "cloud 9," I called my dear friend Karen who is a real spiritual networker. I explained that I would like a catch up and ask her advice. She too was blown away and said she needed time to think of how we could do this. We were under no illusion that without proper planning it would fail.

Perfect planning, prevents pi** poor performance.

Our mission was to get spiritual information to the masses and fill a 50 minute slot. The interviews would need to have people who were confident in front of the camera, professional, knowledgeable in their subject matter, had excellent communication skills, passionate and dependable. I was to be the interviewer! No pressure then!!!

Karen turned out to be a real gem and our friendship grew stronger as we bounced ideas around about potential interviewees. There are so many avenues into spirituality and the relevant subject matter, that that too needed to be closely examined. Law Of Attraction, healing, positive mental attitude, self-awareness, diet, health and well-being, meditations, how to find inner peace and many other subjects such as colour therapy, acupuncture, mindfulness and information about the aura and the chakras were all relevant.

We needed to seek out the best person to interview from a particular subject and I truly believed that that is what we achieved. I am forever grateful to Karen for many aspects of our friendships, though this was outstanding.

Another outstanding and monumental figure in all of the planning of the shows was that of Colin Clarke. He had brilliant business acumen and advice and we regularly chatted about a huge variety of subjects. He was kindly, though assertive and I have to say I owe him a great deal and am very grateful for his friendship; full of truth and integrity.

One fine morning in our usual manner we arranged to meet in the local Sainsbury's café. As usual hot chocolate and cake were on the menu! We chatted easily about our lives and our families and I told him I had been offered the show. He was delighted for me and asked "How are you going to plan the interviews?" I replied that "I was going to research the subject matter closely, ask my guests for a list of questions which they would like me to ask through the show and what they would like to promote – if anything."

"No" was his advice as I looked on dumbfounded. My mind raced, as I was trying to think how on earth I would manage if I didn't follow this simple format. "Your intuition has got you this far, you need to go with your instincts, by all means chat to the subjects beforehand and gather information but, when on set, you MUST ALLOW THE INTERVIEWS TO FLOW."

It made perfect sense though I had already visualised myself on set with a list of prompt cards and questions to ask the person being interviewed. To be honest his advice made absolute sense and for that I am forever grateful.

The planning and preparations were lengthy and very time consuming. Some people were definitely in, whereas others were definitely NOT. I recall my first interview with Pauline Tomlin who was amazing as we discussed Law Of Attraction and her life-coaching business. It gave me such confidence as we chatted so easily on set, just as though we were sat on someone's sofa chatting to them in their own lounge; which is exactly what I wanted. I followed and trusted Colin's advice which proved to be priceless. It meant, more than anything else, that I *had to trust in myself.*

The other interviews with Mark Abadi, Peter Uglow, Dave Binder, Mandy Pearson and Rachel Bartholomew, Steve Jack and Julie Dodgson were truly fabulous too. I learnt so much from each and every experience. Harry and Steve were delighted and the shows received great reviews. (Note: The video clips of the show are available on YouTube. Just type in "Mary Curtis interviews…."). Steve Jack is now known as Christof Melchizedek. Pauline's blog is http://insight-fulangel.com

TRUST

"You will be a failure, until you impress the subconscious with the conviction you are a success. This is done by making an affirmation,
which clicks."

Florence Scovel Shinn

Financially, I was hoping that this, in time, would create abundance. However, as the months went on, I became aware that my resources were drying up and the planning and the time it took to rehearse and chat with Steve and Harry had taken up so much of my energy, that when I decided that the time was right to close that particular chapter of my life; whether temporarily or permanently, it seemed like a huge weight had been lifted from my shoulders.

I loved doing the shows, chatting with guests and prospective guests. However, I was certainly becoming aware that in the last few weeks of June, that my work was almost done. A natural cycle in my life had come to its natural end and, as always, I had to listen to that feeling. Of course as with any chapter in our lives, natural closure can lead to fear.

Recognising the fear was itself an insight. Why would I fear something if it was the right thing to do? Being aware of the ego minds' trickery, I knew I had to navigate around the fear, rather than bite into it, which would actually fuel it further. I checked all my options patiently using wisdom and discernment, and slowly but surely, moved from a place of fear, to a place of balance and a place where my soul felt at ease.

There was an element of this, as, in June, I had been offered other prospects within the channel, potentially doing another show with another presenter, etc. I wondered whether I was doing the right thing? Was it merely that I was getting tired? Would I lose out on other opportunities if I walked away? I decided that I would honour the interviews I had already scheduled and then see what the outcome would be from there. I would check my intuition and feel what was right for me after Ramadan.

There was much spiritual wisdom and esoteric knowledge in the interviews that had already been recorded, so I was more than satisfied that the viewers had much food for thought. Most of the information I had wanted to share was already available in the interviews. I knew that the remaining two would indeed mean the shows *completion.* I had gained much from the experience on a personal level, and although I had enjoyed it, there comes a natural closure for all things in life, to resist this is merely to cause ourselves pain and unnecessary upset, in some way shape or form.

I had Christof's interview and an interview with two wonderful ladies; Rachel Bartholomew and Mandy Pearson relating to their book "Mindful Eating" already booked in the diary for filming. Through Ramadan there would be no filming for a month, as the studio was so busy with charity work filming. I knew I was ready for a very welcome break.

Filming Christof's interview was fabulous and The Universe showed me clearly that I had made the right choice to finish what I had started. We arrived at the studio and began filming within 15 minutes. The shows are all pre-recorded so if there are any mistakes at all we can simply do a re-take. We began, it flowed beautifully and we were done, dusted, delighted and finished within the hour!

It was a perfect example of being in the flow and trusting all would be well.

Afterwards we drove through to Preston for a lovely meal, before he had to leave on the train for London. We were both delighted at the content of the interview and couldn't believe how easy it had been for us both. He asked me again whether or not I was happy to help on the Limitless retreat in Ibiza in a few weeks' time. He was waiting for other bookings so that once he confirmed the numbers, he would know for sure that it was feasible for me to attend with him. I tuned in intuitively and explained that I could see myself staying with him and Roxy; I could in fact see myself lazing around his pool! And, so I knew, I would definitely be going, whether or not it was in a professional capacity or one of a social trip. Either way, it felt right and I was both excited and delighted too. My idea of a perfect afternoon and a wonderful interview in the bag too!

So, it was by now the middle of the year, the planning and filming of the shows had taken up so much of my life up to this point in the year, that I was wondering what I would do with my new found time. I was delighted too as being in the flow of life, some people refer to it as "The Vortex", meant I knew that all would be well and I would allow that space to naturally be filled with something else. I felt that the experience had helped me towards motivational speaking in that it had greatly assisted my confidence and credibility, but I was still very aware of my financial security too.

I had spoken to my dear friend Dave Binder and said that I felt one of the main reasons, if not THE ONLY reason I had done the show was in fact, that I was meant to meet Christof. Certainly from our first meeting I had received so much healing and awareness. I knew he was a massive key to my spiritual unfoldment and further development.

He had kindly invited me to London on his Limitless weekend as a gesture of thanks for the interview. I had attended at the beginning of June, which gave me great insight into his work prior to my interview with him. Much had been achieved and despite being initially invited as his guest, I ended up working with him.

It turned out to be a wonderful weekend. I asked friends for advice regarding accommodation and my friend Beth had put me in touch with two gay men, who kindly offered to put me up for the weekend. They were my chaperones for the weekend, looking after me on the underground and giving me confidence to travel. I am indebted to them both. Ian even made me a birthday cake too!

That weekend will stay in my memory bank forever. Deep friendships were forged and many of us are still in touch.

When we all introduced ourselves, one member stated she was from Staveley. At break time I asked her if she meant Staveley, just outside Kendal. "Yes, why, do you know it?" "Yes, it's one of my favourite places and my favourite eating place is Wilf's too." She was well and truly gobsmacked! Needless, to say, I visited many times last year and we even saw a Kingfisher too; much to her delight as she had waited over 11 years to see one on the river. She was truly pleased to see him though in all his glory and majesty as he sat there in the trees!

TRAVEL & TRANSFORMATION

"Ordinary people believe only in the possible. Extraordinary people visualize not what is possible or probable, but rather what is impossible. And by visualizing the impossible, they begin to see it as possible."

Cherie Carter-Scott

2014 had already been a very powerful year of transformation, unexpected blessings and surprises. At the beginning of the year I had no plans regarding holidays or short breaks. Returning from London in June had left me feeling refreshed, rejuvenated and my body, mind and soul replenished. I love to travel and it is truly a passion of mine. My son Matthew had left for Australia in October 2013 and I missed him dearly. I knew that he had spent Christmas without his family and we had all dearly missed that precious time together.

In order for me to spend time with him, I had to look at the finances; I would need to have at least two weeks with him, practicalities meant that the costs would be in the region of £5,000 for the flights, spending money, accommodation costs, money to cover my bills, etc. whilst I was away. Being self-employed certainly has its benefits and although I had produced the book and the meditation CDs, so that I would have a passive income, it just wasn't enough to cover these costs. Thus travel was something which would have to wait...or so I thought! The story would unfold further.

I had only the intention to push forward with my work and become a motivational speaker or certainly to put as many things in place to lead me to this place. My trip to Switzerland in November was still very fresh in my mind and I wondered if I might go back there sometime in the coming year. I looked forward to the prospect although I knew that what would be, would be. Peter had paid for my trip and when I had worked out there, I earned enough to cover my costs and thoroughly enjoyed myself. However, I was well aware that I needed to get my finances in good order and very soon, as my overdraft was getting bigger.

So, in relation to travelling, I had a blank canvas and I knew it, yet I felt that The Universe would guide me, just as I had been guided with my travels to Switzerland and The Lakes in previous times. I was, and am, a firm believer that we are always in the right place at the right time anyways, so I trusted that The Universe would take care of things, and, as usual I would go along for the ride and go with the flow.

ARBONNE

"We can change our lives, we can do, have & be exactly what we wish."

Tony Robbins

I have many beautiful clients over the years and when I watch them flower, it's truly priceless. One such young lady had had a tough time with lack of confidence, which had affected her in many ways. She was coming from a dark place into a much more, lighter life. She was smiling more and certainly more open in her consultations with me.

One evening I received a text from her mother to say that her daughter was doing a presentation and would I please go along to support her. It felt right. I was actually free that evening and called my mother to see if she too wanted to come along. She duly agreed and I collected her whilst she asked me what event it was we were actually going to?

"I've no idea" I replied, explaining that said young lady needed support and that I wanted and actually knew I had to be there no matter what it was! Mum is used to me now and knows that I just follow my nose. She sat there and smiled. We arrived at the hotel and were offered a drink and I was surprised to see my dear friend Dawn.

The presentation started and I was delighted to be a part of the audience watching her as she explained that she had joined a network marketing company who sold top quality make-up, beauty, hair and skincare products at cost price. They were all natural, green and the company had recently achieved 100% vegan status. I was hooked! The business plan totally made me smile and I knew *I was definitely IN!*

Even my guides were telling me to join and sign up!

The presentation continued on to say that the company gave lots of support, positive mental attitude and also Law Of Attraction were encouraged to its members. This was indeed a win. Win. Top quality products at cost price, 100% vegan and coaching and camaraderie thrown in for good measure! Non-brainer!

I joined Arbonne and have been impressed with EVERYTHING! I needed a new foundation anyways and had already been paying top price for other brands which had mineral oil as a main ingredient. Up until that evening, I did not know that said mineral oil was a waste product from crude oil, which is not even fit for car engines!

There is NO law preventing oil companies selling this to beauty companies for pennies, despite the fact that it is like liquid plastic on the skin and does NOT allow the skin to breathe. We absorb a huge percentage of whatsoever we put on our skin and any inappropriate products will clog up the liver with toxins! Wow, what a revelation.

Not only did this business make perfect sense it would be a brilliant complementation to my current business and would give me an opportunity to learn about products and thus educate others too!

Another link in the chain was cemented and within weeks I had several consultants under me and many preferred clients too. All loved the products and the team building days were incredibly inspiring, yet an added bonus!

I love it when a plan comes together!

If you wish to order any products from the company, please use my ID number 441225383 or http://www.marycurtis.arbonne.com

ABUNDANCE

"Worldly riches have been feared, despised, condemned, and even hated by spiritual aspirants, because of ignorance of how to be in them and yet not of them, how to possess them and not to be possessed by them."

Annie Rix Militz

Arbonne managers are trained to look and coach their staff through LOA. I was asked by Dawn what I wanted from the business and we discussed goals. She explained that it would not happen overnight and like all other businesses, would take time to mould itself and grow; although some people had reached the top levels within months.

Obviously my spiritual work is my main goal although the two fitted together and most of my clients are aware of wanting healthy products for their skin and hair anyways.

It made perfect sense and I had lots of ideas how to promote the products and raise awareness. One particular chat with Dawn stands out a mile to me, even now, over twelve months down the line. "I'm putting more effort into Arbonne than my own business" I said to her. The pennies were beginning to drop into place. I had, by this time, been in business over 14 years and **NEVER ACTUALLY REALISED**! I did what I did, because I loved it and was very good at it...that realisation in, and of, itself was like a bolt of lightning to me.

To be honest it was also upsetting. Why had I not realised this before and pushed myself forwards? The story would unfold. I was still using the affirmations daily of *"Success, freedom, peace and love."* Therefore, anything that was standing in the way of that meant that I would have to work through those obstacles to achieve said affirmation. Arbonne was showing me the cracks in the mirror!

Several days later Colin called and sat me down for a business chat. He was straight to the point, as he usually is, and asked me directly what I had earnt in the last year, knowing that I had had my accounts done. I gave him the figures and he became VERY assertive, as he stated clearly that I should, at least, be earning two or three times that amount.

Colin is a great advisor and, being responsible for the business planning of a very successful holistic dental practise in Preston, has a great reputation/résumé behind him. I was listening intently whilst at the same time, fearing that I really would have to shake myself and get on with changing my attitude. He continued….."You need to put your prices up too." I sat there and squirmed like a worm. He was certainly not going to take **NO** for an answer. "£60 per treatment….you know you are a very talented and professional lady. You have a huge well-earned reputation and you've trained most healers across Lancashire and the North West. It may mean that you have less clients as you put your prices up, but it will mean you will get what you are worth and deserve. If you see two leaflets with healing advertised and one charges £60 whilst the other is £40, which is the better?"

More dominoes were dropping and he did have a point. Have you read "Business for Dummies?" Did I look like I had? "Nope" I replied. "Right then, tomorrow morning, WHSmiths in Preston. You have a mission. We will catch up soon to discuss your progress."

No pressure then! "God" had spoken and I needed said kick up the pants! He was indeed right with everything he said and I needed that kicking…. well, I had probably needed it for quite a while. I bought said books and started reading! Boring as sh*t…..Still haven't read them to be honest!

Two days later, my dear friend Clare called and said *exactly what Colin had said WORD FOR WORD! The Universe was well and truly providing me with a well-deserved wake up call.*

Time for action and the time is now. I was close to tears with the realisation that to charge more meant that I would indeed be beginning the process of standing in my power. I knew financially that I had no choice and I knew it was Universal guidance. I needed some new business literature anyways and Clare agreed to produce them for me listing my new prices.

Throughout this process our friendship deepened and she's such a great, motivated lady and such a motivated lady too. Said leaflets & business cards looked amazing and I was thrilled. It was time to move forward.

IBIZA RETREAT

*"There are only two ways to live your life.
One is as though nothing is a miracle. The other
is as though everything is a miracle."*

Albert Einstein

"Good Morning Journal"

The following is the entry to my journal which was dated 24th July 2014. Following on from having met Christof to interview him for the TV show and having worked with him in London on the three day Limitless retreat, I was subsequently invited to attend a week-long Limitless retreat with Christof in Ibiza.

My flights were booked and I arrived a day before the retreat was due to begin. I knew life was about to change.....

Great to meet you (addressing my new journal), I was told on Wednesday morning; 23rd July that it would be the last time I would be "ME" as I knew it. This did raise some fear I admit but the greatest feeling was the absolute "knowing" that I had to be there on Ibiza to attend the retreat and assist Christof in all aspects at all times.

My guides had told me this before, although I knew that this time, it would mean change for me on a profound level – like nothing I have ever experienced before. I honoured the fear within me, as to deny our emotions only leads to denying a part of ourselves, to ourselves. I had wasted many years doing this and had learnt only too harshly that this was certainly not the way to become more heart-centred. That particular fear, if I had actually given it fuel and allowed it to multiply, would surely have stopped me from getting on that plane on that lovely sunny Thursday morning.

My flight time that morning was 08.30 hours, which meant that I needed to be up at approximately 5am. I knew I needed to leave home about 5.45 in order that I had plenty of time to drop off my phone and diary and arrive at Liverpool airport in good time. As usual my internal body clock awoke me at 4.51am exactly.

The sun was up and it was another beautiful morning. The weather had been lovely for the last few weeks and that is so unusual in the UK! It really did feel like a new beginning for me. Usually my guides give me snippets of what is to come in the future; they show pictures to allow my awareness to grow and to assist my confidence in new situations. However   this particular morning, as with ALL previous times when I had tuned into the retreat, all I got was a huge blank. This is pretty scary for someone who has always had insights into the unknown. Usually they will show me a villa or a place I'm staying, maybe a beach or a chapel or landmark to confirm my being there. *Nothing. Sweet Nothing.*

So, in very simple terms, all I had left was *TRUST*. Trust in my knowing that all would be well and I HAD to be there; come what may! What I had realised through experience was that this nothingness meant just that; I was about to enter into the unknown and experience NOTHING-NESS.

I knew and trusted that I was meant to go and had already met some of the people on the retreat after having shared a three day Limitless workshop in London at the beginning of June. I knew Christof would do what he could to take care of me and that was all I had, nothing more and nothing less.

Trust was my only way forward and after all my precious spiritual learnings, I knew I had to "go with the flow" – without expectation, attachment to the outcome or conditions. There would be no bargaining, pleading with my guides, just simply TRUST. The word resounded in my head as I gathered my thoughts, emptied the bins, made a cuppa and tidied the last few bits around the house, packing the final few items in my suitcase and hand luggage.

My dear friend Dawn had agreed to have my phone and diary which meant I would have *no distractions* whilst away though I have to say that during the 3 day London Limitless workshop with Christof the work was so intense, that I certainly could not have answered any enquiries from patients and clients anyways. She was definitely the best for the job and I was incredibly grateful. Thus, I would have NO outside contact with the world whilst away and NO distractions from others. This gave me freedom to concentrate on ME and allow my spiritual advancement, whatever shape and form that may take.

As I drove to Dawn's house in bright sunshine, I certainly felt more than slightly nervous. As I dropped the phone and diary through the letter box, I knew that this was it for me. There was no going back now. Time to face the fear and "suck it up Princess!"

Driving along the motorway towards Liverpool, I became aware of the bulk of traffic and was surprised even at this early hour. I was so pleased that I was no longer a part of the commuter nightmare since I had changed my life over a decade before. Phew! Working from home was such a bonus. Whilst driving, I thought of all the changes in that decade and how my life had evolved because *I had allowed change* and actually had by now become welcoming & accepting of it. I was touched to think about the abundance of my wonderful family and ever-growing number of grandchildren, my friendships, clients and patients too.

Most of all, I was aware of how I had changed. How I had evolved from a life of stress, hassle & drama, to one of freedom and inner peace too. I became aware of how much I valued these things now and how much that value deepened daily.

My guides had mentioned change. Christof was a profound healer and shaman and a heart-centred humble man. He himself had changed his life having previously lectured internationally as a top physical fitness coach. He had realised over the years that the soul is important too and though he could have stayed in that industry and continued to earn thousands, he had instead chosen to follow his heart and soul. *This then led him to teach from the soul to the soul.*

He had been asking The Universe for unlimited abundance and wanted to work with those in positions of leadership who could influence people; by making them aware of the immense benefits of living a harmonious life. They then in turn could bring this to their clientele and employees creating harmony in the workspace too. This was quite a thought and an incredible vision, one that could indeed be ground-breaking & revolutionary. Imagine employers teaching awareness of energies; positive mental attitude and the Law Of Attraction, not to mention personal awareness and personal responsibility?

He had asked me to attend the Limitless workshop in London at the beginning of June following my suggestion that I interview him on my TV show "Living A Dynamic Life". Now he had asked me to join him in Ibiza to work with him and to meet some wonderful new people and assist them through life's journey. Where was MY life's journey going? Where was life taking ME?

What was it that I wanted to manifest? For years I had looked for the perfect partner. Working to find my spiritual self, I had found my inner child who had been locked away for over 40 years. Through finding her whilst training as a life-coach my contentment had deepened and strengthened. I had changed massively in the previous year and had learnt to see life through the eyes of a child once more. I had learnt to laugh even more and to be even more child-like.

My journey towards **completion** had begun and was nearing **completion**. I was very happy and contented. I was in the process of allowing and not forcing things into my life. My stress levels were reducing too, as I became more accepting of all things in life. My life no longer contained any drama and my health and well-being were fantastic too.

I have a beautiful family, a lovely home, a job I love and friends and family I deeply care for and they in turn for me also. Life is great and knowing that through my book and my work I have received some awesome reviews and wonderful testimonials, in the last decade and more. I had indeed touched all those who had met me or had some form of communication\treatment from me, so I too was deeply moved in all aspects.

Whilst driving to Liverpool airport I thought of the TV show which was also doing well and reviews were very positive; this too was evolving and I had had a lengthy discussion in the studio a few weeks earlier about positive changes.

I continued to enjoy spending time with my beloved family and granddaughters. Matty my middle son, continued to enjoy his new life in Australia, although I dearly missed him daily. I thought of him often and tuned into him, checking his state of well-being.

Financial freedom would mean that I could visit him and stay for a few weeks, sharing new experiences, hearing his voice and having a daily hug or three! He is 6" 7" so hugging him is a fabulous experience, as I curl into his chest and he still over hangs around me. Find someone who is almost a foot taller than you and enjoy the experience. It's totally awesome.

My thoughts took me to my evolution. I was now happy in myself and happier than I had ever been. This feeling was deepening daily and my connection to The Divine was strengthening too. By listening to that connection, I knew where I was meant to be and who I was meant to be with. I loved myself now and so never felt alone or lonely. Did I want that special someone in my life? Someone who could assist me through life's journey and someone I too could assist? To be supported and nurtured felt right, and, as I tuned into the feeling, it allowed my heart centre to expand, and it felt warm and comforting too.

Arriving at the airport I parked the car, thanked her; my car I mean, gathered my luggage and walked inside to the departures lounge. Checking in was easy and I was looking forward to breakfast at "Frankie and Benny's" and the usual hot chocolate. I had enough time although would not be waiting around for hours before the flight and announcements were made to board. Nervous flutters in my tummy came and went.

The flight was full and most were youngsters going for the typical Ibiza experience of drink and sex. They were very noisy and disruptive on the plane! For those of you that know me well you'll be aware that this is my idea of hell, as I love quiet spaces and times. I kept reminding myself to remain calm and stay in the heart-centre, whilst they got more and more drunken, louder and louder and more and more rude to the cabin crew! The flight otherwise was smooth and the views over the ocean and the mountains amazing. Landing meant that I would be free of their noise. I looked forward to collecting my suitcase and then I could escape when Carolina collected me.

I was greeted warmly by Carolina and a piece of cardboard reading "Mary Limitless Retreat". This was it, the adventure was about to begin. Christof had emailed the day before to state that I would be going straight to the villa where the retreat was to be held and that I would see him the following day. I trusted that The Universe had it covered although I have to say I was slightly disappointed as it would have been lovely to meet and greet him and I was also looking forward to meeting his beloved Roxy too.

Carolina and I connected instantly; her warm smile and French accent immediately put me at ease. We packed the car and chatted, as though we had known one another for years, about healing and a thousand and one subjects. Carolina explained that I was the first to arrive that day and I thought to myself that at least I had my journal and my books so being alone in the villa would be fine. I knew the Universe had it covered and that I would be fine regardless. Trusting The Universe meant that I had totally surrendered the outcome and any and all expectations on my first day on Ibiza.

Then when she explained that she was taking me directly to Christof's villa and I knew it was all in divine order. I was so excited now. This was it. My eight days on Ibiza had begun, what was to follow I had no idea but here I was enjoying the sunshine. I knew there would be miracles to come and of that there would be many. I was thrilled as we passed through the countryside and I felt that I was being greeted by the palm trees and the olive groves too. The sun's warmth was wonderful and although England had been warm in the previous weeks nothing compared to this.

Then I caught the sound of the cicadas. Now I was truly delighted indeed and smiled from ear to ear. It's a sound that is very personal to me and really touches my whole soul and in fact my whole being, it did from the very first time I heard it many years earlier in Greece and I guess it always will too. There is no particular reason for this, I just simply love that sound. I knew that I had done the right thing in coming and taking Christof's kindly opportunity which I knew was also from The Universe and part of The Divine Plan.

This was meant to be, an invitation to return here after almost 6 years away and was wondering if this too would be another 360 degree turnaround?

I was looking forward to seeing Christof, meeting Roxy and seeing his new home. His previous lifestyle meant that as an international speaker he had travelled for over twenty years. He had not had a solid base previously and I knew this meant the world to him. The simplicity of being settled and to have somewhere to call home were his personal desires which he had wanted for many years. How many of us take our home for granted? Do we really think that living that kind of lifestyle is full of glitz and glamour? This man craved a base and he certainly deserved the best too.

As we pulled up and the security gate was opened, I was delighted to see a row of palm trees line the driveway. There was a lovely garden to the left and a POOL. I love swimming and always have, the feeling of homeliness struck me, I felt safe and very welcome indeed here. I was thrilled to be welcomed by Christof and some other attendees; Greg and Izzy. I knew, I knew them both immediately and just as I arrived they were making their way to the beach. We exchanged "Hello" and "Goodbye" and then Christof explained that he had some work to do via Skype. I was to make myself at home and take a swim if I wanted.....he would be a couple of hours and Roxy would arrive later that afternoon. WOW. It was all happening.

Caroline helped me with my luggage into the bedroom and hugged me goodbye as she had other airport collections to make. I promptly changed into my swimming costume. I always have a great book with me as I love a good read and I made myself comfy on the sun lounger by the pool, started reading and was getting more and more used to the heat before deciding to go for a dip. I felt like the luckiest girl in the world! I was under NO illusion that working with Christof would be easy and that it would be a demanding week, managing the attendees and assisting them to open their souls. I knew there would be many emotional moments for them and possibly for me too. So, these precious few hours alone would be my sanctuary, before the working week started.

Looking around at the scenery, the mountains and the palm trees made me think that I could quite happily live in Ibiza – certainly live in a warmer climate. I adore the outdoor life, being able to swim in the sunshine and dine outdoors too. I read a little, swam a little, soaked up the sun and was already turning a lovely shade of the Mediterranean skin type.

Peacefulness filled my being and I was totally at ease. I was in the flow or "The Vortex" and I knew for sure that I was meant to be here. Enjoying these moments alone was soul food to me. Christof continued to work and knowing that we had worked together in past lives and that I would learn so much from him and the other attendees throughout the week was thrilling. I love listening to other peoples stories; how and what has shaped their lives and brought them to this current place. Being able to help them on their Soul's journey would be so fulfilling – knowing that you have made either a very simple or huge impression on someone and that they can then live a more enhanced life is truly a magical feeling indeed.

Later that afternoon Roxy returned and I was so delighted to meet her. We knew we had known each other before and the feeling was one of absolute comfort. We chatted easily and prepared smoothies and herbal teas. Greg and Izzy were due back any time and Christof explained that he had quite a surprise planned for us! We would all go and enjoy time on the local beach and then later that evening we had been invited to a roof-top party in a five-star hotel in the centre of Ibiza! Wow, this was really becoming something of a holiday and a marvellous opportunity to experience many different things.

We chilled on the beach that afternoon. Getting to know Christof better and how he and Roxy had met, learning that Izzy was also a Homeopath and listening to Greg's life story were all inspiring for me. We were all comfortable in one another's presence and we all knew and felt that deep connection on a soul to soul level; soul companions indeed.

Following our adventure on the beach we all got dressed up to go to the party. Christof thought it a good idea to show me the villa where the retreat would be held before the big adventure began the following day. So, whilst en route to the hotel, we called in at the Solaris villa. It was stunning and such a powerful, light vibration of healing energy stuck me. The gardens were designed beautifully with Buddhist statues and deities to Ascended Masters throughout the grounds. There was a platform where we would do yoga daily and outdoor furniture where we could all sit and share our days' learnings. There were also two yurts; one was for Christof so he could get changed for the healing ceremonies, the other was for one or more of the guests to sleep in.

My mind raced as I thought of how I might like to stay in the yurt. Having had my fear of worms and slugs over the years had meant that I had never been able to camp outside. Together with the great British weather, the thought of camping had never appealed to me. However, here I was with a yurt, endless sunshine and Solaris explaining that it would be cooler in the yurt in the evenings than the villa itself. Was this an ideal opportunity for me to clear and heal the fear once and for all?

Me being me and the fact that I'm always up for a challenge, considered the possibility of me actually having the courage to stay in the yurt, away from the comfort of the villa and yet to be able to look up at the stars and be closer and thus open to Mother Earth. Once again, I decided to go with trust and knew that if it was meant to be it would be. I was getting used to the yurt idea and it was certainly growing on me! I made the decision that if anyone else requested it as their living quarters then I would sleep in the villa itself. We checked out the other areas of the villa before saying our goodbyes.

Arriving at the five-star hotel was amazing – the interior décor, the staff and even the lifts were out of this world. From the roof top was a panoramic view over the harbour. As the night went on looking down at the lights from the boats, the mountainsides and the shoreline made me feel enriched. It was lovely indeed. Greg and I had a complimentary neck, back & hand massage. The music was live and the people seemed very nice. I'm certainly not a party animal, nor am I a particularly social creature to be honest, but I was thoroughly enjoying the experience.

We had been told that another couple would be joining us that evening. They had flown in from America for the retreat and would meet us after 8.30pm. Once again, when we met them the soul companion "knowing" between us was truly remarkable. Within minutes Sky and I, called each other soul sisters – knowing that we had in fact been sisters before and her husband, a brother to me. Now the excitement for the retreat was really building. It was hardly any wonder that my guides had given me NO insight whatsoever on what was to await me!

We had all agreed that we would have a huge day tomorrow so an early night would be called for. After dancing, singing and laughing together we said our goodbyes. As we drove through the evening back to Christof's villa a feeling of **completion;** or at least the beginning of completion began to creep over me. Just what was in store for me?

I slept well and must have my Grandad's genes, as he was known to sleep anywhere at any time! He once fell asleep standing at the side of a light house but that's another story! As I drifted off, I could feel my spirit guides pulling close, feeling that they would be right with me throughout the coming week.

A new day, a new dawn and that afternoon we were due to meet the rest of the attendees. I was excited though slightly nervous and wondered just how much help and support I would be able to offer Christof. Christof, Roxy and the others were up and about by the time I awoke. We shared a healthy breakfast of smoothies and herbal teas and the plan for the day was explained, as we would be leaving mid-afternoon. This meant that we had time to swim and chill beforehand. Perfect. More pleasure time and more time getting to know the others.

Christof and the boys were busy in the garden lifting weights and exercising whilst we three girls looked on and felt very tired! After lunch we would be heading out to Solaris. A full week was planned and I wondered how I would cope. Fear was certainly within my being though I knew I was here for a reason, if not several and I would stay the course; come what may.

I was aware that my right ear was feeling uncomfortable, though not painful and I thought it strange, as I hardly ever feel pain or suffer any illness now that I listen to my body and am on the spiritual path. I had been swimming though hadn't dived from a great height, so nothing explained why I should feel this way? I just paid attention to it and sent it healing. I had my Homeopathic remedies with me and certainly one of the best healers in the world.....the story would unfold!

Arriving at the villa for real this time was quite a powerful experience. This was it! The time was NOW! Kelly and Jacqueline whom I had already met whilst in London were there to greet us, as were Sky, Kay and Leah. It was lovely to re-connect with them all. I was so excited. They explained they were sharing rooms and I was welcome to join them in the villa if I wanted to….this meant that the yurt was vacant! I was delighted and explained that I would stay in there.

Kelly offered to help carry my luggage, as we walked to the yurt, which was quite a way away tucked in the corner of the grounds. As we walked we chatted easily and I explained my accommodation choice due to the worm phobia. Kelly and I got on easily and had done so from when we had first met in London, a few weeks before. She too is very psychic and "sees" more than the normal person, having a range of vision to include spirits and energies. As we placed the bags inside and admired the surroundings, we recognised what a knowing we had & that it was going to be a life-changing week for each and every one of us. As we walked back to the villa she suddenly stopped, she looked across at me and said she had déjà vu, that we had all been together before and that we had all lived together as a community…..the one where we were all murdered; which had led me to experience worm phobia originally. Wow. This was a huge realisation and revelation. We agreed to say nothing to the others; although I said I would inform Christof and then he was in the know should anyone else perceive déjà vu.

Christof wanted us all to get the best out of the week and as such we would be having a week without sugar, caffeine and other products which affect our vibration such as meat and alcohol. This would ensure our blood was alkaline and the PH not acidic which causes all sorts of pathologies – not to mention "brain fog". Thus, it would be a diet of organic fruit and veg, fresh herbal teas, water and nuts, seeds, pulses, etc. To be honest, I have a good diet and haven't eaten meat for over a year. Alcohol never really appealed to me either, although I was at that time partial to a hot chocolate and salt and vinegar crisps!

We introduced ourselves that afternoon and held a welcome ceremony. Christof and I interviewed each of the attendees, so that we knew which areas they wanted to improve upon in their lives and what they needed to clear emotionally, which would allow them to go forward in life. It was very interesting and gave us a good insight into what might surface for them throughout the week. We also asked about their physical health and well-being as this is always symbolic of spiritual & emotional well-being and balance. The body will never lie – no matter what the pathology, pain or symptoms. Certainly as a Homeopath and a psychic I had an advantage in this understanding. As a healer we can clear the emotional baggage that has caused it in the first place and as a psychic "see" the past life connections too.

Christof was grateful for my help and support as we gathered our information. We decided upon who was a priority and thus decided upon the order of the healing ceremonies. The first would be held that evening.

The days would commence at 9.30am sharp after a healthy breakfast and yoga was the ideal way in which to exercise the body; which would be daily for approximately an hour. We would then all share what was coming up for each of us – any emotions, feelings, etc. There were lessons throughout the week on how to let go of conditioning and how to improve self-awareness and personal responsibility. By doing all these things, we would each become more aware of our soul's journey and our life purpose/creative talents/abilities/strengths and vulnerabilities. By recognising patterns of behaviour and our emotional responses to certain situations we can begin the process of self-mastery. Hence the title of the retreat: *Limitless*. We are indeed all *Limitless* beings, it's just that we think limiting thoughts, play the victim and get swamped into life's general crap.

Times of change are never easy, as we push ourselves through barriers and boundaries and out of our comfort zones. Inevitably, we benefit from these times, although change can and is often challenging for us. Being asked to be a part of this change for myself and knowing I had the power to assist others throughout the week was indeed amazing. I was going to embrace it with a completely open mind and heart. My guides had told me the previous day that I would be changed forever. Throughout my life my guides have advised me correctly, so I knew that whatever their advice, it would be accurate.

Eating outside is a real pleasure to me and we howled laughing and joking through most meal times. It's amazing the variety of foods you can make with vegan ingredients. Some of the sweets were out of this world. It was such fun being with the group and sharing our own stories. Sometimes inevitably emotional issues came up for release, we all respected one another so just encouraged the release in the easiest possible way. Having a good diet myself, I rarely craved anything although some of the others really struggled with thoughts of meat and coffee.

The lady who owned the villa often joined us and she was a delight. Even on the first day she noticed how well we all got on considering we were from far and wide across the world. She herself had run many groups and never known a group to gel so quickly and so deeply. Kelly and I just looked at one another and kept our thoughts to ourselves.

Each and every moment to me was precious; spending time with like-minded people, being in beautiful surroundings and on one of the most spiritual islands; Ibiza. The energy here is very high; most people think they are attracted here for the booze and the party side of things. It touches your soul – no matter what your background, religion or spiritual disposition. I loved everything about this place and I made an effort each and every night to send my affirmations to The Universe at sunset, knowing that because the vibration here was so high, then they were much more likely to be heard.

Christof had a variety of trips planned and I intended to enjoy each and every one of them to the full. Despite the fact that I was working with him that week, I was also here to embrace everything that was on offer. I love travel and I love new experiences too. Although I had visited Ibiza before, some 6 years previously, this was a whole new level, as I had changed so much in that time. Most days I was the first one to get up and this meant that I had ME time before the days got crazy busy. I spent much time just tuning into myself and listening to nature, after all I was staying in the yurt, so as complete with nature as I could be too. Even the showers were outdoors. A black rubber bag was held up over the shower itself, so that the force of gravity allowed it to flow when the tap was opened. I had never showered au Naturale before and I have to say that I loved that too.

One of the trips was to old Ibiza town in the evening. We were dropped off and given our rendezvous points and times. We naturally split into groups and I was enthralled at the history of this wonderful place. It was so wonderful to laugh and share thoughts with people who were fast becoming life-long friends. We wandered easily up to the top of the hillside and I realised that I wasn't even out of breath. I didn't even feel tired in the slightest. Looking down on the harbour was awesome. The lighting on the harbour, the boats and cruisers was spectacular. I personally have a thing about looking out over landscapes at night and love the lights against the darkness.

As we wandered around we passed many eating places. The smells and thoughts of normal foods tempted us all. It was funny as the boys salivated when we passed dishes of steak/chicken. I thought it was really funny and then….we passed a restaurant where the guests, sat at tables outside, were eating seafood paella. It really is an absolute favourite of mine and I laughed at myself because now I understood what the others felt as I craved the paella. It soon became a joke amongst us and we continued along, searching the streets and exploring the old town.

Christof had given us strict instructions to be back on time, etc as we were then going to a beach party on a private beach. For those of you who know me, I'm not and never have been a beach party girl. In fact I'm not even a party girl really. I'm certainly not a drinker and although I love to dance, it's usually around the kitchen! So another experience presented itself to me and I had already decided that I would definitely give it a whirl.

We arrived after a long drive down a very bumpy beach road. Huge bouncers allowed our entry and we gathered on the beach. My taste in modern music is limited let's say and whatever was being played was crap. Not having been on the party scene I thought this was quite normal although everyone agreed, maybe my taste in music isn't so bad after all? Oh how my children would have laughed at me! Mum at a beach party in Ibiza!

The worm phobia has constricted me in many ways and one which I have regretted, is that I had never been able to lie on the grass or any flat surface at night (for fear that one might crawl onto me). I had always wanted to lie down flat on the earth and look upon the stars and the evening sky. However, here I was in Ibiza, with stars above and a beach where I could lie and fulfil this need in my soul. As I lay there that night looking up at the stars something in me changed. Despite the noise of the music, the people and the general hub, all I remember hearing was the sound of the gentle waves on the shoreline. Blissful doesn't really cover what I'm explaining: although it comes near.

Returning to the villa that evening was truly magical for me, as I said "Goodnight" to the others I felt much lighter and happier in myself than ever before. I returned to my lovely cool yurt and snuggled down for a good nights' sleep and another joy filled, though incredibly busy day tomorrow. I was still aware of the pain in my ear. My right ear was getting worse and now my left had also begun to feel uncomfortable too. Nonetheless at this time neither was painful, so I just made a mental note to have a healthy awareness.

The first healing ceremony the next day was a magical experience as they always are with Christof. They are always held at the end of the day and into the evening. We all assisted by sending positive energy to the person receiving the healing and holding a sacred space. Christof always calls in his Spirit guides and sets the intentions clearly for the best possible outcome. The benefits of healing are truly magical – I have had many miracles myself in my work. This work was compounded with all of us working together as one.

I was able to assist Christof as I offered psychic protection and also shared what I saw when the energies began to lift from the physical bodies. Often I become aware of past life trauma which can also be released too. Needless to say it's a beautiful experience for all those present and Roxy's compassionate energy shone through for us all.

Returning to my yurt was quite an experience. It was dark and I was several hundred feet away from everyone else. Christof and Roxy would be returning home to their villa so I was left holding the fort as it were.

The stars shone brightly, without the artificial light that obscures their presence in my usual Lancashire home. It was so quiet and I felt a deepened peace that I have rarely felt before. My first night in the great outdoors would be truly memorable. I celebrated inside my soul at managing to honour and move away from my fears; the fears that had revelled so much information to me all those years ago during an E.F.T. Emotional Freedom Technique workshop. Despite this, I promised myself that if in any way I felt unsafe in the yurt, then I would take the spare bedroom upstairs in the villa with everyone else.

Curling up inside my blankets, with the nothingness outside was truly magical. I had said a silent prayer to The Universe under the stars before zipping up the yurt. I lay there feeling tired and wondered if it had been heard. Since reading "The Power Of Your Subconscious Mind" I often went to sleep allowing the words freedom, love and success to float into my consciousness then to take me to dreamland.

As usual, I awoke in the early hours for a pee. There were compost toilets further down the garden and in the dead of the night I ventured out. It was calm and peaceful. No fears touched my being and I truly did recognise that I felt more whole-hearted than ever before. Returning to bed again I soon drifted off, looking forward to another day of magical experiences and learning from Christof.

I'm always an early bird, so as usual was awake well before 8am. I walked to the villa and made myself a cup of herbal tea and just sat quietly in the garden listening to the birds. No-one else was awake and to be honest most days started in this way. I was often the first up. I decided I would take my second cuppa up to the yurt, sit outside and read or write in my journal.

Later we would be doing the yoga and then meditating. After that we would be "in class" learning even more. There was so much information to take on board about healthy eating, the chakras, acidic verses, alkaline blood, not to mention lots of others add-ons that Christof threw in for good measure. We were all learning from one another to be honest. It was lovely to sit out in the open air and be in nature whilst learning, there were sun canopies arranged over outdoor furniture and it was truly marvellous.

The pain in my ear suddenly began to increase to such a point that it suddenly became unbearable. I was in absolute agony. The right ear drum felt as if it would burst and the left was not too far behind either. What was happening? How could it suddenly worsen like this so quickly? As I struggled with tears of sheer pain, Christof said that "as your vibration increases your ears will often become painful". Too bloody right!

Tears streamed down my face and I found it virtually impossible to speak. Christof noticed my tears thank goodness and asked me to explain what was happening. It was very difficult to even comprehend, never mind explain, as suddenly my heart centre was ripped out. I helplessly pointed to my ears and then my heart centre and my throat too. Although I've had many weird and wonderful experiences over the years whilst on my spiritual journey this was amazing; and certainly less than pleasant. The pain from both ears was now unbearable and the pain in my heart area beyond words.

The tears continued to flow; by now I was inconsolable and in agony. I remember Christof standing over me doing healing whilst I just cried and cried and shook with pain. He chanted the familiar shamanic chants and someone was asked to run and get his rattle and crystals too. It felt like I was there in part only, as I was almost becoming delirious with pain. What the hell was happening to me? The pain in my chest continued to worsen – just when I thought it couldn't possibly get any worse! My chest felt like I had a shot gun wound and it was completely none existent. There was a hole of approximately 6 inches round and no skin, ribs or anything. I could see right through my own chest!

The pain was unbelievable. Christof's chanting increased as he stood over me calling in all manner of light beings. I could see a wide variety of them; Buddha, Qwan Yin, Christ, Babaji, Sai Baba, Isis, Bridget, Mary mother of Christ and Mary Magdalene too. They were all offering their assistance to me and saying they were willing to work with me anytime I requested their help and assistance. They placed themselves in the open wound and worked to heal it. It's funny that grief has always been an emotion which has completely overwhelmed me in this lifetime.

Then I saw again the vision of two people kissing with the sunset in the background. I knew one was me and the other I could not recognise; neither from the side profile nor the energy field. Who was he?

My guides and the Ascended Masters kept repeating *"It is time"*, *"You are ready now"*. I was being asked if I wanted to live here on the island and work one week in four. I agreed despite being in my current state of sheer agony and distress. I could see myself in the not too distant future selling my house and moving on. This was really what I wanted, to live more and work less. I knew in those moments how much love and support The Universe was offering to me. I would have time to write, to research and to simply just BE.

Throughout all the pain and the tears I recognised my inner child, that lovely little girl and she came and sat on my right knee whilst Christof continued his work of healing me. The Higher Beings came towards me and were stating their thanks and blessings too. I saw many I did not recognise such as Mayan, Hawaiian and Aztec Gods too. Throughout this intensity, I saw the faces of all those I had loved and been separated from; my son Matthew, daughter Emily, my grandad, Sal, Mark, Kevin, my ex-husband Chris too.

There were many I did not recognise, as it was like a fast forward movie. The times of separation and loss, through death, or just differing circumstances was tremendous and the feelings of loss and grief hurt like no pain I had ever before experienced. It really was as though two huge cymbals had crashed together cracking my heart centre wide open. The totality of the grief was so intense.

I guess that really was the moment when my heart centre was indeed ripped out and opened so I could become even more heart centred. One of the last pictures I saw was of myself with this man again and hearing the words "You will work together & heal across the world".

It all happened about 13.30-14.00, on the afternoon of the 28th July 2014. It's a day I will never forget. As Christof finished the healing, he asked Greg and Kay to help me to my feet so we could have a group hug. I barely felt conscious to be honest and only vaguely recall being held up whilst Christof played "The Eye Of The Tiger" for me. The tears just continued to flow and I was exhausted, mentally, spiritually, physically and emotionally. I felt like I had a royal battering indeed.

I needed to lie down and try to recover. As I lay there in the sun I could barely hear Christof's voice as he continued with the afternoon lesson. I was struggling to stay awake and knew I had to make my way into the villa to where we held the healing ceremonies. That's where the energy was at its highest. I would be safer there whilst my soul, maybe my whole being upgraded. It took me so much energy to pull myself up and move from that sofa to walk the 100 yards into the house. I collapsed onto the settee and slept. I was aware however that I was surrounded by guides and all manner of Higher Beings who installed healing codes into the soles of my feet. I could feel the codes travelling up into my legs and beyond. I slept and slept. The words love, courage, strength and wisdom kept running through my head.

Later that afternoon, the rest of the group came to check on me, I vaguely recall being asked if I felt fit enough to go to the beach with them. I really had been looking forward to it all day and already had my bag packed. I hadn't got the energy to even sit up! I was gutted as they left, though knew I honestly needed to just be still and sleep whilst the upgrades took place.

Waking only for fluid and toilet breaks was how that afternoon passed. Later on, I awoke and felt I needed to eat. A smoothie and some salad had been put to one side for me and I managed to sit for a while. Solaris appeared and was sweeping and washing the patio. I was too exhausted to assist and was truly glad of her understanding. My eyes began to close and I had no strength to resist as I passed once again, into a deep sleep, being aware that my whole being was being worked on and upgraded. The body needs to rest whilst DNA is cleaned and de-cluttered. Even my aura felt larger and brighter too.

At 7.30 that evening I awoke feeling very sweaty and knew I needed a shower. Did I feel I had energy to stand whilst I showered? I walked in what must have looked like a drunken stupor to the yurt for my clothing and managed a quick shower before sleep crept once again into my being.

Sometime later that evening, the crew returned, the sound of their laughter and loveliness was touching to hear. They were eager to see how I was and it was lovely to feel their love as they checked on me. "You look like shit" I recall was one comment – though said with the kindest regard and thoughtfulness. They asked if I wanted anything and refreshed my water jug. They said they'd all missed me and asked how I was feeling.

It was getting late and they were about to get ready for another healing ceremony. I needed my bed and they needed the room. Christof and Jacqueline held my arms as I "walked" to the yurt. I was well and truly knackered. Their kindness that night is something I shall always remember. As I drifted into another deep sleep, I knew I was surrounded with Higher Beings as was the whole yurt.

It was 8.30am before I next awoke. I didn't feel my usual totally vital self, although I was much improved. I knew I would have to be gentle with myself and listen to my physical body; even if there were some fabulous trips out and about Ibiza.

I walked slowly to the house and made myself a cuppa. Jacqueline greeted me warmly. She asked about my well-being and said I looked much better than I had done the previous day. She explained that the healing ceremony had been awesome and I was truly sorry that I had missed the experience. We slowly wandered down the garden for yoga. Christof arrived and checked on my health and well-being too. I assured him that I was listening to my body and he said I could just duck out, if I needed to rest at any point.

One by one the rest of the "family" as we called ourselves by now arrived. They showed their concern and I felt their genuine sincerity too. I was deeply touched and as Greg and Izzy approached I apologised for not having been able to attend their ceremony. They said they'd all felt the presence of my soul regardless of my physical absence. It was such a lovely thing to say and as the others had confirmed the same thing I was touched.

I did as much yoga as felt comfortable and listened carefully to my body's needs. Later that afternoon we were doing some dance work so I had already said I would do what felt right. My energy was building, though I knew I wasn't yet up to full speed. The day continued and little by little I improved. The dance work and body movement was awesome and I really enjoyed myself too.

After lunch Christof had given us a rest break for siesta. There would be no healing ceremony that night. He announced that he had a trip planned for us to paddle a canoe out into the sea, to watch the sunset. By now, I was feeling much better, though unsure I was able to attend. Besides I had never paddled a canoe before and although I'm a good swimmer, wasn't absolutely sure I could make it. Christof suggested we all reconvene after siesta. My yurt was lovely and cool, as I curled up for my afternoon nap.

Upon awakening, I felt well enough to push myself into another new experience. I was really giving this retreat my all and allowing myself to experience as many new opportunities as possible. There would be no healing ceremony that evening, so once home from the beach then I could return for zzz's. Following siesta few wanted to attend the kayaking at sunset. Leah took some convincing and eventually Leah, Roxy, Christof, Izzy, Greg and I left for our evenings adventures. It wasn't yet dusk and it was still warm. Neither Leah nor I, had ever kayaked before and I can honestly say that we laughed and laughed, as we struggled to get out into the open water. I took the rear position as she directed us. Paddling left meant we went right and vice versa. Christof and Roxy howled at us as we paddled around in circles for ages before we truly got the hang of it all. We almost headed into a cave at one point and banged against several of the boats that were anchored off shore.

The feeling of freedom once we got into open water was amazing and feeling the wind through my face and hair was fabulous; especially bearing in mind how awful I had felt the previous day! I was enjoying each and every precious moment and soaking up the sunshine too. We paddled into open water and had the opportunity to snorkel. Leah felt safer in the kayak but once again, I was ready for an adventure. Miracles do happen and despite wondering whether or not I would upturn the boat – with Leah in it, I managed although not exactly in a lady-like manner to get into the water.

Swimming and knowing how deep the water was just inspired me to swim more and watching the underwater wildlife truly beautiful to behold. We were told it was time to leave and our guides came to help me get back in the kayak. I gathered some seaweed as a gift to my companion Leah as I attempted to board. Leah begged me not to tip it up as I tried without success to get back on board.

After numerous attempts, bearing in mind that everyone else *but me* were now back in their said kayaks Toby decided that I needed a hand. By this point, I couldn't stop laughing and as such was totally unable to coordinate myself back into the said kayak. Toby asked "Are you ok if I put my hands on your bum to help you aboard"....my swift reply through giggles was "just do it".....by this point everyone else was also in stitches too. Completely unladylike I was thrust into the boat and Leah was relieved that I had in fact NOT tipped her into the said water. By the time I had reassembled myself the other kayaks were several hundred feet away. The sun was beginning to set and we paddled faster in order to catch up.

The others had stopped to rest and watch the sun go down on the day. I was so thrilled and excited knowing that I had achieved yet another goal. As we gazed into the colours of the sunset we both shared a very special silence. My affirmations, I knew, had been heard and were registered by The Universe and I was feeling ready for anything.

Returning home that evening I was filled with a really deep sense of satisfaction. I had pushed through many fears and achieved much in such a short space of time.

Throughout the week the miracles kept coming. Many began to re-remember that we had in fact once been part of a spiritual community & we were part of a larger global community. In fact, one evening Belinda remembered that we were **called "The Diamonds Of The Light".** How amazing it all was, we enjoyed our reunion and have stayed in touch. Soul companions know no boundaries across time & space. Leaving the following Friday was very sad, though we all promised to keep in touch. Each and every one of us have grown and gained so much in less than a year.

Thank you Christof.

PORTUGAL

"Generosity is a sign of our reliable
connection to abundance"

Following the chat I had had with Colin and Clare, regarding my finances, together with the positive input I was receiving from the Arbonne team, the money was rolling in.

Life was on the up or so it seemed, I had loved Ibiza and felt very much in the flow. In September quite out of the blue, my guides instructed me to go to Portugal. It was strange, as I have wanted to visit Porto for over 14 years. I was most surprised and yet obviously delighted that I would at least be visiting a place where I knew I had to be and in fact, had known, for over a decade!

Usually my guides give me clues as to why. I often do Earth healing whilst I am visiting a place, sometimes I know and recognise that I am there to collect soul fragments. There have been so many miracles in my life when I have followed their instructions that I simply "go with the flow."

I am happy to travel alone and wondered perhaps was it that I would meet my new partner whilst I was there? I still received not even a glint of a clue, so I just began looking on the internet for holidays. Nothing was jumping out at me, so I wondered whether or not to use Co-operative Travel, as I had used them previously to book travel to Luxor, Egypt.

Upon answering the telephone, I chatted easily with a chap called Matthew. It was so easy and flights and hotel were booked.

However, unless I was willing to travel to a London airport, which I certainly was not, then Porto was out of the question and thus all, in all, after checking in and asking my guides, Lisbon was my destination the following week. As Matthew took my details for the booking, he recognised my name and we discovered that he was from Manchester, had seen, and READ, "The Goldfish That Jumped," I was so thrilled.

I was excited and slightly confused however, as I still received absolutely NO information from my guides as to what would await me when I arrived in Portugal?

The flight was easy and when I arrived in Lisbon the midday sun beat down and gave me a huge welcome. After looking through holiday brochures, I just wanted to get amongst the city, so rather than order a taxi to the hotel, I thought that I would get a bus or train. Actually, when I walked from the airport there were no taxis anyways and no-one to ask. Not even a bus was in sight either. Matthew had said it would be easy! I do not speak the language and had never actually been here before at all. I didn't know anyone, here so was a completely "new girl on the block" so to speak.

I headed for the underground! It was very busy and I really didn't actually know where I was going. Everyone kept pushing in front of me and I just accepted what was to be whilst I waited...deciding what I would do. Should I go back upstairs and try to get a taxi or a bus? I asked The Universe for help as I realised that this was all a little too crazy for me! Straight away a very tall Dutch chap approached, asked was I in the queue and asked for a ticket "Down town." Well that made perfect sense and so I asked for the same after he left. I had just come up my Master plan....I would follow him I thought!

As I received my tickets and turned to go, he had disappeared. I asked The Universe again for assistance, as I followed even more steps down towards said train line. The hustle and bustle I had expected to find was nowhere to be seen! I honestly didn't know what to do and there were four train lines potentially to catch. Not quite as simple as I had thought! In the centre of the area was a stand selling products. I had NO choice other than to go and request their help and pray that they spoke English and would take pity on a very confused maiden!

I approached and was greeted with many smiles so that was a definite bonus! I asked if anyone spoke English when this chap answered in a Lancashire accent to say "Yes." Imagine my surprise when he asked if I was from Yorkshire! "No" I explained, "where are you from?" "I'm from here although I was sent to Stonyhurst college as I child until I was 16 years old." Said college is only about 15 miles from Preston. We chatted easily and laughed at the synchronicities, as he explained which coloured line to get and that I needed to change and he also suggested that I go to the hotel first and leave my luggage.

So, the Universe had shown that I was meant to be here. I continued to ask for help as I followed his directions. As I sat on a very busy train there was NO room for my suitcase, so I just held it tightly, very tightly. In fact, every time the train stopped, the wheels decided that the bloody suitcase was in competition with said train and could travel at super duper speeds too! My ARM!!!!

Once again I was saved. A lovely chap came to sit beside me, who was very evidently gay and held said flyaway suitcase for me. I was reminded of my friends Ian and Steve, both gays, who had kindly looked after me whilst I travelled on the London underground the year before.

I both thanked him & apologised in English and was so delighted when he spoke back to me, in English, asking where I was going. I explained that I had never been here before and was keen to get to the city to see the beautiful sights. He explained that he too was changing at the next station, getting off at the stop before mine and offered to carry my suitcase. WOW. I really was being looked after.

He was really kind and advised me to always watch my handbag, that many restaurants had two menus; one for the tourist (and it was obvious I was), and one for the locals; which of course would be much cheaper in price! He continued to explain that there was a train line by the shore in Lisbon and showed me on my map its location, advising that I visit both Belem and Cascais. He said the train line ran right by the coast and the scenery would be stunning. There were also places that under NO circumstances was I to even venture into as they were rough! The other chap from Stonyhurst had also advised the same. How wonderful and synchronistic too. We wished each other well as he left the train and we smiled at one another, a deep, knowing smile.

I arrived at my stop and when I had mounted the stairs into the sunshine just "knew" I had to be here. I followed my nose and headed to where I thought I should be. Excitement filled my soul and my inner child was thrilled too. I was aware that I was, by now, both hungry and thirsty. It had been a very early start that morning to the airport and I was flagging. Although my plan was to bumble for about an hour, I was becoming aware, especially in the heat of the day & with a huge suitcase, this would not be possible. I managed to find a vantage point from where I could see the surrounding countryside and ocean too. It was magical and most impressive too.

I asked for help again from my guides and walked a few yards ahead stumbling onto a local restaurant. I asked if they spoke English and promptly sat down. The menu looked fabulous and one particular staff member spoke extremely good English and asked to take my order. I also requested water and a hot chocolate too. It was delightful indeed. Following the meal she asked me if I wanted a taxi and I thought that that was very considerate indeed. Within minutes I was on my way through the city, passing so many beautiful sights and trying to remember the direction was taxi was going, so that I could book in, freshen up and get straight back out again. I was certainly going to enjoy each and every minute of this magnificent city.

Booking in was easy and my room comfortable enough too. It was slightly out of the main city, though I would be happy to walk in to the town daily anyways. I freshened up and tried to retrace the steps of the taxi! It soon became very evident that this was impossible as there had been many corners, twists and turns! I gave up and followed my nose, again going with trust.

The architecture was lovely and I was thrilled to be out in the sunshine too. Listening to the language and just bumbling, I enjoyed the many sights and soon came to the square. I had walked for over an hour and decided it was time for a rest and a spot of people watching too.

What a beautiful place indeed, there was so much to see and do here. I was thrilled and ordered some fruit juice whilst I rested my weary body and allowed myself a welcome break to recharge. I had decided that I would look for the main railway station and planned a trip along the coast. Sitting there just relaxing made me realise how my life has changed so much since I became a spiritual warrior. I also became aware of how relaxed I was after so many years as a stress head too!

Later I walked along the sea front and admired even more architectural wonders across the city before returning to my hotel room, via taxi, of course, at around 9pm. I was shattered and looking forward very much to my adventures the following day. I had decided to get the open top bus and to travel on the city tour the next day. This would enable me to get my bearings and enjoy this magical place. I was up early, as usual and left the hotel just after 8am. As it happened, I had asked the hotel staff in which direction they would advise me to walk to the city. It was amazing and simply out of the hotel front entrance, walking straight ahead and down one of the many Lisbon hills.

The tour bus was great and I enjoyed another blissful and peaceful day. I hadn't been aware of any healing that was needed, nor had I actually met anyone in particular. Why was I here? That afternoon I travelled to Belem to visit the sights and loved each and every one of them. The stunning scenery was truly outstanding and I really could have stayed longer. I had only booked a short break from Friday to Monday, so time was already running short. There was so much to do and I decided that one day I would definitely return here.

Following the advice of the gay chap on the train and my friend Bryan, I booked my rail tickets the following morning to Cascais. No longer was I afraid of trains or the underground, thanks to the help of Ian and Steve in June of 2014. As I sat on the train, I watched the waters go by, as we passed further from the city centre. Within minutes we were looking over mountains and such marvels with the sea to the left. We arrived and once again, following my nose I found my way to a lovely café before making my way to the beach. I hadn't thought to bring my costume and towel and would soon regret that decision!

I pottered around and noticed a harbour where I watched huge jellyfish and marvellous boats and yachts. I love the sea and all sailing vessels too. The sun beat down and I was already gaining quite a tan. I was so grateful that I had come here and listened to the advice that I had been given. Further wanderings took me through some beautiful gardens and the flowers, trees and shrubs were so lovely. I was in my element and wished that I had just booked my whole short break here!

After an afternoon lazing on the beach with a good book and NO costume I decided to venture towards the restaurants for an evening meal. I found a superb vegetarian restaurant and as I love to eat outside, I was delighted to sit in the street. The food was awesome and then I was told they had a rooftop where I could also enjoy a cake and some freshly prepared fruit juice. I certainly didn't need to be asked twice. I knew the view alone from up there would be fabulous too. I spotted some men who had flown in on the same plane as me and there was nowhere else to sit, so I joined them all. They were from all manner of locations in the UK and many backgrounds as we chatted easily about their lives, etc.

As the sun began to set I knew I needed to head back for the train and to the hotel. We said our goodbyes and I was still wondering why I was here? Was it merely just to enjoy myself? Nothing came to mind, despite me asking my guides, whilst I travelled back on the train looking out over a most stunning sunset.

Monday morning came all too soon and my plane would be leaving about 1pm. I had time if I was up early enough to catch the train to Belem, as I wanted to visit the Tower. I knew it wouldn't open until ten, although I thought I would just sit nearby and marvel at its architecture and the energy it held. So, that Monday morning that is indeed what I did. Just sitting in the bright, beautiful sunshine and watching over the Tower. I could feel a connection here but unless I wanted to risk missing my plane it was not an option to visit this day!

I travelled back to the hotel, waited for the taxi and met up with the same chaps I had eaten with the previous evening as we all waited for the plane. After an easy flight, my son collected me from the local airport and we chatted about his weekend, whilst I had been away. It was strange as I hadn't met anyone significant, felt any energies, nor had any insights, other than that I had had an altogether fabulous weekend. I could certainly become accustomed to this way of life though!

I vowed to return at some point in the future and still wanted to visit Porto.

UNEXPECTED SURPRISES

"Motivation is what gets you started.
Habit is what keeps you going."

Jim Rohn

My love of travel is certainly a passion of mine. So having visiting my beloved Ibiza, Portugal and Glastonbury in 2014 I really thought that that was it for me. The autumnal season had arrived. Thus the weather decline means for all of us, that unless we travel further afield then it's time to put the suitcases in the attic! Put away the shorts and the tee-shirts too!

Little did I know that when I had bought my suitcase from Debenhams that it was soon to be used again!

My youngest son Phil had had a busy year establishing his own business and needed a holiday for personal reasons. Being 23 years old – a great deal younger than myself, he'd asked two of his closest friends if they would like to go with him to Salou, in Spain. Unfortunately for them, they couldn't make it. Fortunately for me, although I was in fact his third choice (some would say lucky three), I was invited along.

I have visited several parts of Spain before; Barcelona and Alicante. To be honest I hadn't even heard of Salou. So, me being me, I looked on "TripAdvisor" and found the variety of nearby places we could visit. I certainly "knew" that I was meant to go, although I certainly had no idea how it would unfold. Phil had taken complete charge of the holiday and it was already booked; I knew nothing of the hotel, accommodation whereabouts in location to the beach/local facilities etc.

So once again I was completely following my intuition and going on trust. The flight was for 6am in the morning. For those of you that know me well – I am definitely NOT a night owl. Usually 10.45pm is the latest time for me to close the day and hit the pillow. Many asked me would I stay awake through the night from the previous day as obviously we had to be at the airport by 4am, thus leave Preston by 3 ish! We were using the Jet Parks Plus facility so therefore needed to allow an extra 30 minutes anyways. The thought of staying awake all night certainly did not float my boat. I entered the land of zzzz's about 9.30pm, knowing the alarm was set for 2am and that Phil would phone me if he hadn't heard from me, to say that I was already awake!

Phil was actually working that evening, so would only finish about 2.30am, so I was due to collect him at 2.45am. The plan was to then zip down the motorway and off we would be on our sunny travels. As a Hypnotherapist, I can self-hypnotise and thus had set my internal alarm clock. Usually I'm awake much earlier than I need to be, so I trusted that my inner clock would in fact work a treat. Indeed it did, I was wide-awake and bushy-tailed by 1.30am. By the time I had showered, sorted out the last of the washing, cleaned the loos and emptied the bins, (all the usual exciting things), I was actually ready for Phil, five minutes *later* than schedule!

He had had a quiet night at work up until five minutes before he was due to finish. The usual typical silly incident, which was both unwarranted and unnecessary, though had meant he was ten minutes late for our rendezvous. Within minutes after explaining what had happened, we were on our way to Manchester. My body was letting me know that it wasn't very happy to be awakened at this UNGODLY hour, I can assure you.

Our swift arrival at Jet Parks and the fact that there was a bus ready and waiting for us was really lovely on what was a very cold, chilly October morning; confirmation that The Universe was with us. After the luggage check-in and passport security checks, the priority was to do the things that we only do specifically in airports: perfume testing, looking through the shops, gathering an abundance of magazines, which we wouldn't normally read and for me it's a hot chocolate with eggs benedict; usually at "Frankie & Benny's". Today however, I settled for a hollandaise sauce sandwich and of course a hot chocolate too. Phil was thrilled though obviously much more tired than myself.

We waited to be informed which of the departure lounges to go and sit in, making our way upstairs as directed. After walking what seemed like miles…. I needed the ladies room and as I opened the door to go inside, had not realised that there was another lady behind me and I swiftly closed the door in her face, rather than holding it open for her. Honestly anyone would have thought it was 5.30am!!! Needless to say, I apologised.

The flight was smooth and easy. We gathered our luggage knowing that our hotel transfer was taken care of and we would just need to look for someone holding up a sign with our name on it once we got through the airport. Phil thought he was really important! Sure enough a happy, smiley face greeted us and the couple we had spoken to in the airport lounge were also on our coach. Off we set and arrived within 20 minutes at our designated hotel apartment. By this time we were both exhausted, Phil certainly more than me, so I unpacked whilst he slept.

The sun was shining brightly and it was already very hot and sunny. Looking over the balcony downstairs, I could see a pool and just enjoyed looking at the lovely inviting water whilst I waited for "Sleeping Beauty" to awaken. My dear friend Cathy had kindly leant me her copy of "The Shack" and I was keen to get started.

I sat on the balcony reading in the bright sunshine, listening to the quietness of the birds and the occasional child's laughter. How lucky I was I thought! Being the end of the season, I had assumed that the hotel would probably be half-empty and that would explain the quiet. Little did I know that the story would unfold?

Those of you that know me well are very aware that I spent several years living next door to the neighbour from hell. When the children were younger and of school age, she would regularly play her music, usually Oasis, over and over again, until at least 3 or 5am. The children would regularly be disturbed by it, not to mention me! If you were really lucky or unlucky, as the case may be, then you could often hear the din through the walls of my house, the adjoining house and maybe even the next one! Not much of a surprise that I moved into a detached bungalow! LOL.

Anyways, Phil slept on whilst I read and soaked up the sun. The apartment was basic and I was pleased that we had had a safe journey. I was thoroughly engrossed in the book though, after about an hour, became aware that I was beginning to feel very tired. The zzz's were calling me and I needed sleep, so I nodded off just before twelve. I awoke to loud music and someone talking very loudly. Wondering what was happening, I ventured on to the balcony to see that it was obviously a holiday club, rather like Butlins, Pontins, etc. and the red t-shirts rather than redcoats were organizing bingo and a music quiz. Not much choice other than to sleep through it then?

It's surprising what you can get used to and eventually I dozed off again. Phil was completely out cold and unaware of any noise at all. After about 90 minutes I awoke and went back to read my very engrossing book. I could feel the sun on my skin and knew that as usual I would be tanned in no time at all. Not knowing our whereabouts in location to shops etc. I didn't want to venture outside without Phil - especially as we only had one key between us. I had packed some snacks so managed on those whilst he continued to slumber!

Eventually my hunger pangs increased to the point that I needed to awaken "Sleeping Beauty" and did so very gently…..explaining that I was starving! A few minutes later we were making our way to the local shops and restaurants. We were booked in a self-catering apartment, so purchased some essentials before looking for a nice place to eat.

I had promised myself paella…long story! Whilst in Ibiza we had a diet of smoothies, juices and salads, throughout the week to cleanse and detox. Therefore, no meat, fish or other snacks, etc. One evening, whilst there, we had visited Ibiza old town. I had laughed at the two guys who were on the retreat with us, as they kept talking about how much they missed chicken and meat, especially steak.

As I eat a really healthy diet I was not really affected by the raw food diet, or so I thought until I saw someone dining with the biggest bowl of paella I had ever seen. From that moment on I had promised myself, whilst drooling, that once I got home, I would find a wonderful restaurant in which to eat the said paella. Needless to say, I hadn't found one and being in Spain was salivating at the mere thought!

We were in luck and here it was…..seafood paella, my absolute favourite. The waiting seemed to take forever, although we both knew it would be fresh when it arrived. It was certainly delicious and I savoured each and every mouthful. After eating, we made our way back to the hotel and after putting the shopping away, we walked down to where we thought the beach was located.

My intuition was right and the breath taking beach was located, literally less than a ten minute walk away. The scenery was indeed stunning and the views wonderful, encompassing mountains and coastline. Surrounding mountains were lovely to behold and the ocean a lovely clear blue. The water was shallow and inviting. I love swimming, but for now at least, would have to make do with a paddle. I had checked the times of the local sunset, now I had also found a beautiful spot by the sea where I could watch and meditate from, knowing what time to return. (Meditating at sunset, dawn and just after noon are very powerful times to send Universal requests to the Divine).

Looking around the whole surrounding area, it was clear that the locality had been built just for the tourists. It was really a concrete jungle. It saddened me to be honest, although I do realise that one man's meat, is indeed, another man's poison. I would make the most of this place and enjoy each and every moment.

We sat in the last of the afternoon sun and just enjoyed the whole ambiance of the place. Phil had worked many hours in the run up to the holiday so it was nice to see him relax for once. Eventually we walked back to the hotel and called at the reception desk. We saw leaflets advertising a variety of trips in the locality. We had noticed on the way from the airport, many buses advertising trips to Barcelona and had both stated that we would like to go. We asked for details and the receptionist explained that we would need to be up early to get discount tickets from the hotel reception to give to the bus driver. We had a plan. Or did we?

Looking through the brochure upstairs in the room, I noticed there was a trip to a place called Montserrat. As I read further, it explained that it was known as the Holy Mountain, that there was a holy cave in which Mary Magdalene had appeared. Now my attention was indeed powered up! There was also a boys' choir – I love singing and the BLACK MADONNA. I had researched this many years previously and got a shiver right through my body as I read on. My soul was calling me to go. The plot was about to unfold.

Philip isn't as spiritual as me; he is only 23 after all, when I mentioned the trip I was very surprised that he actually said he would like to come along. The problem was that the trips were listed for Monday and Wednesdays only. I was desperate to go and knew it would be a very early start, bearing in mind he was still exhausted and we were both adjusting to the new time zone. However, he was determined, so we made enquiries and had another twist to come.

The following morning, our first full day in Salou, we were up early and I ventured to reception to buy the said vouchers as instructed at 8am. As she looked behind the desk she said they had all been sold and not re-stocked, as the season was virtually over. The bus company had a shop down the road, so she advised I check if it was open and otherwise check at the red box kiosk, on the corner further down the road. So I had instructions and a plan, or so I thought at least. The Universe had other ideas of course! The story was about to unfold.

I ventured down to the travel shop. It was closed, as was the red ticket kiosk on the corner. There was no-one around to ask and there were no signs relating to opening times, etc. The bus was due in about 30 minutes and it was the only one listed in the brochure. I ventured back to the hotel, explained my unproductiveness to Phil and we both said that the best thing to do, was to go to the bus stop near the kiosk and buy a ticket on the bus. Little did we know that you have to obtain your tickets first!

When we arrived there were many people waiting and the kiosk remained unmanned. Five minutes to go! Phil is relatively horizontal and just left it all to me to organize. Eventually a man came to the kiosk. He was chatting to the locals and began selling them tickets, they obviously knew the system, and we were left waiting at the side. The bus arrival time had passed and no bus had, as yet, arrived anyways.

So, two numpties who do not speak the Spanish language, who do not know the system....Spanish time means the buses are usually up to 30 minutes later than advertised and it is altogether a "Carry On" moment, or two, or three. Despite trying to get served, the locals know the system.

The Montserrat bus arrived and then left. Then another arrived....and left! Then the third one arrived and the guide asks for English passengers, we still haven't even got a ticket. IT LEAVES. Eventually, now that most of the crowd have managed to get on the bus, Phil and I get actually get the chance to ask the chap in the kiosk if he speaks English. Yippee, he does and he's actually very clear as he states that the buses have gone for the day and the next one is due on Wednesday!

Plan B came into action. He pointed out that the Barcelona bus was due in about an hours' time. Phil looked shattered though agreed that we should go to Barcelona for the day instead. At least now we had some understanding of the Spanish system. Rather than waiting to buy tickets again on Wednesday for the Montserrat trip, we would buy them *now.*

An hour later we walked down to the said bus stop, tickets in hand and waited for the Barcelona bus, which was 20 minutes late. The bus arrived and we were told that that particular one was for the Russians, ours would be later. Evidently different nationalities went on different tour buses, another wait. Ten minutes later, our bus finally arrived and we were off on our first adventure.

The trip to Barcelona would take several hours and we were due home early evening. The guide explained what we would be looking at in the city and how much time we would have to ourselves for shopping, etc.

Barcelona is a beautiful city and I have to say we were very pleased to see the sights from the coach. The trip itself took us to a beautiful hillside vantage point, overlooking the harbour, ocean, city, suburbs and surrounding area. Although there were many hundreds of tourists, we really thoroughly enjoyed the experience. Phil and I were surprised at just how lovely the whole area was. I trusted that we were obviously not meant to be in Montserrat that day, and, that in fact, Barcelona was to hold its own treasures for us. I was looking forward to seeing the Holy Family church. The day was truly turning out to be fabulous. It was nice to spend time with my son and just BE.

As we drove through a variety of streets and looked at the various architectural wonders I was thrilled. The whole feel of the city was magical and inspirational. However, as the guide began to explain that we were approaching the Family church and that we would drive past before parking up, so that we could have an hour to walk around the perimeter of the building - I was very attentive indeed.

If you haven't been to this amazing celebration of design and wonderment, then I would recommend that you at least google it. The energy from the building is out of this world and even the most sceptical, would probably feel something. The drive-by alone was amazing. Minutes later we were actually stood nearby with throngs of tourists. What a celebration of artwork and worship to the divine. The craftsmanship was truly out of this world and beyond anything I have ever seen. For me that in itself was touching, though I have to say that the whole essence or presence of the place was truly awesome. I made a promise to myself there and then, that one day I would return and spend a whole day/weekend here.

As we walked around sacred symbols & geometry were everywhere. It is truly a special, touching place indeed and the history of its origins a story to behold. The church to date hasn't been finished and costs are astronomical. Some people have amazing vision and determination, as did the architect who originally designed this magnificent monument. We were both touched, on a soul to soul level, as I am sure were all the other tourists. The queues of visitors waiting to get inside the church wrapped themselves around the sides of this work of genius. Our allotted time certainly didn't allow for an internal look although our imagination could merely guess at its inside wonders and treasures.

For me a place like that holds such a high vibration of positive energy that an automatic upgrade takes place, allowing the person within that aura to be enhanced. Almost like a de-cluttering of unwanted thoughts and emotions, old habits, etc. I was certainly being upgraded and loved each and every moment of being near this magnificent building. The Universe was sending us a clear message confirming that we were indeed meant to be on this particular trip.

We were then to meet back at the coach and were visiting other parts of the city before our homeward destination. About 90 minutes later we were dropped off in the city centre and had a couple of hours to explore the sights. We opted for some lunch in a local restaurant and I was delighted that paella was available. Phil and I chatted easily, whilst we ate the local cuisine. We were thoroughly enjoying ourselves.

We decided that we would just bumble around and not go too far from our rendezvous point. My purse had broken and I needed a new one. As we left the restaurant we both noticed a shop with genuine leather purses and wallets. Again The Universe was having its way with us, as Phil purchased a wallet with the "OM" symbol and I got a multi-coloured purse. I knew it was a sign, welcoming new abundance in my life and moving on. In fact, my guides said very loudly "This is to welcome abundance in your life and a new chapter. You WILL welcome abundance into your being." The story would unfold further, especially in the coming weeks and months.....!

Water and water features are a particular love of mine and today would be no exception as I had spotted water fountains not too far from our bus stop. Phil was tired and we both agreed to just chill and relax by the fountains. Although it was such a busy spot in the city it was truly fabulous and we sat in the sunshine enjoying the moment. We had agreed to have a cuppa before leaving for our two hour journey home. As luck would have it, we found the very best café in Barcelona; especially for hot chocolate. We watched from the square surrounding the fountains. The Universe looked after us once again.

The journey home was peaceful and I was by now settling into the Spanish way of life. I was in the moment, had a deep knowing that I was meant to be here and that over the course of the next few days something magical would happen. I enjoyed looking out over the countryside as we journeyed back to Salou. Just as I had in Ibiza, I had meditated on the sunset and was thinking of my affirmations once the sky turned a beautiful orange. As soon as I could see the magnificent colours of the sky change, the affirmations went off to be heard by The Universe....and I knew they would soon be answered.

The day ended on a wonderful note and Phil and I wandered back to the hotel contented and delighted to have had such a lovely day. We decided that tomorrow we would have a lazy, restful day & simply check out the local area and the other nearby beaches.

The following day after a very disturbed night's sleep, due to a very noisy hotel and walls that were far too thin, (I shall leave that to your imagination)! I awoke looking forward to spending time with Phil exploring. He is not an early riser, so I was quite contented to write the book on my laptop and/or read. However, although time was getting up towards 10 am, Phil was still asleep. As I gently nudged him awake, he explained that he felt very ill and suggested that he have a few more hours sleep, in the hope that he would feel better.

I had got to know the area a little and I do have a fairly good sense of direction, so I just bumbled down to the beach and read. "The Shack" really is an addictive read and I was so contented within myself that I realised how much I have grown. No longer was I worried that I was alone on a beach. To be honest, I was barely aware of the other families and couples. Contentment is something we all strive for and I was delighted to be honest to simply BE. I was enjoying the relaxation and listening to the waves. I was still and at peace with myself completely.

Years ago, there would certainly have been a time where I would have had to have been on the go all the time. I would have walked from one part of the coastline to the other rather than be still. Maybe that's why I had gone to Portugal? Maybe it was simply to recognise that deep inner peace and BE-INGNESS? I sincerely felt at one with everything and certainly with nature here as I had done there.

Time is very precious to me and here I had an abundance of it. I had written over a thousand words in the book earlier that morning and had time to read. Once again, I had taken the decision to leave my phone at home with dear friends and for that I was very grateful.

Phil indeed slept most of the day. I checked on him regularly and left him to sleep and get well. It was ironic that he had booked the holiday, I had gone along for the ride and I was thoroughly enjoying myself! I walked and pottered about between different beaches and continued to relax and just BE.

The following day was the Montserrat trip and I was hoping Phil would feel well-rested enough to come along with me. We had another disturbed nights' sleep and I was pleased that he felt he could manage our outing. The said bus arrived in Spanish time which was over 30 minutes later than scheduled and we duly set off.

Montserrat is also known as Holy Mountain. The coach trip was approximately two hours and Phil rested whilst we drove. As I soaked up the Spanish countryside and listened to the guide explain how the day would be planned, I could feel an inner pull to the magical mountain.

Journeying through the countryside was lovely and I thoroughly appreciated the views. After over an hour I had an incredible urge to look to the other side of the bus. There the mountain stood in all its glory. My heart centre was expanding and I could feel my vibration increasing. Although I wasn't physically shaking, I felt my whole being, being drawn to this magical place.

Excitement grew in my soul and I knew I had made the right decision to come here. The nearer we got, the more the power and strength I could feel from the Holy site. Soon we were right beside the mountain and the trip included going up on the funicular. As we gained height, the views were astounding and so amazing. I was stunned and thrilled. Phil was evidently in his element too and delighted that he had felt well enough to attend. The train progressed further and eventually we arrived at the station. Instructions regarding times and meeting places, etc. were made clear, as we were due to visit another village by the coast after this trip.

There was indeed so much to do; the monastery to visit, the cave of Mary, listening to the boys' choir and the Black Madonna. I really felt drawn to visit the cave where Mary was said to have appeared. Phil and I set of and eventually arrived at the cross of St Michael! We had misread the signposts! It was a beautiful spot and we could both feel the energies of this holy place. The views were breath taking and astounding too. Time was against us and we decided to travel up the mountain and then catch the funicular back to the meeting point.

As the heat of the day intensified, we both sweated and walking up that particular part of the mountain was very challenging. We urged one another on and there was much laughter between us. Once again the views were truly awesome and we gained so much from being on that sacred mountain. Finding the railway station for the funicular was not easy. We were beginning to worry about timings and being left behind. However, as always, I was listening to my intuition and being carefully guided to move forward to the left. There it was. Luckily the funicular was due within the next few minutes and we waited patiently in the queue.

We absorbed all the breath taking views as we waited. Once aboard the funicular we soaked in the vast countryside and the peacefulness of the surrounding valley. I was thrilled to have had such a lovely experience, but felt that there were so many other things I needed to do here too. Being so aware of my soul's guidance, I found it difficult to acknowledge that I actually felt disappointed at all the other wonders I had missed.

As our coach departed I looked back at the mountain in the distance and felt regret in my soul; actually in my whole being. Then the mountain seemed to say "Come back soon, you haven't received what you came for." I was shocked, as I really didn't know what to think. We were only here for a week and it was passing quickly. There were no other trips shown in the brochure and I had no plans to go away on holiday again before the end of the year. I wondered what I would do and struggled with the thought of the cost. So, how would this come about? There was a sense of urgency, in the message from the mountain and it played on my mind throughout the homeward journey.

Life works in mysterious ways. We arrived back at the hotel and I felt sad. I always go with my intuition, trusted and knew something would show itself in due course. I was tired at the end of the day and we just chilled and rested that evening.

Once again our sleep was disturbed and I was glad that being an early bird meant that at least I'd had plenty of sleep, before the early hours of the morning antics gathered pace and awoke me. I shall once again leave that to your imagination.

When I awoke, I just knew I had to return to the mountain – coach trip or otherwise I would have to find my own way of getting there. Again I was relying on TRUST alone. I wandered down to the chap in the bus kiosk after 9am and explained I needed to return and asked his advice. How truly wonderful this Universe is when we listen to the inner guidance. "There's a trip tomorrow" he stated, "Oh" I said "...it's not in the brochure." "No, it won't be because your brochure is in English and the trip is for the Russians....so you'll have to go with them. You know how to get around and the guide speaks perfect English, so she will inform you of times, etc."

I almost fell over and couldn't believe it! It was promptly booked and I was so excited. My soul heaved a sigh of relief and I knew it was RIGHT. Phil was delighted when I told him and humbly stated that he "Knew" I'd be returning. How did he know? Apparently, when I questioned him, he had said that he knew the previous day when we were leaving, that I would be back within the following few days. He also said I should go alone as it was necessary for my souls' growth. Not bad for a young lad of 23 at the time.

MONTSERRAT TWICE OVER

"An extraordinary life is all about daily, continuous improvements in the areas that matter most."

Robin Sharma

So, that bright Thursday morning, I set off for my second trip to Montserrat. I was so excited and filled with healing energy. As usual the bus was late though this time I knew what was to be expected and I already had my ticket in hand too! I listened to the Russians, as they chatted between one another. The bus came and the guide was lovely. She put me at ease immediately and actually came to sit with me for about 20 minutes chatting about all sorts of things as if we had known one another for years.

Once again as we neared the Holy Mountain I felt the intensity of the energy. This time it seemed even stronger. Today was definitely going to be a very special day indeed! I'm even shaking now as I write this piece in the book! How truly amazing life is, if we just look at and feel its beauty.

Upon arrival, I wandered off as I knew the layout quite well. This time I would have about 6 hours in this magical location high up in the mountains. I was guided to queue for the Black Madonna statue. You can touch her and send your personal prayers/requests. Mine were flooding right through my whole being! As I neared her, after queuing for over an hour, I could feel her energy pulling me. I was actually close to tears. As I touched the statue, I heard her very clearly say "You now have EVERYTHING that you need in life to complete your dreams and achieve all you wish to achieve." Bloody Hell....no mistaking that then!

I had wanted to listen to the boys' choir too and Phil and I had missed it earlier in the week. The exact moment that I touched her they started singing – surely yet another sign from above? Confirming my truth and that life was about to get better.

I walked past the statue, bearing in mind the lengthy queue behind me and just listened to their beautiful voices. Tears were in my eyes; my heart and soul were on fire.

As they closed their performance I walked towards the cave of Mary Magdalene and stopped half way along to eat lunch. The views there are some of the best that I have ever seen in my whole lifetime and together with the sun on my ever tanning skin, I was feeling blissed out.

As I continued on to the caves where she is said to have appeared, I could certainly feel something! I knew I was being upgraded with divine energy. I stayed there for quite a while on this special day; after all I had several hours to kill. When I left, I felt different and "cleaner." I had certainly been moved to experience this place.

I continued to walk up the mountain as it felt so right and visited her viewing point. Although the path was actually quite dangerous in parts, there were many other tourists who kindly offered their helping hands. As I approached what had been her living quarters, I could certainly feel something beautiful touching my soul. I waited here for quite a while, just simply taking in the magnificent views and the feelings.

Making my way down to the station to board the funicular I was in a very meditative state. I felt sad to be leaving, though hoped one day that I would return.

Boarding the coach, it was obvious by the Russians jovial mannerisms, despite not understanding one single word, that they were happy. The guide asked me how my day had gone and had I visited and achieved all I had wanted to do? "Yes" I explained and she could clearly tell how contented I was. The drive back to Salou was lovely and I hoped Phil would be getting better. I sent my affirmations up to The Universe as sunset appeared. It certainly had been an altogether, truly magical experience indeed.

When I arrived back at the hotel, Phil was pleased to see me and could see that I was glowing. He was chuffed for me and I was delighted, that he did in fact, feel better!

The following morning as we chatted over breakfast Phil announced that he could see a brand new car on our driveway at home!? I told him to get lost, as I loved my Saab, also known as "Black Beauty," had it regularly serviced and I expected to get several more years out of her. He continued, saying very adamantly, that he saw a black, brand new spanking BMW on the drive. We actually almost argued.....The Universe would indeed have its way and less than a month later, said black BMW arrived!!! "Black Beauty" Mark Two had made her appearance!!!! This was another step towards abundance.

Our holiday would come to its inevitable close a few days later, though we both returned refreshed and rejuvenated to the UK. Oh and somewhat tanned too!

It was almost the end of the year, so many surprises and unexpected events had occurred and blown my mind to be honest. It was amazing how the year began and how it ended too. I am self-aware enough to know that I still had issues relating to abundance, that I needed to clear.

My dear friend Tony was seeing a therapist called Chris Gelder, he kept raving about how amazing he had been in facilitating Tony's "letting go & moving on" process, or "healing and peeling," as we often call it in healing circles. After a lovely walk by the canal one day, Tony asked me to seriously consider allowing Chris, to assist me in my clearing and de-cluttering journey through life. I was aware that Paul had brought me thus far, but I am also wise enough to know, that Tony wanted what was best for me and is an incredibly intuitive man too. Not to mention a dear and trusted friend.

As I tuned into Paul's energy, I received an easy, calm, relaxing response, to the question of who would be the best man for the job; at least for the time-being. When I tuned into Chris's energy, I was filled with intense fear and almost terror! "Right then, feel the fear and do it anyways" I told Tony. "I'm going to make an appointment to see Chris." Once again the story would unravel itself as I trusted my inner judgements and intuition and certainly that of one of my best friends!

Trust, trust, trust……

360 DEGREE TURNAROUND TO HEAVEN

"Life's too short" is repeated often enough to be a cliché, but this time it's true. You don't have enough time to be both Unhappy & mediocre. It's not just pointless; it's painful"

Seth Godin

So, 360 degrees indeed; the wheels of my life have indeed been turning, as you have read in the last four years, since I wrote "The Goldfish That Jumped". My daughter, husband and three of my favourite granddaughters, (All five are my favourites and I tell them frequently), moved down south to Kent on Mothering Sunday 15th March 2015.

The events leading up to this were very rapid and to me it was obvious The Universe had given them its blessing. It was an easy move and a very swift one indeed. At the end of 2014, both my daughter and her husband were ready to move forward in life. By now both were highly qualified in their careers and wanted a better life for the girls. Preston did not hold the answer to their prayers of fulfilling their lives; or that of the girls. It was time for them to move on.

They still wanted to go to Australia with Matty, although current finances were not sufficient for that to happen. The time came when they knew they had to move, as the house they were in was rapidly becoming too small with three youngsters. The fact that my daughter was, at the time a hoarder, did nothing to improve matters. Russell decided they needed to de-clutter their home, in order that they would have more room. Several trips to the charity shop and tip created space for them. Within a few weeks, he also decided to move the furniture around so that it was positioned against the walls, rather than placed in the middle of the floor space; which blocks energetic flow.

When we look at principles of Feng Shui we can see that a cluttered home means a cluttered mind. Thus, an uncluttered home, creates an uncluttered energetic flow.

As Christmas loomed ahead, they knew the girls would get gifts there would naturally be a need for even more space to be created. This meant yet another weekend of decluttering. Then in February, after over 20 years of being addicted to coffee, my dear son-in-law decided to quit. The inevitable energy he released by letting go of the addiction was truly amazing. He and Emily had decided that they needed a bigger home and would like to move to a better area.

The Universe was listening.

Russell applied for several jobs and waited for a response. He was very keen to work in Kent as the job was almost 10k more than his current wage. As my daughter is a nurse, she would find work anywhere. The requests to interview him came thick and fast. He was offered interviews within the week and got the job offer the following Monday. You can imagine the panic and concern from my daughter as the realisation sunk in.

Handing his notice in Russell had no regrets, though he knew they must find suitable schools for the girls, childcare for the youngest and a new home in Kent. The Universe acted swiftly, within six weeks they were packed up and on their way. I'll never forget that day. There were many tears and a whole heap of emotions too.

Watching my son Phil drive them off and Russell follow on in the car was really quite monumental. My parents were with me and I was glad not to be left standing alone on my driveway. The feeling of emptiness would surely have consumed my being otherwise.

Emily and the girls had stayed with me for the previous eight days, so I had had a full house with lots of busy times, as she was planning their move and sorting out the packing from their previous home. It had been exhausting for us all. Now they were on their own journey into the unknown.

I guess any normal mother would have been anxious under the circumstances, though I knew and trusted that The Universe had worked so fast that all would be well. I totally trusted that they were cared for and would be absolutely in love with Kent immediately. Indeed they were and as the girls settled in their new school too all was perfect. Emily found a wonderful childminder and the rest is history as they say. She also applied for four nursing jobs; was offered every one and took the perfect job offer she had wanted.

I had a knowing that I would visit them within a month's time. This would have given them time to settle and time for me to adjust to their leaving too. Certainly I had missed them and having that intense trust in The Universe, brought me intense comfort. I now had more time to do what I wanted to do; even though Grandma duties had been very precious, life was now changing, yet again.

A NEW DAY

"You've got to wake up every morning with determination
If you're going to go to bed with satisfaction"

George Lorimer

In need of my granddaughter fix, I booked my train tickets to Kent with the help of my son & daughter in law. I felt pleased though scared at the unknown. The thought of the train journey still raised unresolved fears although they had lessened considerably. "Face your fears and do it anyways" kept running through my head.

So, Thursday 2nd April, I set off on the train to see my beloved family. I was very emotional indeed. The mere thought of them meeting me on the railway platform, brought tears to my eyes. Waiting on the platform at Preston station was such an emotional one. Feelings of fear, excitement, love and the great unknown, ran through my being, as I waited on that cold April morning. I knew that once I had arrived in Euston, I needed to transfer over to Victoria. The thought alone of the London underground still brought up fear in me. This time no-one would be there to meet me and show me the ropes as it were.

TRUST, TRUST, TRUST….

The train ride from Preston was easy and I settled to read India Drummond. The scenery changed as we got further south and my soul was vibrating faster, as I knew I was getting nearer to my precious family. Dear friends had told me it was easy on the underground and that I should just to follow everyone else as most fellow travellers would be heading for the underground station. It's certainly easy to do anything when fear is not a feature…..my heart felt like it would thump its way out of my chest and my poor adrenals were on overdrive too!!!

My prayers for help went up to The Universe….at least I had hoped so? I reached Euston and asked for help at the "Information Desk"…..yes, this was it! "London underground to the right at the rear" he stated. ARGH….I was unsure whether or not I would need to buy separate tickets for the underground, so I queued up like a numpty and wondered how many other people amongst the crazy hustle and bustle were newbies at this?

Everyone rushed everywhere and it really is an overwhelming experience. I was told I didn't need to purchase another ticket, to use the one I had and go through the barrier, to keep to the right hand side and off to the right from the escalator! Crikey this really was it. If I wanted to see my precious family, I now had no choice.

Whilst on the escalator, I chatted easily with a young man behind me, who looked like he knew what he was doing. Needless to say, when I fell over my suitcase as the escalator came to its end, he helped me up and we laughed! He too was going to Victoria, so we got on board the train to said station and he helped carry said luggage – without falling over!

Arriving at the station I was thrilled. I had faced my fears and achieved my new mission….now all I had to do was catch the over ground to Charing. Piece of cake….very soon I'd be met by my daughter and granddaughters; I had plenty of time for the loo and a quick chai latte before the final leg of my journey.

The relief when I sat on the seat of that train was intense. Tears began to fill my eyes, as I swiftly looked around me to see if anyone was staring at me. Just over an hour to go. Although the India Drummond book I was reading was completely addictive, I had never travelled this far south in the UK, so I decided to look out from the window and take in the scenery. To be honest it was truly lovely; moving through the busy city, then into open countryside and passing orchards.

I counted the stops one by one...Harrietsham, Lenham, and then Charing. I had paid close attention to all the stops, the train stopped only for a few moments at each destination, before moving on towards Ashford. There would be no time for mistakes or dawdling about that was for certain. Thoughts of what I would say, fears that they might not be there, all ran through my brain. What if?...... I thought of all the other passengers who might be watching from the windows, as we were reunited and how many tears I would cry! Would they see me first or would I see them first?

"The next station will be Charing....." I was already up and ready. As the doors opened, I looked to the right and saw my daughter with the three little beauties. As I disembarked they all ran towards me shouting "Grandma"....How I managed not to cry I honestly do not know! We hugged and hugged, within moments, they were telling me of how much they loved it here and how much they loved the sunnier, warmer weather too!

Emily stated there was a local park and had packed us a picnic, so we could catch up and eat, whilst overlooking the church. The girls could rest and play, before we walked the mile and a half to their cottage. The whole feeling was that of complete & utter peacefulness. The buildings were a mixture of modern and ancient,

242

yet were perfect in their differences too. Being reunited with Emily and the girls was just like having never been away from them.

We chatted easily and promptly downed the picnic. I always remember that Emily refused to learn to cook when she was a youngster and actually refused to do many other kitchen chores either!

"I'll marry a chef Mother, so don't you worry, as I won't need to cook"....she did and now she's a much better cook than me! I was really taken with the buildings here and keen to get to know the area, where my daughter and her family were living. I asked if she minded if we bumble around before heading back. "Of course", she agreed and I was so aware of a deep peace that had descended over and into my whole being.

As usual; me being me, I found a cosy tea shop and suggested before we leave, that we sample the delights of the village café and their cakes! Knowing my daughter very well, she promptly agreed and the four of us snuggled into the corner table. The hot chocolate and sizeable cakes were a treat. It means so much to me that I now have the money to spoil my family as and when I choose. Russell called to say he had finished work earlier due to the holidays and agreed to meet us. It was so lovely to see him too.

There wasn't enough room in the car for us all. Emily, me and the eldest two girls offered to walk home; thank goodness for Russ; as I didn't need to drag the heavy suitcase!

Walking through the countryside was such a delight to me. They were obviously settled and very happy. The girls' laughter and delight spilled through in their conversation and silence too. They were excited to show me the way and eventually their new home.

We laughed, joked and chatted as we walked through the countryside. I felt so at home here and was very surprised at just how deep this feeling was throughout my being. My whole body relaxed more and more, I knew I had to be here. Some things are just RIGHT. This was absolutely right.

Right for them and right for me too.

We eventually arrived at the corner of the lane where their cottage was located. Only another three quarters of a mile to go. It was so quiet and blissful, the countryside green and lush. We had only passed a few houses and the surrounding hillsides were already inviting me.

Arriving at the tiny row of cottages was truly lovely and I was delighted to see their new home – knowing without a doubt, that they had made the right decision to come here against all odds and all logical thoughts. They had followed their hearts and here they would settle. The house was lovely and felt welcoming. They still had some unpacking to do and were essentially still settling into village life. The girls showed me around and I was thrilled.

The garden outside led to a woods and they loved playing here and making dens. To the rear was a disused sand quarry, which had a lovely walkway around its perimeter. A walk for another day I thought. I took my suitcase upstairs & settled myself in with a cup of Lady Grey. We chatted about the things we could do over the weekend and I made it clear that I was happy to babysit, so that they could go and have some quality time as a couple together.

Looking through the front window, I had felt a huge energy vortex from a place I just knew I had to visit. The whole area was so high in beautiful energy and indeed, I would later find out that they lived very near the pilgrims walk from Canterbury to Glastonbury. No wonder the energy was of a high vibration!

Emily was left cooking a superb dinner, whilst Russ and I drove to the local village for supplies. Driving through the countryside was awesome and once again the contrasts of architectural design filled my senses. I was definitely in love with this place. We arrived in the village square for bread, ham and other bits and bobs. Esmae was with us and, as she wandered freely through the shop, I was struck by how easy she found all the items and how comfortable she obviously felt to be able to wander around on her own, out of our sight, yet knowing we were in the same shop – something I had never previously known her to do whilst she was in Lancashire.

Everything had changed for the better for all of them, despite a few hiccups in the beginning. I was relieved for them and was looking forward to my time here.

We enjoyed a lovely quiet evening and I was ready for an early night too. I slept under the skylight on the floor in the girls' room, peaceful and contented. What pleasures would tomorrow hold?

NEW LEARNINGS

"An extraordinary life is all about daily, continuous improvements in the areas that matter most"

Robin Sharma

The following morning, Russ was once again eager to show me places and sights. However, there was not enough room in the car for us all to travel together. He looked on Google, to see what events were going on locally over the Easter holidays. We established a rough plan! "Make plans, make God laugh," as my dear friend Dennis always used to say. How very true. "Let's just go with the flow" I said. We were off to Leeds Castle that day, then the races and a hike other days. A plan was formed.

Leeds Castle was amazing, the grounds, trees, lakes, peacocks and the castle itself. Could this place actually get any better? We were having a fabulous time and I was pleased to see them settled and happy. I offered to take their youngest daughter off for a walk, as she was getting tired and grouchy. We wandered through the grounds and I felt I had been here before. It all felt so familiar. We had arranged to meet up again in just over an hour. It gave them time to enjoy the eldest girls and of course this meant being able to do different activities, otherwise impossible with an almost two year old! I loved bumbling around, just allowing this peaceful feeling to deepen, into my being more and more.

The said time arrived and we met at the café near the adventure playground. In the next play area, were jesters showing children and adults how to spin plates, juggle, etc. I watched on in delight and my

246

inner child was thrilled. Russell too, was obviously loving each and every moment, sharing with his family. The girls were lapping it up, laughing and messing around as all children should. I stood to Emily's right happily watching over them.

I heard Gracie to my left shouting "Grandma, look what I've got for you," and turned to see her holding up a red wriggling worm, of no less than a foot long. Tears began to well in my eyes immediately and my heart pounded in my chest, crying out in intense pain. My whole being shook, as I turned to my daughter, and, as calmly as I could, told her very quietly to get Gracie away from me. "Are you ok mum?" "No" I said as I moved quickly to the right creating space between myself and Grace.

As Emily gently explained that "Grandma just doesn't like worms," and took care of the situation, the tears flowed and I was aware of being consumed with a feeling of immense grief. Yet, I wasn't abreacting (abnormal reaction) as I would have done years ago had someone approached me with a foot long worm. What the hell had just happened?

So, I obviously hadn't cleared the whole worm phobia picture, as I had thought after all? What could I possibly have left uncovered? I had figured out who my husband had been, my community, the traitor, the torturers....what could I possibly have missed?

I calmed myself within ten minutes – no screaming, freaking out, panicking, running off, shaking violently from head to toe, no trying to vomit, no hyperventilating....yet the *deepest grief* that I had ever felt filled my soul. What the hell was this about?

I had been working intensely on my deepest fears with Chris Gelder, since Tony had suggested we meet up in January. I knew I had to text him that evening. If there was anyone I trusted enough to get to the bottom of this, it was him. An appointment was made upon my return and he agreed to send me healing, as did Tony, when I told him what had happened.

Upon our return home I was exhausted, whether it was the fresh air, the walk, the whole relaxing holiday thing or perhaps the grief, I honestly didn't know. We once again had a lovely meal, cooked by Emily and I was fast asleep before ten.

The following day Emily and Russ needed to go into town to get footwear for the girls. I stayed with the youngest and we played and laughed. I was exhausted....once again, was it just that I had completely relaxed, or was it the deep grief that was causing the tiredness?

After another marvellous lunch, we planned to go to the races later that afternoon. I said I would stay home with Lavender, whilst agreeing to meet up with them later, once she had had her afternoon nap. Nothing worse than a grumpy toddler and I was tired anyways, I dozed on the sofa whilst she slept. Besides, it was giving Emily and Russ precious time with their eldest two, who had never even been to a race course – let alone watch a live horserace.

Eventually Lavender and I walked up to the racecourse, just in time to catch the last race! They were thoroughly delighted and had had a great day. They had also won on both races, so everyone was happy. We all walked around as the stall holders begin to pack up and people left the field. Everyone was friendly to us and I was surprised as usually we think of the North/South divide. It was certainly not in evidence here.

The race course was very close to the pilgrims' walkway and I could "feel" the energies very strongly. I suggested to Emily and Russ that the following morning, I would happily take Lavender in the backpack to check out the route. This would give them a welcome break and me time to explore. I was excited as I love walking and adventuring too.

Another evening of bliss and easiness followed. Emily and Russell had still not sorted out the TV and this was absolute heaven to me! For those of you that know me, you'll be aware that I hate noise for the sake of it and am contented to listen to music and chat. Perfect.

After another very restful sleep, I was feeling more refreshed. The next day I was thrilled to wake up with my granddaughters and have breakfast with the family. Simple things in life are often the best and this absolutely was indeed. Just after 10am, I set off for the walk, asking Russell to drop me off with Lavender. I would telephone later, once I had had enough!

Following Emily's maternity leave, I had had my grandma duties once a week with Lav. Bobs. We were and are very close, I was looking forward to spending time alone with her again on our walk. Despite being on the wrong side of 45 and nearly 50, most people assume that Lavender is mine when we are out! Quite pleasing really! Anyways, I sung to her, whilst we walked and she happily repeated what I sung from the backpack. We arrived at the stone cross and settled down with an apple.

The scenery was beautiful and touched my soul. I thought of how wonderful it would be for all the girls to grow up here, away from the hustle and bustle of their previous Lancashire life. It was funny, as I had never even thought of moving away when they were younger.

So many thoughts passed through my mind, whilst we just walked and took in all the surroundings. It was so lovely, and even as I write this chapter, the clarity of my recollections remaining amazingly clear to me. I felt a truly deep soul connection here and knew that I had lived not too far away, maybe in a past life or one in another dimension of time and space. I just KNEW IT.

We pottered along happily, singing and laughing. I really believe that children are little sponges who take in everything we tell them. So, I decided to say numbers in French, which Lav Bobs promptly repeated. I then started to say some Greek words too, before realising that my Greek was shockingly rusty! Ah well, at least a few smatterings meant that if she heard them again sometime in later life, I knew she would find learning the language easier.

We continued onwards and I can honestly say I was in my element. We found an old telegraph pole to sit on and I got Bobs out of her backpack, so she could sit alongside me. Joy and bliss completely filled me and looking down at Bobs, I felt a deep sense of peace and completeness. She would grow up here in this wonderful place for as long as was meant to be and despite the fact that I missed them all dearly, I was also delighted that the new chapter of their lives was as awesome as this!

Eating our tangerines and having some water, whilst sitting in a field laughing and sharing was fabulous. I had no idea where the nearest village was and although I was by now getting tired, with the weight of the back pack, I was happy to bumble onwards to see what the day brought. Lavender was happy to walk and we made our way towards Charing.

The weather was good and it was getting warmer, as we walked along the "Pilgrims Way." She was glad to be out of the back pack and toddled along happily. Being a grandmother is truly a most magical thing! I was getting hungry and wasn't entirely sure we would make the next village. I had been watching out for landmarks and was aware that we were close to where Emily & Russ lived.

After walking about half a mile, Bobs was getting tired, so I carried her for a while. She chatted and laughed, then got quieter and quieter. Time to head to the main road, to meet daddy, bundle her in the car and then she could sleep at home. It was a perfect ending to a long morning.

Russ collected us and dropped me off in the village of Lenham, where I found a lovely quaint tea shop. The Ploughman's Lunch on the menu looked very inviting, so there I sat in the square in the beautiful sunshine, with a hot choc and a fabulous salad. I felt as though I had died and gone to heaven. I was falling in love with Kent and was thinking how on earth would I manage to up sticks and live in this beautiful part of England. My business was in Lancashire, though my skills transferrable...all I knew was that somehow, I would find a way; if it was meant to be and The Universe would guide me!

The ancient church across from the square, was calling me in throughout my luncheon. Once finished, I wandered over for a look inside. It was lovely and again filled with a great peacefulness. I looked at the lovely features and appreciated all aspects of its beauty. I decided to sit and meditate in a seat where the sunbeams filled the space. I would ask The Universe for guidance and just sit and BE.

Within a few moments an elderly gentleman entered the church and came over to me. "Were you sleeping?" He enquired, "No, just meditating" I replied. He was in his 80's at a guess and he chatted easily about the village, the damage the church had sustained during the war. Then he enquired about my origins, as I certainly do not have a southern accent! I explained that my daughter and hubby had moved here, with their family, and he said they would love it here. I explained I loved it too and wondered whether or not I was meant to be here. We chatted easily for quite a while longer, before he said he ought to go and wished me luck.

I remained in that beautiful place for quite some time longer, after quietly thinking, praying and digesting all that I was feeling and experiencing. I eventually left, after an expression of thanks to The Universe and decided that rather than call Russ, I would walk back. It was by now, very warm outside, I enjoyed the sun on my back and my face. I loved walking those precious miles, although, I have to say that I was surely glad to arrive back at the cottage, to a cuppa and the loo!

Everyone had enjoyed their day, Emily and I said we would later go for a little jaunt after dinner. Yet again, it had been another day of blissfulness. I was becoming aware that the following day would be my last, before my early departure on Tuesday morning. Although I can honestly say I had been "in the moment" the whole time, I felt time had flown.

Emily and I enjoyed our little walk and chatted easily when the girls went to bed.

Precious times and very precious memories.

My last day was lovely. The weather was fab again and we had decided to check out the public footpaths through the fields to the next village. The countryside was stunning as was the variety of wildlife...just awesome. To be honest, we weren't entirely sure what all the birds of prey were, although we were definitely delighted to see them flying above us.

Checking out the village and the houses, the architecture and visiting the church, were all once again lovely experiences too. We found that we could do the Pilgrims walk home and en route passed a "shrine" dedicated to those walking to Glastonbury. Once again I had Bobs on my back and walked ahead, so that she wouldn't get bored, as Emily and Russ walked more slowly with the eldest girls. Thoughts of how much I had loved each and every moment, and thoughts of coming back, were running through my head. I truly felt at home here and had no doubts, about how easily I could settle here either. It's true that home is where the heart is.....my heart loved this place.

My last night in Kent was once again fabulous, though everyone was a little sad – especially me, that I was leaving early the next morning. My train departed at 07.57am. I knew it wouldn't be too long, before I returned and kept that thought, as I later drifted off into slumber land.

Upon awakening the following morning I felt quite sad, though as the train was due to depart just before 8am, there was very little time before I left. I watched over my sleeping granddaughters and committed that picture of both their peacefulness and loveliness into my memory box. I vowed I would return and do all I possibly could do, to achieve this as soon as possible.

Leaving them was hard, as I kissed and hugged them all, whilst Russ placed my suitcase in the car. He kindly dropped me at the station. It was a most beautiful, stunning sunny morning. The railway station was just like one out of the scene of a 60's drama…..beautiful and simple country living. It was obvious that very little had changed on this station in decades. Whilst I was waiting for the train, I was emotional and tears sprung into my eyes. Russ had already left for work and I was here alone; yet felt as though I was being watched over from afar.

I was looking forward to passing through the lovely countryside, whilst at the same time saddened to be leaving my beloved family too. I was also looking forward to seeing my other sons and granddaughters too. A few stops down the line, I heard the voice of my guides clearly; "You will be here before Christmas". "Wow" I thought, that would indeed be marvellous. As we neared Victoria station I heard them again "We will sort this sooner than that, as you need to be in Kent to do your healing work". Exciting times ahead I thought!

The train rattled along towards London Victoria and most people were commuting for work. There were a wide range of people, some in suits, some young and seemingly care-free, some older and more serious. I felt kind of out of place, yet also, that I was in a protective bubble too.

Having by now let go of my fears of trains and the underground, I was ready to change stations to Euston and headed for the nearest café, where I ordered a Chai Latte. As I sat there, I wondered what would actually become of me? Would I, could I, actually live in such a beautiful part of the country? How would I support myself if all or most of my clients were in the North West? It all came down to trust and I knew I had to simply go with that TRUST.

TRUST, TRUST, TRUST

The train journey from Euston to Preston was also very easy. I had requested The Universe to send a local bus too, once I had walked to the bus stop from the railway station. I live so close to the station, it's not worth getting a taxi. As ordered from The Universe, the said bus arrived within three minutes and I would in fact be home before 1pm. The day was glorious and sunny. I unpacked and made a cuppa, still feeling rather dazed from my adventures. I decided to visualize moving down there and how this was to be achieved.

I sat in my beautiful garden by the fruit trees, at the rear of the house, soaking up the sunshine and honestly felt The Universe was with me. I visualised my beautiful home finished; the windows needed replacing, the exterior of the house needed painting and the log store and garage needed sorting too. Was I really ready to sell up and move down south? I wondered just how much equity was in the property. Could I *really* do this? Could I *really* consider leaving my beautiful home, friends, family and my beautiful life? Truth be said, I love Lancashire and love walking locally. However, here I was; knowing that this was absolutely right for me and was a necessary part of my life's journey.

The local park is beautiful with a mile long tree-lined avenue. I meditated in the garden and sent my requests clearly up to The Universe, to hear and act upon. I then decided whilst the washing machine got busy, that I would take a walk for further inspiration. I truly love being in nature, and both Avenham and Miller parks are teaming with positive energy. So, this was me then. This could well be one of my last walks in the beloved park. Decision made, it felt very clear and right for me. This was it and I was moving to Kent and would do all I could in my power to get the house finished and move on to a new adventure.

SYNCHRONICITIES

"Silence is the richness of the soul,
Loneliness is its poverty"

May Santon

The previous year, I had made enquiries about new double glazed windows, as some had blown and some were looking shabby. My son Phil had bargained a good price and when I got home, I received a phone call from the company, saying that they were happy to come out to the property and re- assess the windows which needed replacing – was I interested? Too bloody right I was! The appointment was made and a date set for them to come and re-measure said windows.

Logic always plays a part in these situations and I reasoned with myself that the house needed finishing; whether I moved or not. It had been something which I had visualised for over a year now. Knowing the workings of The Universe and Law Of Attraction; all I needed was to just visualise and let them take care of the rest. So that's what I did!

Also the previous year, my dear friend Andy had decorated the interior of the house and we had discussed his doing the exterior too. We had agreed a price and when the time came for him to start, the weather had deteriorated and we both agreed that the following Easter, would be a suitable time for the work to begin. He had been brought up in the South and the following day he called with his lovely southern accent to say that he was fully recovered after recent surgery and would love to start the work ASAP! So, The Universe was showing me that all was going to plan.

The garage and log store needed sorting too, so I decided to write to the local builder as I did not have his number and would ask him to come to quote for the work. Phew, everything was easy! He called within a few days and promptly started the work a couple of weeks after. Once the log store was cleared and tidied, I knew it was all coming together.

Andy and I had already purchased the exterior paint the previous year. We checked through the garage, as to what we had and what we could use. We tidied as much as we could out of the garage and I realised that in fact, I had been tidying and de-cluttering since December. Had I known this was coming? We sat down for a cuppa and I discussed this with Andy. I explained that I had thrown over two black bin liners of old paperwork away, de-cluttered my wardrobe and also gone through my sons old clothes, etc! Maybe on a soul to soul level, I had had a knowing? I had had enough experience of this already since re-awakening and it did all make perfect sense.

As we were sat chatting, I re-remembered that when Emily, Russ and the girls had left several weeks earlier my guides had clearly stated "Won't be long until you leave either." I had forgotten, though I had also had a vision: that I too was packing up my belongings, my life and moving! Andy had guessed that I would move down there anyways, as had three other, very dear and close friends too.

The reality was beginning to set in. It dawned on me that The Universe had known about this, well before Russ had even applied for the job! Well, time to crack on and get the house finished then!

I'm a sensible soul and realise that although The Universe has a divine plan, no amount of rushing is going to speed things up....especially if we get stressed in the process, so we may as well accept, rather than resist.

Needless to say, Andy started the decorating within the week and the date for the windows was set for the 30th April. I was wondering how I would pay for it all and again, just surrendered to trusting that The Universe would take care of it all.

There was nothing else I could do now but TRUST. I knew that everything in my home had already been de-cluttered and was either staying or going with me. All surpluses to requirements had been removed! Time and patience were all I needed. My dear friend Tracy was also moving and our birthdays are on the same day! Yes! The Universe was having its way! Work on the house would be finished within 6-8 weeks..... or would it?

BEGIN WITH THE POSSIBLE

"Begin with the possible;
Begin with one step.
There is always a limit,
you cannot do more
than you can.
If you try to do too much,
you will do nothing."

P.S.Ouspensky & G.I.Gurdjieff

"Begin It Now" (ed. Susan Hayward)

I returned from Kent on Tuesday 7th April. I had already requested an appointment with Chris to uncover why I had even reacted, when Gracie had held up the worm the previous week. I was due to see him in his office at 10.30am Friday 10th.....I was terrified and knew something was about to be revealed!

So, as cool as a cucumber, as Chris is, and utterly professional, he asked me exactly what had happened and what I had already cleared re the worm phobia and the dungeon, etc. For those of you who have not read my first book "The Goldfish That Jumped" I had had a fear of worms throughout my life and had always said to my mum, even as a child: "Please don't ever let them touch me, because if they do, they will kill me".

I never knew or understood why, though the fear was so acutely real, why I was terrified of both worms and slugs. Whilst on an introductory course to *EFT; Emotional Freedom Technique several years earlier, I had been chosen to be a guinea pig for my phobia from a group of approximately 16 people. Whilst tapping out my fear, I suddenly became aware that I was in a dungeon, being executed and tortured. The worms were on the floor in with the straw and once I had been unhooked from the wall, beaten and tortured, I was killed….the worms having touched the skin on my right knee, as I was pushed to the floor; *thus it had become my belief that if the worms touched me, I would die*. Falling onto the worms was my last memory in that lifetime.

EFT is a very effective healing technique, which involves tapping on a few acupressure points on the body, in order to release unresolved emotions and fears, whilst at the same time, repeating verbally the fear and said emotions.

As a healer, I felt that I had to move through the fear and I had sent healing to all aspects of it; well, at least up until now I thought I had! The more I healed it, the more I would have recollections and gradually the fear lessened, so that, over time, I could walk on grass without footwear and also do the gardening, without having to wear gloves. So, the fact that I had reacted to my beautiful granddaughter holding up her prize worm at me, meant that I had obviously not quite cleared as much as I thought.

It was a combination of personal responsibility, self-awareness and the fact that I cannot practise what I preach, if I cannot deal with my own fears as a therapist. This makes me a hypocrite with my patients and clients, not to mention myself, so all of these factors had led me to call Chris. This was the perfect man and a dear friend for the job. I knew that he would hold my space and support me, no matter what was to be revealed from my subconscious mind.

The fear itself, that I still felt, was showing me that there were still hidden aspects that were now ready to be revealed. I was wise enough to know, that I had to move through them, otherwise they would indeed hold me back. For those of you that know me, I'm always ready to face a challenge! Rightly or wrongly!

Chris sat me in his magic chair, got me into a relaxed state and then asked me what my body felt like. I had a pain in my right arm…to be honest it bloody hurt! It looked like a tube was in there – almost like a blood transfusion? I was confused and did not understand as I certainly wasn't in the dungeon? What was this all about?

"Go into the pain, what is it trying to show you" Chris's gentle, yet assertive voice was coaching me. It was then that I saw the lifetime. I was aged about thirty and a male engineer working on the canal basin in Manchester.   Slowly, the story revealed itself, in between my sobs, the pain in my arm and intense pain in my heart centre. I saw myself as a manager of men, building the canal and I supervised them. I became aware that I had originated from Newcastle and was such a talented engineer, that I soon got bored of a job. I had worked in the shipyards there and had moved, when I got this job offer, to manage the building of the canals.

As the memories flooded back, I became aware that I was deeply in love with my wife and we had met in Newcastle, been married for several years and then moved here. I adored her and she really was my soul-mate in every sense, besides being my best friend, lover and soul companion. When I saw her in my mind's eye, the love poured from her to me and through and from me too. It was truly amazing. My heart centre was getting more and more painful, as Chris gently coaxed from me the details.

The men I worked for were very wealthy and gave little or no thought to our safety. At that time there were no health and safety regulations in place. I managed the men and became aware that I had seen many injured, some even die, through lack of safety measures. I had held many of their hands, whilst my men had been in tremendous pain and agony. Despite pleading with the bosses very little had changed, though I kept trying. I was a very happy man and always cheery. No matter what job we did, or how boring it was, I kept the spirits of the men happy and jolly. Any disputes and inappropriateness, were dealt with as soon as they arose, the bosses left me to it to be honest.

I was paid a very good wage, though the men were paid a pittance, many had huge families and many mouths to feed. I knew and respected them all personally, though certainly did not allow shoddy workmanship and lack of teamwork. I worked them to the best of their abilities and felt that I had got the very best out of each, and every one of them; both personally and professionally.

To be honest, the memories I had, made me feel that I loved the work and the men too. Yet, I was greatly disheartened that the standards of care were so lacking from our employers. A picture opened in my mind's eye, showing my dear wife bringing me lunch, as she always did. All the men knew her and they knew the love and respect that we shared. One of the bosses was deeply angered by our love and was very jealous. Often when she called at the yard, if I ever caught a glance at him, he would have a nasty snarl on his face. Despite his wealth and the fact that he was well-known for having lots of women to his bed, he was clearly a very unhappy man.

It's funny how clear past lives can be whilst under regression and the intense detail they can reveal. I knew this man's eyes and I know who he is in this lifetime. He is now one of my best friends and certainly one of the kindest men I have ever met.

Suddenly the pain in my heart and my arm worsened as Chris continued to hold my space. The story unfolded once more. My beautiful wife had called with my lunch this particular day and had our baby son George in her arms. He was only a few months old. I adored him, he was strong and such a loving child, intelligent and always interested in everything that was going on around him. That particular day we were working in a different part of the canal basin and had to sort out how we would obtain and maintain the water levels. There was a pit which was deep and huge where the excess water could be stored, in case it was necessary to re-establish the water levels.

The engineering involved was well ahead of its time and I was delighted with the way it had worked too. She was eager to see the new project and had once again brought yet another delicious lunch. As she neared our location, I waved and smiled and was making my way over to them, when the other men showed her the depth of the pit and were explaining to her how it all worked. She thought it was great and just as I neared her she looked down into the pit with our son in her arms. As usual, as strong as he was, he was wriggling and giggling in her arms. As he moved, being as strong as he was, she lost her grip on him and he plunged several feet into the pit of cold water. The basin was inaccessible; after all it had been built to store water, there was no reason why anyone would ever need to have access. My heart flipped and I looked in horror as the men's faces and the cries of anguish filled the afternoon air.

There was absolutely nothing any of us could do. We stopped the machinery and eventually, slowly, but surely, one of my men who was called Marco, scaled down into the pit. He retrieved George's little blue, swollen body, later that afternoon and my wife howled and screamed as I held her close, thinking that we would both die with grief.

It was an awful recollection and tears flow down my cheeks as I write and edit this; the memories still as clear, as they were on that fateful day. The bosses had heard the commotion and had come out to see what was going on. I saw the look on his face when he realised what had happened, there was a smile of pleasure, that finally something would break my spirit.

We wrapped the body in a blanket. Grace, my wife, was screaming and shaking. Suddenly she stopped and became deathly silent. "Let's go home with George" she said. She nodded in respect and gratitude to all the men, who had tried to rescue our son and who shared our grief and pain.

She carried him all the way, as if he were simply sleeping in her arms. My arm wrapped around her shoulder and I just held back my tears wondering when the shock of the reality would bring her back to me. The yard was not far from where we lived, though it seemed a lifetime before we actually arrived there. I lifted the latch and we sat down, all three of us.

She remained in shock for two days, checking on him in his cot and wrapping him up. It was strange and I honestly did not know what to do, other than play along and WAIT. One the third day she awoke and went to his cot, to see if he was crying for his feed. The smell of the decomposing body was by now becoming overwhelming and putrid.

Whether it was the smell, or the very bright sunshine flooding in through the windows, after several days of rain, I will never know, but suddenly as she reached into the cradle she let out the most awful howl I have ever heard. "He's dead" she screamed over and over again. I held her close and allowed her to scream and kick and scream and kick, some more. The smell was making me sick and it was all I could do to hold her tightly without vomiting from the stench. Eventually she fell asleep, into a very deep yet peaceful sleep, which took me by surprise. I had to move the body and wrap George in appropriate cloths. As she slept soundly, I tended to his body and my tears fell silently as I clutched him to my chest. I said my quiet goodbyes and went next door to our neighbour, who was an undertaker of sorts.

He took our dear George and I asked him to keep the body, until my wife had awoken and could say her goodbyes to him too.

His funeral was short and sweet, although every single one of my men came to show their respects and support. Again the boss was displeased, but he knew that they would NOT be returning to work that day at all. His face was grimaced at the funeral and yet there was also something about him which was beginning to soften too.

I stayed away from the yard until Grace was stronger and her family had called to stay with us. She blamed herself for the accident and the guilt was crippling her and ripping her apart. I felt neither guilt nor shame. I certainly felt our loss and the grief, but I still had the woman I adored by my side and was happy to have her regardless.

Eventually, I returned to work and despite my boss hoping that the incident had lessened my spirits, I proved him wrong. The camaraderie the men showed just got bigger and stronger. Grace soon returned to her usual routine of bringing my lunch and the men always looked over her whenever she was in the yard.

Again my right arm began to ache and I could see what looked like a rubber tube seemingly coming from the vein? It did not make sense. With Chris's further coaxing, I moved forward several months ahead, in time to a scene where Grace had once again come to the yard. She was still grieving our loss, though had brightened somewhat. Life had continued and we were so very much in love, despite everything.

There had been a recent delivery of wooden sleepers, I had asked the bosses for certain safety procedures regarding the stacking and storage of the wood, as it wasn't safe. As Grace neared me the whole pile, it just came crushing around her without warning. She was crushed from the waist down and, as she lay dying, I held her whilst my blood flowed through my arm into her arm. I knew it was useless anyway and despite the efforts of all my men to remove the logs, she died within the hour. As I held her hand, she whispered that she had just realised that morning that she was pregnant, despite dying, her excitement relating to the pregnancy shone through.

I lay with her long after she was dead and her body cold; the logs still covering her lower body. The men were silent as they kept removing the wood that had crushed my beloved. This time even the boss looked on with genuine sadness. Blood covered most of my legs as I lay there with her. All I could think about was her, how much I loved her and how much she filled my whole being with love. George had been an extension of that love, and, though I loved him dearly, nothing compared with the love I felt for her.

Once the logs were removed from her body, the men looked to me for guidance and I just requested them to leave us on that fateful day, until I felt I was ready to carry her body to the nearby buildings. I still recall how I felt, I wasn't lonely or shocked. It was a very strange feeling of emptiness, nothingness.

I guess I lay there for maybe an hour, maybe more, just talking to her, telling her how much I loved her whilst holding her cold hand in mine. I carried her body, eventually, to the nearest shed, and placed it on a make shift bed, which we used if the men ever needed first aid. I stayed with her for a while then walked to the neighbour and asked him to remove her body and sort out the funeral arrangements.

Everything was in slow motion and I went home to a house that was empty and lifeless. I kept looking for her and watching the door, hoping that it would open at any time. I could smell her around me and actually feel her with me and yet it was strange to me in my confused state, that she was not physically present.

Another very simple funeral followed and the men all attended showing their remorse and respect. This time, even the boss shook my hand and actually showed emotion and regret - knowing that had he listened to me this could have been avoided.

After several more days I returned to work. I looked for her every day at lunchtime and just quietly beavered away. I felt my love grow for her daily, even though she was not around. I still feel that love now. Throughout the session with Chris, I had sobbed and cried. He got me to replay the scenes where both she and George died, so I could cuddle my son and my wife, say my goodbyes and bring a happy outcome to the actual outcome. I even forgave the bosses. It was another move towards freedom of having restricting and resisting abundance in this lifetime. I had seen what abundance and money had done to corrupt my bosses in that lifetime & how they had no intention of using money wisely.

Since George's death, I had stayed away from the "pit" as we all called it. One afternoon however, whilst I was working there, I saw something catch my eye. We had emptied it for maintenance works. Buried deep in the mud, were several items of gold and silver. There was a chalice and various other items. I bundled them up and although I declared them to the bosses. They just shook their heads and put me in touch with a man who might know their value.

My time had come to move on. With the wealth I acquired from their sale, I moved to London, worked there for a while and then moved to Kent, where I settled and stayed in an old white cottage, which I renovated and loved. As a young widower, I was looked upon by many a maiden, though I was still in love with my wife and never had another intimate relationship. I went on to live a very simple life as a blacksmith and carpenter, working whenever I felt like it, or when someone wanted assistance. I died an old man who was very contented, still feeling Grace's presence around my being daily.

As I came out of the regression I saw a huge jigsaw. There were two tiny pieces missing and, on the table besides it, was a brand new completed jigsaw. What did this mean? **Completion?** Was it significant of the ending of one chapter in my life and a whole new beginning? I had no idea. Time would surely tell. For now, as I sat in that chair, I was exhausted and still feeling the full intensity of the grief. I needed to get home to bed and rest.

Yet, I still wondered how this all tied in with the worm phobia? Was it because I had moved and lived in Kent in that lifetime and had just returned from there? Or, was it because it had happened that my granddaughter had held the worm up to me whilst in Kent? Neither felt right, though at that time I was too knackered to care. I just wanted to drive safely home and sleep.

THE REAL DEAL

"The great and glorious masterpiece of life is to know your purpose – "

Michel de Montaigne in A Bag Of Jewels.

The love I felt for Grace stayed with me following that session, and I can still feel it now as I write. To be honest, since I felt it, it has never left me. I have felt it daily since then – almost like a comfort blanket.

Within a couple of days of having seen Chris, I got a skin rash, which covered part of my lower back. It was slightly itchy, though not a problem as such. Whenever I have felt insecurity of some sort over the last few years, it has flared up. Something was brewing, the words of Paul my life coach, ran through my head; "The body won't lie" was being repeated and repeated. I had tried to meditate on it, Chris and I had discussed that the mystery as to why I had overreacted to the worm a few weeks ago, still remained unsolved.

We had already discussed maybe trying again through Hypnotherapy and an appointment was booked for the 20th April, which was a Monday. Chris had agreed to come here, as he preferred to get away from his office for a change. I was more than happy and when he arrived we chatted easily and shared a cuppa too. He loves Earl Grey and I'm partial to Lady Grey. As usual, we had a good catch up session and shared many things. I have learnt so much from him over the last few months and love being in his presence.

"Ok" he said, "Let's get cracking" in his usual jovial manner. I had explained about my back and we agreed to just let it flow, as we had done in previous sessions.

"Breathe three deep breaths in and relax" I was so used to this that within seconds I was relaxed and chilled as I sat in my armchair, comfy in my own lounge. By now the sound of Chris's gentle voice was so familiar to me. If there was anyone I trusted completely to unravel this, it was Chris. Despite knowing that when I had previously worked on this, I had re-remembered that awful scene in the dungeon and felt so awful that I was terrified that I might just return, I knew I had to follow Chris's lead, trusting that he would keep me safe and guide me through the scenes, to bring clarity and peace.

"Go back to that moment when Gracie held up the worm to you whilst in Kent recently." Immediately I was back in the dungeon; to the lifetime were I had been a spiritual leader, teacher, shaman & healer. My people had been murdered in front of me, body parts all over the floor and there I was, barely able to stand, as they had beaten me so badly in my back that my ribs were fractured and the kidneys damaged and bruised; the pain in my back was excruciating. I was sobbing and crying, moaning with deep emotional pain. Chris continued, asking what I could see and feel. Being a hypnotherapist we are trained to deal with what we term an abreaction – an abnormal reaction. This was certainly a fully blown abreaction and he was in control of guiding and assisting me through this.

My right arm began to hurt beyond anything, I have ever experienced in this lifetime, despite having had tendonitis and a variety of other pains following a whiplash injury several years before, when the sensory and circulatory nerves were trapped in the right hand side of my neck. I was weeping at full pelt now and almost screaming in pain, whilst I wriggled and writhed in the chair. Chris coached me through what was happening and I could barely speak, as I whispered that my right arm was in agony.

"What's happening to your arm?" he continued. As I looked down I could see it was battered and bruised at the top. When I looked at the fingers they were being cut off, piece by piece. The pain worsened and I winced in agony once more. As professional as he is, Chris immediately clicked his fingers, told me that the pain had disappeared and that I was now disconnected from the pain, although I could still have full awareness of what was happening.

"What's going on?" he continued. My sobbing had stopped once the pains had gone and I just watched over the scene as it unfolded below me. I was close to death by now. The torturers knew that the information they wanted about the location of the other spiritual communities would not be forthcoming, no matter what they choose to do to me. They struck me again in the back, by now my soul was getting ready to leave my physical body. I was exhausted and welcoming of death. I knew and understood about death as a spiritual teacher. After all I had taught it to my people. My loved ones would come to me in spirit form, to take me to the other side and I knew that I had absolutely nothing to fear at all.

As I seemed to move from my physical body to my light body, I became very confused. I had had my eyes closed throughout the session, as I always did with Chris. There was a man standing in front of me in spirit, the love I felt from him was so very familiar to me. I'm guessing that the look of confusion was spread across my face, so Chris asked me what I saw. "There's a man here to take me to the other side, but it's not Richard, my husband."

Richard was the first of our spiritual community to be murdered that fateful night, I was the last. Why was he not here to welcome me to the other side? Yet the radiance of love I felt from this man, as he stood there with his open arms, was amazing, and far more loving than Richard ever was, despite the fact that Richard and I had shared so very much.

"I don't understand" I continued on to Chris, "It should be Richard; I know I was never unfaithful to him and I know that I loved him." It was a few moments before the mystery would unravel itself as to who this stranger was. The love was so intense and then I recognised it as that of Grace, in the lifetime where I had been an engineer. It was the love of the soul I was feeling and I knew this love.

We often change sex between lifetimes and there was absolutely no denying this completeness. I was being welcomed into the loving arms of a man I had loved as my FIRST husband Peter. Long before I had even met Richard, we had met and married, sharing so much love and wisdom. We had taught spirituality together and were completely in love with each other and honoured in our community. We had lived then in Ibiza. We actually lived on Es Vedra, and, as the healer and shaman, I had made the island invisible to others, so that we would not be found!

Whilst the pictures unfolded in front of me, I explained to Chris what had happened and what I had SO clearly blocked out and denied from myself for centuries! We had been married for several years, when he had ventured on a trip to foreign lands, as there had been an emergency to meet with others of our kin. I was heavily pregnant with our first child, so had been advised not to travel. He was due back within the fortnight that the baby was due, so I was comfortable with that, although something nagged within me.

The story unfolded, he never returned and was presumed lost at sea. I was devastated completely & went into labour immediately, upon hearing the news. The baby was almost at the due date anyways, so my attending healers and midwives were not too worried, although my grief intense meant that I cried throughout the whole labour. It was relatively quick for a first child and within six hours our dear son arrived. He had the cord wrapped around his neck three times and whilst passing through the birth canal, it had choked him. I had lost my beloved husband and my newly born son. I quickly slipped into a coma; probably induced by the shock of both deaths. I was tended to and watched over for several days, before I returned to consciousness.

My life would never be the same. Thinking that I could protect myself from further loss, I closed off part of my heart centre and vowed that even though I was only in my twenties, I would never again love as I had, neither would I ever have any other children. These vows I made to myself and they left karmic imprints in my aura, reminding me that no-one could love me, as he had once done.

Chris asked me if I was frightened of dying and I explained that I was happy to pass. He was contented to guide me through the passage of death and bring a close to the worm phobia once and for all. I filled the dungeon with light, and, as I did so, I remembered that whilst being married to Richard, who had in fact been my second husband, I had lied to him, refusing to have his children, despite the fact that he was desperate to start a family.

My excuse was that I would never have children with him, in case we were ever caught and tortured, explaining that the children could be potentially used to blackmail us in to giving away the details of the whereabouts of the other spiritual communes. It had all been a lie; to hide my pain and the loss of both my dear son and my husband. I became aware in the final moments of that session of regression, the awesome power of denial and delusion. I sent healing to Richard and moved into the light with Peter.

As Chris coached me and allowed me to return to my normal state, as the Mary I am today, I became aware that Peter would in fact be a long term partner in this lifetime and was the guy I saw in the pictures from the sunset in Ibiza. Now the story was all unravelling and finally making perfect sense. I thanked Chris and we chatted over another cuppa, before he dashed off to his surgery locally. I felt shattered and shaken with the revelations. I needed time and patience to digest all that I had now uncovered, knowing that it had in fact been a huge letting go, which would allow me to move on in my current life.

THE FINAL PIECES OF THE JIGSAW

*"Be at peace and see a clear pattern and plan running through all
your lives,
Nothing is by chance."*

Eileen Caddy, Footprints on the Path

The regression, on that remarkable Monday, left me full of grief, Chris said it was the most emotional I had ever been whilst in a session with him. I was very tired, so I had rested as soon as Chris had left. I listened to my body that day, as I had learnt to do over the previous years.

The following day I still felt uneasy. This was quite normal, I told myself, having a walk in one of my favourite places, to try to shake off the feeling. I love Rivington and thought that by walking up to the Pike, I would feel much better and free of these feelings; of being lost and disconnected. I sat on top of the hill looking out over the surrounding area and felt nothing. The views from there are usually amazing and always bring a smile to my face and my heart. Today was certainly different. I called in my guides for assistance, which usually helps when all else fails. Still nothing.

By now, I was close to despair, as the weight of these emotions and feelings dragged me down and lowered my vibration. There is a quiet spot to the right of the Pike and the pigeon tower which few people know, so I knew it would be quiet and peaceful there. The intensity of the feelings, were making me feel most uneasy. I thought of one last thing that might help; I would do some EFT on myself. "Feeling lost makes me feel sad and uneasy" I repeated as I tapped out the emotions. They lifted slightly but still the bulk of them remained and weighed heavily on my being.

Nothing changed, and, despite meditating on it to uncover what it was trying to show me, I was now beginning to feel really overwhelmed. I decided that I would just have to get on with it and make the most of the day, as I always do in these situations. To be honest, since becoming more spiritually aware, I rarely had a bad day so it was quite an unusual situation for me to be in.

That night still feeling very uncomfortable, I honestly couldn't settle, so just gave in and went to bed early. My phone, as usual, was on silent downstairs. I didn't even feel like reading, as I walked up the stairs to the land of z's.

Wednesday morning I still felt unsettled, as I checked my phone I saw there was a text message from Chris from the previous evening, asking how I was and that he had a spare couple of hours between 11-1pm that day; did I require another session with him? He just knew! I was so grateful and called back to say that I felt so uncomfortable and unsettled within a feeling of being lost and sad. "See you at 11 then" he said down the phone, after I mentioned that I had done everything I could possibly do to shift this feeling.

Laughing and drinking our favourite teas, we settled into easy banter and Chris listened as I explained my feelings. Within minutes, as was usual, I was under hypnosis and calmly being asked about my feelings. With my patients and clients, they very often feel lost/sad when soul fragments are missing. This can happen for many reasons as I have previously explained; we give vast parts of our soul away in our family life, with partners and our children. We can often do it in our careers too. However, for whatsoever reason, it had never crossed my mind that this could be soul fragmentation.

Chris took me deeper and the pictures began to unfold. I had tummy pain and my head was most hair sore. The further I tuned into my body, the more I was becoming aware. I was a young lady in her early twenties dressed in a very tight corset, which was becoming very painful. As I tuned in, I was aware that I was married and with child; it felt like approximately 16-20 weeks of a pregnancy, which was why the corset was distressing me. I was worried for the unborn child and my head was sore as my hair was pulled back so tightly, it hurt. I had lovely curly, auburn hair and was very beautiful indeed.

I was taking a gentle stroll in the gardens, when many people came running over to me screaming and shouting. I was aware that I was in a palace; I could smell smoke and hear the crackling of burning wood. As it unfolded, I knew it was London, and yet, despite being in England, I could not understand what they were shouting about. As I wandered through the garden, I became aware that I was of royal blood. Suddenly someone grabbed me by the arm and it was one of my attendants. As they spoke to me *in French,* I realised the reason I was here, was in fact, to learn English and, indeed as French royalty, it was expected of me. My husband was currently in France and I was here for a few more weeks, whilst I picked up the language. At least it explained why I couldn't comprehend what they had been screaming about. My attendant explained that the palace was burning down and we must leave quickly.

Within seconds I became aware that I was dying, as the smell of the smoke increased and by this point I was coughing and spluttering through the session with Chris. He continued to guide me through the scenes. "And how do you feel now that you are dying? Are you in any pain?"

"No" I answered, so calmly that I surprised myself, as I explained that I had surrendered to death, knowing that this was meant to happen and all was as it should be. However, the baby was scared to die and I guess was probably being starved of oxygen, so I just sent light to him.

As I passed out of my body to Source and rising above London, I became aware that I had been a healer in that lifetime. Whilst in London, I had established several very strong healing grids of energy, which would be recharged for use at a later date when the city needed the increased energy. I had also a knowing, that I would return at a later date, to recharge these energetic grids and became aware that most were along the Thames River. I had also left approximately 17 soul fragments, which I would collect in another lifetime, when my vibration had increased sufficiently too. All this, had in fact, been meant to happen and all was well.

As I floated upwards towards source, again the feeling of being confused arose within my consciousness and felt upsetting. Explaining this to Chris once again, he gently coaxed the answers. As I died, I was aware that my husband was in France and though we hadn't been married long, I certainly did love him. If I reincarnated soon, I would be too young to be with him, if I left it for a while, he would all the while be getting older.

What should I do? The pictures fast-forwarded to him hearing of my death and he did not seem too bothered. Indeed, as I looked deeper he was having several other maidens to his boudoir. I was both shocked and then stunned.

The pictures then revealed that before my marriage, I was in love with another man who was seven years younger than me. I was definitely not acceptable that I would be **allowed as royalty to marry him**. As I tuned in further, I became aware that this was Grace/Peter's energy! So the man I had married had been my second choice. Yet another suitor came to mind, who was my dear friend Alfred, whom I have met and known very well in this lifetime. He was my third choice, as he was very much older than me in that lifetime and not royalty so, once again, not a suitor as such. We weave a very tangled web and this one certainly was such a web.

Chris asked if there were any issues which needed healing and as I got a Birds' Eye view of London I was drawn to the London Eye, by the Thames. Soul fragments were located there and also on the nearby bridge, though many were along the river too. It became obvious that I was being guided to visit London in the very near future. *I needed to collect all the soul fragments and put the others to rest.* I would need to go to the London Eye and travel on a boat cruise in order to put to rest this lifetime, recharge the healing grids and allow whatsoever else to surface and unfold.

At this time I was thinking of working in London and had been discussing this with a dear friend of mine. It seemed a simple solution to me, to be able to move to Kent, work in London to support myself and change my life for the better. The commute would be easy enough from there, as I knew that there was no way I could ever live in London city centre.

MANCHESTER LAID TO REST

"All physical disease has its origin in the emotions"

Ian White

Now I was aware that I had healing to do in both Manchester and London. The Manchester life, where I had lost my dear wife and son needed healing first. Chris and I discussed it and he suggested where the location from my description of the canal layout might be. As from previous chapters, you will be aware that I have always had a fear of Manchester for years. There was no explanation whatsoever from this lifetime, although now perhaps I had an answer?

My dear friend Tony knows Manchester much better than I do and he agreed with Chris, that the location was most likely to be north Manchester, near Deansgate. It felt right and Tony had been ill for a few days, I had been busy with work, so, the first available date was the 2nd May. I was nervous to be honest and just glad that the British weather was reasonably kind!

My friend Bev had called to collect my accounts, a few days earlier & she had also done a reading for me. She said that all was well; the second book was to be a priority, and that I would be travelling extensively, teaching more spirituality than healing, I would go and see my son Matty in Oz, would soon come into money and all would be truly wonderful. She also saw a new romantic, long-term partner and much love between us. She saw a new home and said I would move to Kent. I would write several more books and become an international speaker. There were several other things regarding my family and she was accurate in each and every one; as she usually has been in the past.

It was a funny day, I felt weird and very tired after she left. I crawled into bed for over an hour as luckily, I was free for the rest of the day. When I awoke, someone had posted a meditation event locally on my Facebook page. It felt absolutely right and I decided to go. As I drove I knew it was the right thing to do and saw many friends….including Bev! I was stunned!!!

The meditation was very powerful and brought many insights and confirmed much of what Bev had said too. I was thrilled and, to be honest, because I'm usually the one running events, it's sometimes lovely to just sit back, letting someone else take central stage.

Many things were discussed and a basket of healing crystals was passed around to assist us in meditation, should we require one. I had intuitively chosen a crystal which was for deep grief. I held it throughout the evening. Then *blue irises* were discussed and they are certainly one of my favourite flowers. It felt right to purchase some for my healing prayers in Manchester later that week.

Tony and I had planned this several weeks previously, but knew today, Saturday, was indeed the day. He is very spiritually aware and he also felt that as I would heal myself & a huge part of my past, then he too would be healing on some level(s). Chris had suggested laying a wreath, or maybe buying some flowers and placing them on the water. This seemed like a really wonderful idea.

The morning was very emotional, Tony and I met at Piccadilly station. He was waiting for me on the platform when the train pulled in, with his usual huge smile and equally huge hugs too. His other name is "Tony Huggles" or "Teddy Bear," so there were no surprises there!

We chatted easily and discussed plans for the day, where we might go for lunch, etc. We opted for a Chai Latte before, we started towards Deansgate. Whilst venturing through Manchester, following the life coaching sessions, I had found a little florist and we walked towards there once we had had a drink. I purchased the blue irises and some gypsy too.

As we neared the canal basin, I could feel the energy building. This was definitely the right place. We both intuitively "knew," where we had to be, as there are many bridges in the area. As we moved over to the right, we stood on the first bridge, each saying our silent prayers as we each threw a blue iris into the water. It was strange, as I knew I was placing some here for Grace – not yet George, as that had to be done separately, for some reason; thus, I had to keep some flowers over for later. As I looked up, in front of us was a canal barge called "The Kingfisher."

To the left of that, was another called "Nomad Rush." It had only taken several hundred years to bring this healing together after all. Then there was another barge whose title referred to **hugs and cuddles** which we knew related to Tony.

Tony hugged me as I cried; we just stood on the bridge and said our goodbyes. We knew to move on and one of the next barges was called the "Blue Iris." Tony and I are very aware of coincidences, synchronicities and miracles from The Universe, but these were fabulous confirmations indeed. The owners of the barge were available and it felt right to offer her a single blue iris. She was delighted and we chatted easily about life on the water.

We then knew that we had to move on over the other bridge, around the corner, passing a barge called "Gladys Emily," (glad it's Emily). My daughters' name is Emily and I knew that by healing this chapter of my life, it would allow me to be much freer to move to Kent. We then passed "Isis," who just so happens to be a very powerful spirit guide of mine and I connect to her through the emerald energy. I had just that morning, put my emerald and diamond ring back on my finger. I had bought it from Manchester, three years earlier, when I had visited Luxor, Egypt!

We continued on and moved over the bridges. We both intuited where the healing energy needed to be sent and threw in more flowers. I did not know this area we now moved into, although I knew it was right for us to continue onwards. I still had flowers left and was confident that we would find the right locations. I absolutely knew to move to the rear of the canal and over to the left, however as we neared it, the pathway looked inaccessible.

We had to find a way around and indeed, as we got nearer another path led very close to the waters' edge. We followed the path around a bend, as we did so my feet suddenly stopped and I was filled with a deep grief. Tears started flowing and although Tony had wandered just slightly ahead, he returned by my side. As I turned to the left, I just knew that was where little George had perished. As we walked on, there it was, a huge deep round pit just as I had pictured it. I was amazed and felt so very sad indeed. There were many more tears and more hugs from Tony. We stayed there for quite some time. Despite it having been a past life, the feelings were very real indeed and I needed to let these feelings pass. As I threw the blue iris in the water and watched it swirl, I sent healing to the whole area and to the water.

We then moved to the final bridge, Tony had been advised by his guides that we needed to retrace our steps exactly. On the bridge was a manufacturer's plaque from Egerton. Egerton is one of the next villages to my daughter, her husband and family. More confirmation indeed! I had one remaining blue iris left for each of us as we walked near a barge called "Just Imagine."

I knew this was a sign & that by releasing our pain and grief, we both now had to set our new intentions. In fact, we set them in silence, right by the magical barge and we both felt the affirmations being heard by The Universe too. Mine were very simple, *"**love, freedom, success, travel and all things positive in abundance such as motivation, inspiration, enthusiasm and for the books to be completed and successful".***

Our mission had been completed. Although we had said earlier that we would eat on the canal side, we now knew that we had to move on and eat nearer the centre. What a day it had been, how emotionally battered we were both feeling, as we ambled towards the city centre.

What would our futures hold now that we had actively let go of the old and were at least ready and willing to bring in the new with clear intentions?

All that happened on the 2nd May. The book at this time was 40,685k words. Within two days, I had inspiration to write and the total was now 48,795. I had, after all, requested that the next books I write be successful and completed! On Wednesday 1st July, the total was 83,585. I just needed to finish writing the chapter relating to my recent London visit. Testimonials were coming in, thick and fast, they too being added to the contents. On Sunday 5th July, I completed the book and was absolutely delighted with "my baby number two," by now the word count was almost 89k words!

Who could have known the speed of all these magical jigsaw pieces coming together and bringing me towards *completion?*

Ask and you will indeed receive, but <u>always</u> be careful what you wish for!!!

Therefore, if this had come to fruition; within a little over two months, I was wondering what would happen with the other affirmations and their outcome?

LONDON LINKS

"I learned that nothing is impossible when we follow
our inner guidance,
even when its direction may threaten us
by reversing our usual logic, -"

Gerald G. Jampolsky, "Love is Letting Go of Fear"

Through my work with Chris, we had also uncovered links to London. London also needed healing and I knew I had to go. The lives that I was clearing with Chris were so deep, that I discussed few details to anyone at all. The Universe works in mysterious ways and one day whilst out to lunch with my dear friend Tony, he shared his intuition, that I visit the city within the next few weeks!

We chatted easily over a healthy lunch of sweet potato wedges and salad. He laughed when I ordered my hot chocolate. He always makes me smile when he laughs, as that laugh I have "known" for centuries! We have had many past lives together and we have both intuited many. I explained my travel plans and told him it was "really deep stuff," I was clearing as we do in spiritual circles. I continued that the whole trip would change me and make headway for my future too. Little did I know then just how true those words would turn out to be!

He was due to travel soon, so the trip would be a welcome distraction for me, rather than to miss him! He laughed as we continued to share all manner of topics of conversation and then parted ways – both returning to our daily lives.

Over the following days, I was told clearly by my guides, that I had to be in London between the exact dates; 5-7th May. I booked my train tickets – no longer afraid of train travel and was actually looking forward to the challenges that travelling via the London tube would bring. What a turn- around!

The train was on time that morning and so many magical things had already happened. My dear friend Jacqueline and I were due to meet that afternoon. She was leaving for Ibiza the following day. Thus, if I had gone at any other time, it would have been impossible for us to meet.

More unfolding was afoot, not only that, but my dear friend Clare often works in London and had stayed in a very cheap, yet lovely hotel, within easy access of Earls Court railway station, which was absolutely perfect for me. She had booked my room for the two nights stay and I was thrilled at how everything was coming together.

Whilst she is in London, she often meets up with a chap called Ashley, who is also a lover of LOA. They actually attend a LOA group called "Yes" who hold regular meetings. The previous week they had attended one and felt the guest speaker was rubbish. Thus, she had suggested that my name be put forward as an inspirational speaker! She had in fact mentioned my name to Ashley & he had asked her to ask me to meet him for dinner on the Tuesday evening, so that we could share ideas and common ground. Wow. I would be meeting Jacqueline for afternoon tea, then Ashley later for an evening meal!

The rest of the time, I knew that I would be doing the healing work that Chris and I had worked through and discussed at length. It turned out to be truly fabulous. The said train journey was easy and even the tube trip to Earls Court! I found somewhere for lunch and located the hotel very easily indeed. Ashley and I had texted throughout the day. We had arranged to meet about 6pm, which gave me lots of time to chat with Jacqueline that afternoon. She's a real diamond and I love her dearly. We were so delighted to see one another and shared a lovely cuppa in the local village. She was looking forward to holidaying and spending time with her precious daughter. Catching up was wonderful, although inevitably we had to part later that afternoon. I found my way so easily around the tube and bumbled back to the hotel for a rest before meeting with Ashley.

He and his wife loved living the spiritual life and when I tuned into The Universe, I knew it would only be a matter of time before I met her too. Ashley had promised to text when he finished work and let me know his expected time of arrive at Earls Court. Neither of us had met before, so I described myself and he just wrote "Look for a short guy with a bald head and a huge smile."

Meeting up was fabulous, just as though we had known one another for ever! It was truly a blessing and as neither of us knew the area we just used LOA to find our way. "Right which way then?" We intuited right from the station walked about two miles and found this absolutely amazing restaurant that was quirky and enjoyed the whole evening. Chatting easily about all manner of spiritual subjects.....Truly an evening to remember and a friendship that has and will last through lifetimes!

Ashley asked if we could meet up the following evening for dinner too. Clare had suggested that he have a reading & healing with me too, so I agreed. Brilliant, I now had something to look forward to on

Wednesday evening, as I was meeting my friend Ian on Thursday, before leaving on the Preston train.

The following day, I knew I had to visit the London Eye first and heal the loss of Grace. I brought in the energy and allowed it to pass down to the water's edge. I stood there for quite a while, just being, and allowing the grief to pass. Afterwards, I knew I had to go to Westminster Abbey then onto St Paul's cathedral.

As I turned to leave, two young girls were stood close to me and asked if I spoke French. I explained that I did a little, although they struggled to understand me and me them! We soon used sign language and they wanted some stamps for postcards. I offered to post them and they were thrilled. We said our goodbyes and I continued towards the bridge to do more healing as it overlooked the Eye. By this point, I had shed a few tears and just allowed them to flow freely. There was no-one about, as it wasn't even 10am. I looked across at the river and knew that I truly had been here so many times before.

As and when I felt ready, I wandered towards Westminster Abbey. Before I had even crossed the road outside Westminster station, I was coughing so violently, that I had tears running down my face. Luckily, I had a bottle of water in my bag, as I truly thought I would choke. "Definitely karma here then," I thought and once again delivered a healing energy, to resolve whatever had happened previously.

The queue was already forming for Westminster Abbey and thus as it was ever growing, I thought I might as well get stuck in now, rather than wait and queue later. The place is vast and stunning. Once again, much healing was needed, as many of the energies were out of sync. Mission accomplished, I decided to bumble around for a chai latte and something to eat, before venturing to St Paul's cathedral. That is such a magnificent work of art! It was simply stunning and breathtaking. I was keeping in touch with Tony, who was assisting with the healing work too. He had texted to say, that he could feel my aura stretching into the heights of the dome bringing calm and balance. I was thrilled.

I then decided to climb the steps to the dome and enjoy the view It is a true piece of beautiful architecture indeed. Although I enjoyed the views, looking down upon the whole place from a tremendous vantage point, I promised myself that I would NEVER do it again and was so thrilled to place my feet on solid ground again!

I was beginning to feel really tired and just sat quietly in the chapel. I was meditating and asking for advice from my guides. I was told to move to the rear altar and spotted several art forms of sacred geometry which were beautiful; if only people knew their meaning!

I waited until 2pm, knowing I needed to get the tube and return to the hotel, for a much needed sleep. Ashley texted later and we met up. When I awoke, I walked up to the post office to post the cards for the French girls. They were postmarked to addresses in Toulouse. This had kept coming up in several conversations! That evening, Ashley and I were delighted to see each other again and share common ground. The reading and healing were successful and he was delighted. We had a fabulous meal in a hotel, just across from the one where I was staying, later that evening too. It was turning into a well-earned break and jolly great company too.

The only healing work now remaining was actually on the Thames River itself. I knew Thursday would bring a river cruise, before I ventured home. I was due to meet Ian about 5pm after he had finished work. I planned to get the "Hop On, Hop Off," bus to see the city and had seen a sign for the said bus stop outside St Pauls. I got the tube to Blackfriars: well, I thought I did! I ended up in Paddington!

I checked with my guides and they advised "Who said you got the wrong train?" I wandered around and enjoyed the walk by the hospital and the canal before getting on said bus. To be honest, I thoroughly enjoyed it and the guidance was to get the river cruise and travel to Greenwich. I was advised to leave the bus at 12.30pm.

Incredibly at 12.30pm exactly! the bus arrived at London Tower. From there I could then catch the ferry from the pier. Divine timing indeed. Lunch was very welcome and a hot cuppa after sitting on a jolly cold bus! I caught the ferry and once again it was perfect timing, as a huge naval liner was just arriving and was being towed by the tug boats, up into the city. I have to say, I was most impressed too.

I loved Greenwich, everything about the whole place, just felt so homely to me. I'll definitely visit again one day. After strolling around and visiting the lovely church, I had arranged to meet Ian later, although I knew I had to take a trip on the actual London Eye, in order to finish the healing work I had started the previous day. The views are breath taking indeed. I was most impressed.

Time was getting on and Ian agreed to meet me at Westminster station. I was thrilled to see him. We collected the hand luggage from my hotel and then enjoyed a truly marvellous meal at "The Botanist," in Sloane Square.

Ian is friends with the manageress and she was so kind with us. They chatted easily and I was thrilled to hear her foreign accent. She was from Toulouse! My next stop for healing? Quite possibly? Ian and I chatted easily, catching up and enjoying the wonderful cuisine too. Time came all too soon for me to travel home. He kindly agreed, just as he had the previous year, to travel with me from Sloane Square to Euston, to see me off on my homeward bound journey.

After a huge hug from Ian I boarded the train. It was a smooth journey home; I was ready for zzzz's. Mission completed and all healing done. Time for bed and time to see where the course of time would take me now that the blockages were cleared and the soul fragments reclaimed. Little did I know how things would unfold within the next few days?

LOSING MY OTHER HALF

"Every end is a new beginning"

"Begin It Now" (Ed Susan Hayward)

London had left me feeling drained and absolutely knackered. My guides insisted that I rest, informing me **that all the missing soul fragments;** between 17-20, had indeed been picked up back into my aura. They now needed to be fully upgraded and integrated into my physical body. They advised rest, and to be honest, I was so exhausted that there was no other choice anyway!

I returned home after the train journey very late that Thursday evening and just tucked myself into bed when I got home. I slept like a log, although I still woke up tired the following day. I had clients booked in and luckily, as I work predominantly from home, I simply rested in between. I am now finally listening to my body, after having M.E. all those years ago!

The day and evening passed quickly. I was surprised that I had NO clients on Saturday or Sunday, which is extremely unusual for me. I knew it was the magic Universe taking care of me and forcing rest. Funnily enough, as many of you that know me are aware, I am very much an early bird and have amazing floods of vitality in the mornings...usually! That Saturday I was well and truly shattered. I only awoke after 8am which is unusual, in itself and also within the hour, was ready for bed again.

Sunday was a slight improvement, though not by an outstanding amount. Monday I knew I was still under par. The rash on my back had spread across and upwards, though was not itchy, nor was it sore. Being very self-aware, I knew that something was indeed brewing. Chris was away and I knew something was about to show itself, as I had begun to feel unsettled, in a way that I had never felt before. I sat quietly for a few minutes and decided that I would ask Paul Ryder for his help. I booked an appointment for Thursday that week.

Little did I know what was about to unfold. Meanwhile, my dear friend Tracey dropped me off in Rufford and son Phil picked me up later that afternoon. We drove to Southport and enjoyed a Nando's together as we chatted easily.

I rested and listened to my body when we got home. Later, after a quick sleep, I decided to rearrange my bedroom furniture. I had simply moved a very light bedside cabinet and my back locked! I couldn't move, screamed "Ouch" at the pain and froze at 90 degrees! Phil was out and I was all alone, struggling to move due to the severity of the pain!

It was quite a while before I could even breathe enough to gently walk sideways like a crab, hold onto the banister rail and TRY to stand upright. I failed miserably and repeated attempts just had me in extreme pain, so I gave up. The pain seared right through my body and although I took arnica and several other Homeopathic remedies, nothing touched the slightest edge of it. Any, and all, conventional medicines upset my system so much, that I wouldn't even consider taking pain relief or anti-inflammatories.

I couldn't sit up straight, couldn't get comfy, no matter what position I tried and decided to just breathe into it and send myself healing. Again, nothing touched the acute pain. A dear friend had taught me yoga for back ache when I had simply sprained it over a year before and I tried "The Rag Doll." I screamed out in pain and realised that perhaps I had definitely hurt it more than ever before. Needless to say I did NOT achieve said "Rag Doll" position!

As a very positive person, I just assumed that it would be better the following day. I had no idea of the severity of the injury! Unbeknown to me I had ruptured a disc or two and indeed, when I went to bed that evening just assumed that I would sleep well and all would be ok the following morning.

That was **not the case** and indeed the word "assume" means to make an ASS of YOU (U) - and ME. Well, probably **dumb ass** was more appropriate looking back. I had clients booked solid all day. They knew as soon as they arrived, I was in pain, as I couldn't stand upright! Thank goodness I work from home and thank goodness my clients are great people and understood that I needed to sit down through the healings.

I thought a massage might help and put an end to the agony. Booking myself in with a friend I was excited as I thought of how wonderful it would be to move freely once more. Guess what? That wasn't the case at all! It eased and I had a better, though still incredibly painful nights sleep, but was still unable to stand the following day. So much for the power of positive thinking! There was obviously so much more that my body was showing me. Meditation through the pain was not easy, although I certainly gave it my best shot.

I was looking forward to my session with Paul on Thursday and duly booked my train tickets. Looking back as I write this, I am smiling to myself, as I truly had no idea of the severity of my injuries. I just carried on, although I had certainly knew that I was unable to lift, carry, sleep on my left hand side, go for a walk, shop or hike!

Clare has long been a great and inspiring friend over the past few years and she had made an appointment to see me Wednesday afternoon. She looked so surprised, when I answered the door, as I still could not stand upright. I explained about my London trip and that I was due to see Paul the following day. That would then all would be sorted, I would make a full and speedy recovery. She asked how I would get to Manchester in my current state and I explained that I had booked train tickets. She laughed and said that she knew I wasn't fit to travel, she was in Manchester the following day anyway, with her own business and she would take me and park as close to Paul's office as possible, knowing that walking was a challenge for me!

I was deeply touched and relieved, as by now, I was beginning to realise that it certainly wasn't merely a sprained muscle. We arrived in Manchester and had a good chat en route. We enjoyed a fabulous lunch, whilst I struggled to sit still for more than a few minutes and hobbled to the toilet before we left! How funny all this seems, now I look back? She walked me to Paul's office, which took at least ten minutes, compared to the usual five minute jaunt and asked me to call as soon as I was done.

Pauls face was a picture when I walked in. He was very sympathetic as I gently sat in the chair. He asked what had brought me here & I explained that I had the possible intention of moving to Kent, working in London and moving on in life. "Ok" he said, "make yourself small and go into the pain into your back."

What unfolded was a complete surprise to me and really odd as I had NEVER gone into a past life with Paul previously. I closed my eyes, going into the pain and straight away was on a battlefield, well, to be more precise, a minefield. My legs were intact, although they had been sheared off at the waist. I knew I was dying and was trying to reach for my gun, so that I could shoot myself in the head, rather than be captured by the enemy. I was exactly half way between the allies and the enemy lines. I felt no pain, apart from that which I was feeling in this lifetime, which is unusual in itself.

I felt angry that I couldn't reach for my gun, and, as I was explaining what I saw to Paul I was distracted. In the vision, someone was pulling my left arm and I felt confused as to why, and who, it might be on the minefield; knowing that whoever it was, could get blown up at any minute. Astounded, I looked up from my half body and recognised the face as that of my dear friend Tony. I was *so cross* with him for risking his own life to come and gather my torso. As I told him to leave me, he replied "Ummm, and what do you think mum would say to that?" in a really broad Northern accent.

It suddenly dawned on me, that he was my brother. Actually the whole scenario opened up before me with incredible clarity. He wasn't just my brother, but my identical twin. We were seventeen years old, both ginger-haired, tall and skinny. "Mum would bloody kill me, if I left you here wouldn't she, you daft sod?" he continued, whilst yanking my arm towards him. It was then that I noticed his right thigh. There was a bright red blood stain seeping through his clothing.

I was so close to death, thus drifting in and out of the physical world and that of the esoteric. In that state, I knew that he too was dying. The wound was filled with a fast-acting poison and I could "see" the poison spreading throughout his bloodstream, whilst in the esoteric realm.

He dragged me from the minefield into a ditch and snuggled into my half body, as we both lay dying. I remember the uniforms were khaki coloured and our tags were laid open across our chests, so that they could easily be removed from our bodies, once we were located. As we lay there we both thought of mum, a very powerful dominant character, who would at least know, that we had died together on that fateful day.

As we lay dying, I knew that he hadn't come to save me for mum's sake, rather because he was so afraid of dying alone. We were twins after all and had never been separated. We had other siblings, so as I lay dying, I took that to be some consolation for our dear mother.

Tony died a few minutes before I did. It was a peaceful death; he just got quieter and quieter. As his dead body lay at the side of me, I embraced death, knowing that I was going away from this hell hole.

Paul gently asked me where my legs were and asked me how it felt without them. He asked how I would feel in this lifetime without them. I answered that I would not be able to go forward and would be severely restricted. He asked me to locate them on the battlefield. Again the anger rose as I could see the enemy gather them up and take my belongings; my socks, boots, knife and belt, not to mention my trousers themselves and my underwear. "Why are you angry" Paul asked....I looked into the picture for the answer; "Because they are taking everything from me." I replied. "Is that true?" he questioned?

Looking again at the unfolding scenario, I saw them as desperate men who had nothing. They had NO supplies, no food, no clean clothing, no descent footwear and no food. They were helpless and starving. They had been promised much and received nothing during the war. They were exhausted and had lost all hope. Their only thought was to kill. I was totally shocked at this revelation, as our battalion had ample supplies, despite being on enemy ground. The only emotion I then felt was that of compassion for these desperate young men who, like us, knew nothing much of what we were all fighting for and it all seemed incredibly pointless.

It was at that point that I passed over to the other side, leaving what remained of my physical body behind on that fateful day. I remember it all so clearly now as I write, recalling all the minute details.

It explained so much and yet left me with a deep sadness. The next pictures were very odd indeed, as I then saw a huge clock face, rather like Big Ben. I also saw various people stood at *all* the twelve points on the clock. I recognised many, though not all, of the faces and "knew" that they were here to support me through the rest of my life. I then saw a jigsaw puzzle, with two pieces missing and kept hearing the words ***completion.*** Then, once again the pictures changed, this time it opened with a huge bouquet of flowers, a *diamond* and a bottle of champagne!

My guides were saying "It is now your TIME, TIME for you to receive all you have asked for and TIME to celebrate. The TIME is now." I was surprised and quite taken aback too.

So, what did all this mean? As usual, after a deep session with Paul I was exhausted, mentally, physically, emotionally and spiritually too. I thanked Paul and left, taking the stairs very cautiously indeed.

Clare had known intuitively that we were done, as I got out of the doorway, there she was with her beautiful white BMW and a huge smile for a friend in need! We chatted easily on the way home and she was gobsmacked as I relayed the story. It is truly amazing, as she herself had recently experienced first-hand déjà vu, through various E.F.T. and hypnotherapy sessions with me. I was glad to be with someone I could relate to and very glad that she had known I certainly wasn't fit to travel by train!

As we neared Clare's home, I was becoming more and more drowsy, as all the revelations released from my parasympathetic nervous system. I was struggling to talk and she understood, having by now experienced these deeper understandings from our other aspects/past lives, for herself.

She refused to allow me to go home in that state and TOLD me to go straight to bed upstairs. She promised to bring me some water and stated that she would leave me to awaken in my own time. She offered for me to stay the night too, if I so wished.

There are some things in life that you never forget and times like these just deepen friendships beyond normal parameters. I was, and am, eternally grateful to her for her thoughtfulness and kindness. That afternoon, I slept for four hours! When I awoke I could hear the children downstairs and smell a wonderful aroma. A vegetable lasagne was much needed and a decent cuppa too.

When I arrived home later, I was shattered and once again after a heavy session crawled into bed. What on earth did the flowers, the *diamond* and the champers mean? **What of the two jigsaw pieces?**

THE TRUTH REVEALED

"Faith is the bird that feels the light when the dawn is still dark – "

Rabindranath Tagore

Two weeks prior to my back injury, my dear friend Bev had given me a reading. As always, many things were said and she has been very accurate previously, so I know that the advice is well worth listening to. Her words kept ringing in my ear; "You'll be ill with a kidney infection and you must take it easy; whilst at the same time you must enjoy the rest. After that you'll fly, you'll be so busy your feet won't touch the ground, you'll have so many choices, that you need to *carefully, consider each and every one*. Many wondrous things will come to you. *You MUST get the second book finished.*"

To be honest, I think she misunderstood the kidney infection for my back injury, which is quite understandable, especially as the pain was located right on the kidney meridian.

Besides the lifetime where I lost my legs, there were others which needed clearing too. I had already "seen" a hook in my left hip, which I had been working on for several months.

Another came when I did a workshop in Accrington on "Aura and Chakra Clearing." One of my Reiki students "saw" a spear/javelin and kindly assisted me by sending healing.

One morning in the early hours, I awoke sweating, with very painful backache, especially as I had rolled from my right hand side, onto either my back, left hand side or my tummy. I could see a young boy of about 11-12 with callipers on his legs, preventing him from running, or walking comfortably. It was a little like the younger "Forrest Gump" character. Surrounding each and every lifetime and injury, with healing would clear the way to my going forward — otherwise known as *freedom!*

Oscar had seen me twice and helped greatly by giving me simple exercises. Now that I had the awareness and knew the severity of the injury, I would no longer cause unnecessary aggravation. Besides the healing, Homeopathy, acupuncture and massage, I was making improvements daily. In the meantime, the house was closer to being finished and I felt a slight fear, that I knew I would soon be in a position to get the house valued and potentially move on!

Another huge blessing has been that I have had more time, as currently I cannot hike or drive/walk, for lengthy periods. I obviously cannot swim or go to the gym either! Thus the spare time has presented me with other opportunities to do things for myself, which otherwise I might not have done.

My dear friend Jane invited me to join her singing group, "The Skylarks" last year. However, with so many commitments to the TV show, it never happened. Last month, I finally joined and gave *"Little Louise,"* her voice back. **I *LOVE* singing and always have**, so this has been amazing and I really enjoy giving it my all! Just yesterday, one of the group thought I was a professional singing teacher! I'm even happy to do a solo/duet, now that I have found my voice.

This too is another link in the chain to 360 degrees, as I went to school with Jane all those years ago. She actually struggles just to call me Mary as she only remembers me as Mary Louise!

Thank you to Jane and all the "Skylark" group members too.

Yet another 360 degree link came recently, when I was reunited with an old friend I used to work with when I was in the Civil Service. It was right outside the church, next to the school where I grew up! Therefore, once again, due to my daughter, son-in-law and dearest granddaughters, I was in the right place at the exact right time. Great to re-connect Tracey!

So my affirmations *"Love, peace, abundance and freedom,"* are still keys to my spiritual journey. As I write the book now and it nears its closure, I recognise that through the back injury, I have learnt many things. In particular, I am even more in the NOW. I am more present, more appreciative of all I have and even more grateful for the small things; and the big things in life.

Where will this journey take me? My personal feeling is that the repair work on the house, my beautiful home, my personal recovery from this back injury and the completion of the book are all linked. I feel that The Universe will synchronise their completion all at once.

According to Bev, it's onwards and upwards.........watch this space!

Smell you later

Mary or Mary Louise, if you prefer.....

I personally prefer Kingfisher Curtis!!! x

The miracle is not walking on water,

the miracle is not walking in fire,

the miracle is waking up.

That is the real Miracle.

All else is nonsense.

OSHO: Living dangerously.
Ordinary Enlightenment For Extraordinary Times.

BIBLIOGRAPHY

The Wild Wood Tarot — Mark Ryan & John Matthews

The Art Of Forgiveness, Lovingkindness, and Peace. — Jack Kornfield

The Miracle Morning — Hal Elrod

Inspiration — Summersdale

10 Mindful Minutes — Goldie Hawn

Mastering the Laws Of Relationships — Dr Mansukh Patel & Savitri

The Dance Between Joy and Pain — Dr Mansukh Patel & Rita Goswami

Osho   Living Dangerously — Watkins

Believe In Yourself — Dr Mansukh Patel

The Knowing Heart — Kabir Helminski

The BodyMind Workbook — Debbie Shapiro

Pilgrims Guide & Journal — Glastonbury Edition

FURTHER READING

Zero Limits	*Dr Joe Vitale & Dr Hew Ihaleakala Len*
FOOD AWAKENING Nutrition for Now	*Julie Silver*
The Reconnection	*Dr Eric Pearl*
The Soul Whisperer	*Anna-Louise Haigh*
Light-Filled, Loving and Wise	*Anna-Louise Haigh*
Angel Medicine	*Doreen Virtue*
The Forty Rules Of Love	*Elif Shafak*
The Shack	*Wm. Paul Young*
Twelve Lessons	*Kate Spencer*
10 Mindful Minutes	*Goldie Hawn*
Tuesdays With Morrie	*Mitch Albom*
The Manuscript	*Lars Muhl*
Self-Care for the Self-Aware	Dave Markowitz
The Psychic Protection Handbook	Caitlin Matthews
Light Into Life	Dr. Susan Jamieson M.D

ADDITIONAL INFORMATION

HOLISTIC DENTISTRY

For your interest here is a short description of Holistic Dentistry as mentioned in pages 163, 197 and 198.

Holistic dentistry is a contemporary approach to healthcare that looks at your overall well-being and health...not just your teeth! Rather than just using outdated dentistry to treat the symptoms, holistic dentists focus on you as a 'whole person,' looking at the relationship between your oral health and the rest of your body to achieve overall harmony.

Nothing in your body works in isolation...everything is connected. The focus should be on the connection between your oral health and the rest of your body. This approach helps us look at possible causes of the symptoms which can extend to your attitude, diet, lifestyle and stress.

Within dentistry we aspire to serve our patients with holistic, preventable, predictable, long term, quality dental care – which will help you keep your teeth for life and have you looking and feeling good.

A truly holistic approach to dentistry adopts a three tier level of care:

Level 1: Is focused on the patient and any procedure that directly affects the patient' health and care including advanced diagnostic techniques, the materials used in the patent's mouth and complimentary therapies that augment treatment.

Level 2: Is focused on the protocols and procedures adopted by the dental practice to ensure that the practice makes holistic choices on a business level. This may include choice of cleaning products used, energy savings and adopting a paperless administrative system.

Level 3: Is focused on the impact the business has on an environmental level. This includes choices of energy provision and offsetting carbon emissions, ensuring correct water filtration systems, reduced ordering frequency to minimise delivery transportation and forging partnerships with other environmentally conscientious businesses.

At a minimum level dental practices should be a member of the Green Achiever scheme with a view to obtaining Gold Standard Status. At the time of writing only one dental practice in the UK has attained this accolade: Lane Ends Dental Practice in Preston, Lancashire, but it is my hope that more will follow their example and put our environment before business profits.

CONTACT DETAILS

Mary L Curtis: Tel: 07828 929659   marycurtis@talktalk.net
www.journeyintoyoursoul.com

David Lynam: Cover design: hello@davidlynamdesign.co.uk

Emily Griffiths: Original paintings of the kingfisher, rose and diamond.   Tel: 07825 794644